On the Outside Looking Up

Seeking and Following God Beyond the Gates of Organized Religion

Also by Elizabeth Massie:

Night Benedictions

Homegrown

Desper Hollow

Hell Gate

Sineater

Versailles

The Tudors: King Takes Queen

The Tudors: Thy Will Be Done

Sundown

Naked, On the Edge

The Young Founders series

The Ameri-Scares series

On the Outside Looking Up

Seeking and Following God
Beyond the Gates of Organized Religion

Elizabeth Massie

Valley House Books
USA

Copyright Elizabeth Massie, 2016

Valley House Books

Cover art and design and interior art by Cortney Skinner
cortneyskinner.com

Published in the United States of America

All rights reserved. No part of this book may be used or reproduced in any way without written permission by the author except in the case of brief quotations embodied in reviews or critical articles.

"God enters by a private door into every individual." - Ralph Waldo Emerson

"Each one prays to God according to his own light." - Mohandas Gandhi

"Those who believe they believe in God, but without passion in the heart, without anguish of mind, without uncertainty, without doubt, and even at times without despair, believe only in the idea of God, and not in God himself." - Miguel de Unamuno

"Do not believe in anything simply because you have heard it. Do not believe in anything simply because it is spoken and rumored by many. Do not believe in anything simply because it is found written in your religious books. Do not believe in anything merely on the authority of your teachers and elders. Do not believe in traditions because they have been handed down for many generations. But after observation and analysis, when you find that anything agrees with reason and is conducive to the good and benefit of one and all, then accept it and live up to it." - Buddha

"There are many paths to God, my son." - Balthazar, character in the novel and film *Ben Hur*.

"God is with you always. Simply turn your face to Him." - Kirpal Singh

"I believe that life is a journey towards God, and that no one has the right to insist that you go a certain road." - Pat Buckley

"Keep on seeking, and you will find. Keep on knocking, and the door will be opened to you. For everyone who asks, receives. Everyone who seeks, finds. And to everyone who knocks, the door will be opened." - Jesus

Dedicated to all those who long for God, seek God, sense God, and love God, yet have no culturally or religiously recognized name for that relationship. Don't feel you need a name. Don't think you must remain silent. Don't take to heart criticism from those who don't understand, who either ridicule you for believing or condemn you for not believing correctly. Rather, strive to live in the Light God is giving you – openly, honestly, kindly, and with understanding and compassion for the whole of humankind.

Contents

1. Hey There, Fellow Children of God.................................1

2. Concepts of God...21

3. Why Believe?..43

4. Here We Are: Often-Silent, Un-Churched
   Believers Speak Out..59

5. Religious Writings and Human Beings.......................113

6. Free Will and God's Will..141

7. Evolution, Human Sexuality, and other Sciencey Stuff....161

8. Mortal Bodies, Mortal Fears..................................179

9. Death and Beyond...197

10. Obeying, Worshipping, Praying, Meditating..............213

11. Carry On – Life With God....................................227

12. Prayers To God, From His Children........................233

1

Hey There, Fellow Children of God

The Shoulder Tap

As I start this book, I wonder if I'm walking onto a stage in front of a silent yet curious crowd, joining good friends for a chat and a chai, or barreling headlong into a gauntlet of hell-fire naysayers. I suppose I'll find out soon enough. What I do know is that for a while now, God has been tapping me on the shoulder and encouraging me to write this book.

Sure, I know. That will sound egotistical to certain readers. Delusional to some. Blasphemous to others. But when there is a tap on your shoulder, and you're sure it's God, you either go ahead with His suggestion or you shrug it off. So, having put it off for more than a year, I decided not to ignore it any longer. The sense of God's direction is startling and incredibly humbling. So okay, God. I feel Ya. I'm on it. And with Your help I'll do the best I can with this.

Deep breath.

Now when I say, "fellow children of God," I mean everyone. I believe in the Divine familial connection between all people. Believers, non-believers, interested, disinterested. If you aren't a believer, please don't be offended that I'm including you as one of God's children. I'm not trying to convert you. I'm not trying to convince you.

But first of all – really. Who the hell am I to write such a book? I'm no minister. I'm no pastor or preacher. No nun or rabbi or theology student or religious scholar or philosopher. No Sunday school teacher or evangelist or spiritual leader or mystic. I'm just an ordinary, introverted but sometimes outgoing, mostly optimistic but sometimes totally overwhelmed human being. I don't have the professional street cred to write a book on spirituality. I don't have the money to sail off on an *Eat, Pray, Love* worldwide journey of discovery or attend a seminar on religions in a beautiful tropical location. I don't have a year's worth of free time to retreat in the Rockies to meditate on the Holy. Rather, I'm a small town, in-the-trenches writer of a bunch of stuff that allows me piece together a living – horror novels and short fiction, media tie-in novels and novelizations, historical fiction for teens, a bit of mainstream fiction, one lone *Phantom* comic, a couple locally-produced plays, lots of poetry, a little bit of erotica under a pen name (yes, you read that right), and both fiction and nonfiction passages and lessons for major educational publishers.

Since much of my writing is classified as horror/suspense, I initially considered using a pseudonym for this book. I mean, a horror author writing about God's Love? Wouldn't that come across as uncomfortably weird or even flat-out wrong? At first I didn't think I was brave enough to test these waters with my real name, as much as a big part of me wanted to. Yes, I felt the need to share my thoughts on God and religion for a while now. But there stood that hurdle, that stumbling block – should I write as *me*? Wouldn't a book on religion be much more palatable, more acceptable coming from someone with a name not associated with scary fiction?

Maybe.

Maybe not.

My first venture into spiritual writing was a Facebook group called "Prayers to God, From His Children." I wrote this under the pseudonym, S.G. Freeman. I did so because I assumed people would roll their eyes at the idea of a group dedicated to praising and investigating God's Nature that had been created by someone who writes about, among other things, vampires and zombies and ghosts. It's not that I am ashamed of my professional writings. On the contrary, I have no issue writing horror. My horror fiction often explores the human condition, the deepest of human fears and longings, weaknesses and strengths, challenges and hopes. So, no apologies regarding my novels or stories. Still, yes, I *know* the reputation of horror. I've heard the complaints. There are people who lump it all together under the heading of "garbage" or "harmful fantasy" or even "sinful." Case in point: years ago I had a signing in a bookstore for my first novel, *Sineater*. It went fairly well. Those who had read my short fiction were chatty and friendly. Then a woman came up to the table and pointed to the stack of books. "Why do you write things like this?" she demanded. "You're just adding more horror to the world!" While I retained calm on the outside, I felt defensive on the inside. I asked as politely as I could, "Have you read any of my fiction?" She pursed her lips as if I'd asked her if she had ever eaten fried spiders. Then I said, "Not all horror is *Friday the 13th*. It's not all blood for blood's sake. There can be a lot more to it than that." She shrugged me off and walked away. The first of many similar reactions. Oh, well. As some would say, "Whaddaya gonna do?"

An Aside: Two Points of Clarification

One: While I write about them, I don't actually believe in skulking vampires or shambling zombies or hissing ghosts. I don't believe in shuffling mummies or snarling werewolves or possessive evil spirits. They can be fun to write about, though, with all that shambling and skulking and snarling. And they can represent some of the real problems faced by humankind. Through writing scary things, I can, as I prefaced my collection, *Sundown*, look "into the darkness to better understand the light."

Two: I'm not the only horror writer who has a sense of spirituality. Some seem quite devoted to their understanding of the Divine while others explore the Mysteries openly and earnestly. Some horror writers use religion and God as the evil, horrific elements themselves. Other horror writers, without preaching or proselytizing, explore the often devastatingly beautiful, agonized search for and connection to the Divine amid the terrors of the circumstance in which they find themselves. One of my favorite examples of the latter is Stephen King's novel *The Stand*. And, as some already know, horror fiction as a genre has its roots in religion – ancient terrifying tales were created to teach morals, explain the unexplainable, and to keep the flock in line. So horror fiction and religious beliefs have and do rub shoulders. It's nothing new.

Challenging Chats

Back to my earlier Facebook group, "Prayers to God, From His Children." It continued for a full year. I loved composing and posting daily prayers. I looked forward each day to sitting in the silence and letting a prayer form itself in my mind then posting it to share with the members. Some of the prayers dealt with loss or sadness. Some dealt with joy and hope. Some were prayers for strength or courage or enlightenment. Some were prayers of anguish and distress. Some were prayers for those who were suffering to find comfort, help, and peace, and for us to find compassion. There was warm feedback from the membership.

Yet as well as it was going, I felt kind of dishonest that I wasn't using my real name. After many months I came to realize that I shouldn't compartmentalize my life like that. I closed the group.

But the experience had opened a big question in my mind. Why, as someone who wants to be honest with herself and others and as someone who doesn't hesitate to speak out about social, humanitarian, or political issues that trouble me, would I be so reticent as to talk openly about my relationship with God?

Really, why?

I knew the answers. First, because religion is such an incredibly personal issue. And second (a very big second), as much as I feel moved by God in my life, I don't identify with the specifics of any particular religion. I'm an un-churched believer. That can be a strange spot to be in a world filled with religions. When there is no recognizable name for one's personal religion, there can arise skepticism and dismissiveness in those who can easily name their beliefs. And so on I went in my hopeful (clueless?) anonymity, even after I closed the Facebook prayer group.

Most people who have religious beliefs desire a community – large or small – made up of others who have very similar beliefs. Such a community can be comforting, uplifting, and encouraging. Such a community encourages sharing and offers affirmation to the believer. I was and am no different. And since I wanted religious conversation and community without giving out my identity, I became involved for a while in online religious chats. Using a screen name gave me a sense of freedom to say what I wanted and needed to say. I felt a little less dishonest because none of the sites or chats were ones I'd started; I was merely a participant.

So what did I hope to gain from sharing my views on those sites? As naïve as it sounds now, I thought I might find others who knew what I was talking about when I said I was religious but didn't follow a known religion. I wanted to say that I'd discovered that God is real. That God is Good. That God is Almighty. That God loves us. That God wants us to love and help one another.

But it was not such a great idea, those online chats. Can I get a loud "amen!" from those who know what I'm talking about? A "You said it, sister!" from un-churched believers who've also gone the online religious chat route in an attempt to discuss their ideas of God? Worlds collide on social media… people are no longer within their safe isolation. Atheists and agnostics and anti-theists and "nones" and churched and un-churched believers find themselves in a huge, cold glass jar, one we have actively sought out, crawled into, and shaken up ourselves.

One of the first things I discovered during my online religious community search was a blog by a devout Christian. This person was commenting on those who had once attended churches but no longer did. Among other things he posted: "Writing off organized religion because one does not want to put in the hard work of a diligent search for truth or make personal sacrifices does not get one any closer to God." There were numerous comments below that blog that agreed wholly with that assumption. And herein lies the dilemma. It is unfortunate, but some churched people cast un-churched believers in this dim light. They assume we are lazy, uncommitted, or unable to engage in that diligent search for the Divine without their specific religious structure or guidance. Or they believe we are just plain confused or deluded.

Sigh....

(Let it go, deep breath, *om*....)

It seems that online religious chats are more often than not forums for proclaiming, pronouncing, and attacking instead of discussing. For pounding pious chests and calling other people names. When, on any number of religiously themed chat threads, I mentioned loving God without embracing all of a particular religion's teachings, I was frequently blasted, called a heretic or a follower of Satan. I was told I'm going to Hell and was attempting to lead others into Hell with me. I was chastised for creating my own "god" and according to some folks the god I'd created was myself.

"You can't pick and choose what to believe," wrote one poster. "You either accept all the Bible or you must reject it all."

"You're a false prophet!" claimed another.

Then: "I'm glad to preach the Bible's truth to poor ignorant sinners like you."

And then: "Of course God hates! He hates some people and loves others. If you can't accept that, then go off to your New Age friends and have fun in Hell because God hates people like you!"

Devout online believers and adamant online non-believers alike have accused me of delusional, wishful thinking. Delusional, wishful thinking for believing that I could have a genuine, meaningful connection to our Creator without a set of specific theological guidelines. Delusional, wishful thinking there was a God in the first place.

As much as I was tempted (and oh, how I was tempted!) I didn't engage in reciprocal *ad hom* attacks. They're worthless and counter-productive. They only play into the hands of those who thrive on angry exchanges. But yes, the hatefulness caught me by surprise and my responses were sometimes terse. Jagged energy that was both painful and disconcertingly invigorating coursed through me. I'd dig the barbs out of my own hide and fight the urge to hurl them back. That kind of anger, that kind of snarkiness and arrogance generates its own form of addiction. It's a phenomenon that lives and grows well in the cyberspace hothouse. And, as I said, I felt its pull, too. Sometimes, after a particularly heated rash of comments on a religious thread, I'd lie in bed churned up inside, thinking of what I should have said or perhaps what I should not have said. Wondering what new responses I'd find when I looked again the morning, trying to construct my replies in my mind.

Now don't get me wrong. I *know*. Really, I do. I learned, and learned quickly. Such online discussions are an absolute waste of emotional, spiritual, and physical energy. I was under some illusion that I could make a difference or gain something by getting involved; that I could change someone's mind regarding the issue of un-churched believers. Yet however I responded – calmly or tersely – it didn't matter. In discussions like this no reply is right. No comment is correct or even tolerable regardless of how it is stated. It became clear that many who use online chats to talk about religion have no desire to discuss. They want a platform to lecture or make proclamations. They want to have their say and woe to those who disagree. Their negative energies are roused and rewarded through conflict. It's sad. These are children of God who are enthralled by the topic of God yet seem happier to share anger than to share love.

I wish I could say, "Nope, didn't bother me. I'm cool. I don't know them and they don't know me, so why should I care?" And really, why should I care? I didn't know them from Adam (or Eve. Or Steve). I shouldn't care. But I did. I cared because it *is* such a deeply personal, intimate topic. I'd put myself out there and was slammed.

You don't have to hit me with a brick. No matter *what* topic is discussed online, there are people who will become angry and hateful, or look to and hope to become angry and hateful. Religion. Politics. Music, movies, television shows, fashion, celebrities, art, you name it, it's rage-worthy. But I was seeking a place to talk about God in relative anonymity, and in doing so hopefully discover a few like-minded souls. I wasn't there to trash other people's religions but to find common ground.

Bottom line – I learned my lesson about getting involved in online religious chats/spats. I avoid them now, though I'll stumble upon something that makes me want to reply so very badly. I take some deep breaths, say a prayer, and move on.

Yet the desire to discuss my beliefs remained. When you experience something powerful and wonderful, you want to find out if others have experienced something similar. Aren't we meant to share, to talk and learn from one another, to draw closer to each other, to celebrate and mourn and wonder and rejoice together?

We aren't meant to lock away the beauty of our Divine discoveries, are we?

I don't think so.

Of course, there *are* people who boldly shout out their Divine discoveries. They sing about them in church choir lofts or preach them on street corners. They hand out paper tracts to passersby or hold prayer meetings in parks and coffee shops (this very moment, as I'm writing at a little table at our local Starbucks, two men next to me are having a lively discussion about the Bible). Some have "Jesus Loves You" bumper stickers on their cars. Some cry "Hallelujah!" from sanctuary pews or from seats in large convention halls. Some rock revival tents or television or radio stations or podcasts. Some sit on mountaintops with fellow worshippers and raise their hands heavenward in communal prayer. Some gather with fellow believers down by the riverside, singing and immersing and dancing in a public affirmation of their religious beliefs. Some chant. Some drum.

So why couldn't I express myself as openly as these folks (online chats aside)? Not to convert anyone but to just feel free to share it if I felt so moved? Why have I more often than not kept silent and anonymous? That age old answer: because I didn't want to be misunderstood. I didn't want to be judged or trounced or ostracized for not fitting into a particular category, for not following a particular spiritual pathway OR for expressing belief when many around me had no belief. Pathetic, I know. Fear made it hard for me to be open and honest about my God discoveries.

Ah, fear. That great stagnater. The great do-nothing enabler.

Well, pardon my French (apologies to the French...why do we say that, anyway?), but screw fear. It's time to put my religious life out there, openly, honestly, and kindly, not to evangelize or challenge any one else's relationships with God but to claim that part of my being and encourage others who have been hesitant to do the same. It's time to stop worrying about what others might say and to pay attention to the tap on my shoulder. It's time to answer the question, "Who am I to write a book about God?" with another question. "Why not me? Why not any of us who love Him? Why shouldn't we all be free to share our experiences with the Creator?"

Another Aside: A Point of Clarification

I've encountered some adults who feel the word "children," when applied to them, is insulting. A child, as is commonly defined, is someone who is not yet grown, someone who is unlearned and juvenile in actions, someone who needs guidance from an older, wiser figure, most often a parent or guardian. Using that common definition, I'm no longer a child. Most of you reading this are not children.

Yet a more specific definition of child is "the offspring of a parent." Every human who ever lived is someone's child. I'm my mother's child and will always be, even though she has passed away. My grown children are still and will always be my children.

So when I use the term "children of God," I'm referring to us as the offspring of God. All of us, every one of us. I'm not saying we're infantile idiots (though I do feel that way sometimes). Some of us (not myself included) are quite brilliant. But as brilliant as we might be, we still have much to learn. We can still benefit from God's Love and Guidance in our lives.

It's Okay to Say "God"

Those who, like me, have hesitated to share your "beyond the gates" belief in God, repeat after me:
"God, God, God, God, God, God."
Yeah, I know. Saying it out loud might feel uncomfortable. Some of us have avoided saying "God" because it is such an incredibly charged word. It holds so many meanings and draws out various reactions from so many people. Some good, some not so good. Some loving, some not so loving. Some see the name God as Truth, some see it as rubbish. There are those who love the

Name, finding in it acceptance, peace, joy, forgiveness, mercy, eternity, and the power of creation. There are those who despise the word, finding in it fantasy of the worst kind, dangerous, foolish, narrow-minded, delusional, and destructive. There are others who feel or see nothing; to them the word "God" is a harmless and meaningless term. Then there are those who see in it a combination of love and torment, judgment and forgiveness, heaven and hell. Author Richard Bach said, "Next to 'God', 'love' is the word most mangled in every language" which is sad for both words. Then there are others who don't care to discuss God because they feel God is too indescribable to even attempt a conversation. But if I am going to discuss God – if *we* who believe are going to discuss God – we have to at least be willing and able to say the Name.

"God, God, God, God, God."

Let's get used to it. Speaking it. Writing it. Reading it. Hearing it. Let's not let fear keep us from talking about a most real, most important aspect of our lives. This doesn't mean we *have* to say the name; it means we should be free to say it.

There are quite a few names for the One Who Made Everything. Most are religion-specific. For the purposes of this book, since it's not rooted in a particular religion, I'm going with the name God. Or the Creator. Or the Divine. But mostly God. He is our God, whether in or outside a house of worship. So we can and should be able to speak His Name.

Okay. Now let's say this word: "Religion."

"Religion, religion, religion, religion, religion."

I've struggled with that word, too. Like some others, there have been times that I have referred to myself as "spiritual, not religious." That is because the word "religion" has a lot of bad connotations, too. A *lot* of bad connotations. People who disdain religion have a long list of reasons to do so, and their disdain is understandable. Religions have created class and caste systems, have started wars, have burned dissenters at the stake, beheaded them, or torn them apart on the rack, have wiped out indigenous peoples while trying to convert them, have tried to interject their specific morals into governments even when those morals seem to fly in the face of fairness and equality. Yet religions have also built hospitals and schools, cared for the poor, the outcast, and the elderly. Religions have worked to end human rights abuses. Religions have fought against slavery in years gone by and today. Much like the word "God," "religion" strikes many different chords in many different people.

I've come to realize that, for me, "spiritual" doesn't really nail it down. I've come to realize that while I'm spiritual, I *do* have a religion. It might be a religion of one, but it's a religion. It might be an incredibly simple religion, but it is a religion. Other un-churched believers might still prefer to say "spiritual" rather than "religious" and of course they are right in their choice. But those who want to call their belief a religion must be able to do so without being corrected. No religion has a monopoly on that word. Once more with gusto:

"Religion, religion, religion, religion, religion."

So here I am, laptop in lap, preparing to share my beliefs with anyone who believes in God – the Almighty, All-Loving Creator of all there ever was, is, and ever will be – and who loves God but finds herself or himself outside mainstream religion. I'm here to assure you that you aren't the only one and to encourage you to share your views. I'm also here to share with anyone who is curious about those of us outside mainstream religion, with those who believe there can be no true connection to God beyond their particular mainstream religion, and with those who believe all religion is, as one of my friends once put it, a "gateway psychosis." We're on this world and in this life together. We might as well get to know each other a little better. Because in knowing and sharing lie the seeds of understanding. In understanding lie the seeds of patient kindness. In the seeds of patient kindness lie the seeds of peace.

I think peace is a good goal.

Churches and Me

I've done my share of religious exploration over the years, my share of digging, thinking, praying, reasoning, embracing, and releasing. I've been a sincere yet more often than not clumsy seeker, trying to grab Truth by its wildy-flapping hemline and hold on, trying to grasp the concept of God, to touch the Divine Mystery, and to find my connection to it all. I've been a member of Methodist and Presbyterian churches. I've had the chance to worship God in various Protestant churches and several Catholic churches. I've visited Jewish temples and an Islamic mosque. I've read and enjoyed reading about world religions and spiritual traditions. Once, while in Virginia Beach, I attended a free session at Edgar Cayce's Association for Research and Enlightenment (A.R.E.) where we jumped around in a circle and put our hands on each others' heads to offer energies and blessings. I spent a night in a chin-jabberingly cold Virginia mountaintop clearing, taking part in a women's drumming circle around a bonfire, attempting to open chakras, connecting with other women (not sure I opened any chakras, but I had fun so maybe I did). I purchased and completed quite a bit of *A Course in Miracles*. I joined a Unitarian Universalist Church and was an attending member for several years.

Each religious community, each spiritual pathway that I have encountered and explored has been a genuine blessing. They have much in common, even though there are some differing understandings about the Divine, about God. They've all offered something worth pondering, worth considering. Each explores, with a sense of wonder, the nature of the Creator. Each professes a desire to love Him and His creation.

Another Few Asides

First: I realize there are people who might take issue with my use of the word "understand." Some religions teach that we should not depend on our own understandings when it comes to issues about God, but rather the truth as it comes from Him. And I agree. Yet when God helps us understand something, when He moves us, individually and personally, it *becomes* our understanding, and so what can we call it other than our understanding? It was Galileo Galilei who said, "I do not feel obliged to believe that the same God who has endowed us with senses, reason, and intellect has intended us to forgo their use…" I believe God wants us and expects us to wonder, ponder, question, reason, and create in order to make our lives and the lives of others better. He opens our minds to understanding many things, not all of which are found in religious texts or scriptures. Our minds are amazing gifts, not empty bags waiting for another person, culture, or tradition (religious or otherwise) to fill for us. We should use them to consider the world and our actions, to examine what others want us to think. That is by no means saying we can't learn and benefit from the teachings of other people and traditions. We certainly can. But we shouldn't assume that everything another person or tradition teaches is wholly perfect and beyond questioning. We have a great deal to wrestle with as human beings. We always will. And when we view complex issues in the Light of Love, we can discover the best ways to approach and deal with them. God gives us guidance, which can come to us from many sources and through many personal experiences. We can then apply that guidance – that understanding – to our lives.

Second: I use the male pronoun when speaking of God. I do this because in my particular culture, God, more often than not, is referred to as He. I sometimes refer to Him as Father. However, I do not believe God is a man or is male. I also don't believe God is a woman or is female. God is Spirit, genderless, for why would He need gender? Gender is something God devised from the beginning of creation for most species that exist in the physical realm. Yet there is no pronoun that suitably captures the essence of God, so I use that which is most familiar and comfortable to me. I believe this is what most people do. (Oh, and I realize that at this particular time in history, some people are introducing new gender pronouns to use for people instead of the traditional "he" and "she" in order to be more inclusive. These suggested changes/additions have arisen due to the increased awareness of gender identity. The pronouns include "ze," "sie," '"e," "ou," and "ve." I'll be interested to see how this evolves.)

Third: When it comes to life, this very moment is all really we have. We can't go back to the past. We can't skip over into the future. We are in this moment. And this moment. And now this one. Now this one. Each moment is a chance to do something differently, to make a positive change, to get some rest, to exercise our bodies, to take note of the beauty around us, to speak and act out against hatred and cruelty.

Fourth: In this book I'm not dealing specifically with non-theistic or polytheistic spiritual systems or religions such as Buddhism or Hinduism. I respect these religions/traditions but need to keep the focus of this book straightforward and simple.

Back to Our Regularly Scheduled Program

I love God. I don't always follow His Will. Sometimes I ignore His whispered guidance and avert my eyes from the signs He clearly places in my path or on my heart. I often do stupid, thoughtless, selfish things and utter angry, thoughtless words. I get irritable and impatient. My feelings get hurt. I get depressed and weary and self-centered and scared. But I know He is here and He cares. Because of that I love Him as best I can.

There don't seem to be many books that talk about the all-knowing, all-powerful, all-loving monotheistic Creator that don't also bring in the specific teachings of Christianity, Judaism, or Islam. There are times that it feels as if these religions lay claim to the idea of God to the point that He cannot or should not be discussed outside their particular parameters, their particular teachings. On the other hand, it seems that books dealing with more "New Age" spiritual pathways don't often talk about God, or if they do He might be referred to more vaguely as the Source (understandably, as much of God is Mystery), the Higher Mind, or even the Universe. Some New Age spiritual movements see everything as God or each person as God or Goddess who seek to ascend from an illusion of the physical to the true, enlightened status.

So here I am. Too traditional to be New Age and too New Age to be traditional. But that's okay; I'm not big into labels because of the preconceived notions that come with them. Yet if we – those of us outside traditional monotheistic religions who do believe in one God – prefer some sort of title, how about "Now Age?" Those whose day-to-day lives are intimately influenced by their un-churched relationships with God, those who can find value in some of the "Old Age" inspirational teachings but who also believe that God is here now, in this moment, and He continues to reveal His Basic, Most Wonderful, Most Important Truth to us? Though I really don't mind being title-less.

The Basic, Most Wonderful, Most Important Truth of God, and Why We Should Cool Our Spiritual and Emotional Jets

My religious beliefs are simple: God is the Almighty Creator of all that ever was, is and ever will be, and He loves His creation with a profound, unconditional Love and it is His Will that we love and care for each other. This, I believe, is the Basic, Most Wonderful, Most Important Truth of God. And it's plenty. In fact, it's more than enough for a lifetime.

My research has shown that the major monotheistic religions have as a foundation this very same Basic Truth, even as some of their other teachings take different directions. I've also come to believe that God's Basic Truth is not meant to be complex or confusing. He doesn't intend us to turn ourselves inside out trying to grasp a thousand elusive sacred tidbits to piece together in order to find Him. We don't have to learn a secret handshake or password to gain His attention or His Mercy. We don't need to drop a breadcrumb trail through the forest for Him to find us. He is already there. He's already here. As close as our heartbeats, as near as our breaths. There isn't a private God Club in which only those with the one correct style of music or clothing or worship can take part. There is no one "Chosen People." We are *all* His family. We *all* exist through His Power and Love. The Basic Truth of God can be understood by the simplest mind and the most brilliant. It is accessible to all.

We, His children, are never forgotten and never unloved. He understands each of us perfectly. In spite of the dire struggles, pains, and troubles in this life, there are also incredible joys, wonders, and beauties. And this life is but a fraction of existence. There is more to Reality that we could ever fathom, more to the Power of God, His Love, and His Perfect Plan than we could possibly imagine, for the Whole of His Heart and Mind are beyond our comprehension. No one, not one single soul, was created for everlasting torment or oblivion, but to be part of God's Eternal, Beloved Family. He conceived and created us so we could have the opportunity to learn to love one another, care for one another, forgive one another, and come together with one another. We might not learn those lessons, but they are the lessons laid out for us. And God holds each of us in His thoughts at all times, from our beginnings, through our physical lives no matter how short or long, through our deaths and our emergence into Eternity with Him.

However, as beautiful as the Reality of God is or how much the major religions agree on the Basic Truth of God, the topic of God can flare hot and emotional, whether the discussion is over the phone, through the mail, through any of the various social media venues, or in person.

It's happened between me and other believers in person.

Painful. Frustrating. Sad.

Most likely, if you live in the USA, at some point in your life you've heard a rap on the door and peeked out the window to see someone representing a particular religion standing there. You may choose to not answer the door (turn down the TV, hide in the bathroom, dim the lights, get real quiet, or just pretend no one is knocking). In that case, a tract or magazine might be tucked into the door and the rappers will move on. If you choose to open the door, you might likely find one or more smiling faces. They may hand you that tract or magazine and then pose a leading question or ask directly if they can share their religious views with you. They may ask to pray with or for you. They have a relationship with God and want to spread the word. I understand that. God bless them in their dedication. Yet, if you tell them you don't share their religion or tell them you have no religion at all, or if you try to create a conversation rather than listen to the monologue, things might get awkward or uncomfortable.

I live in the country in the Shenandoah Valley of Virginia. Rolling Blue Ridge Mountains to the east, Appalachian Mountains to the west. Beautiful. Up the road not quite a mile from our house is a little Mennonite church. Members of this church have stopped by our house several times. They were pleasant, smiling, not so much wanting to talk but to get their church's magazine into my hands. The first few times (even though I'm not big on door-to-door solicitations; I tend to be the "ignore the rapping" type) I opened the door, took their magazines, and wished them a nice day. They wished me one, too, and went on their way. I didn't even glance at the first few magazines. After one visit, however, I sat down and gave the magazine a thorough read-through. There were some sweet, uplifting, love-based articles in the little 12-page publication. Short retellings of Bible stories complete with illustrations. Some compassionate thoughts on caring for one's neighbor.

But then there was an article explaining why women shouldn't insist on more rights than were spelled out for them in the Bible. They shouldn't preach, they should accept their husband's role as the leader of the family, should not ask questions during church service but should wait and ask their husbands at home. There was also an article that claimed the Bible could be proved by science and that the concept of evolution came from Satan.

Hmm....

Now, these church people seemed to be very nice folks, happy, not angry or pushy. But we definitely had different views on some things.

So I sat down and wrote them a letter. I told them I love the fact that they help their neighbors and raise money by selling handmade quilts and then sending the money to various orphanages overseas. I told them I celebrate their love of God and their desire to share His love with others. I meant it. I still mean it. Then I pointed out, as kindly but clearly as I could, that while we love the same God, there are some aspects that we see differently. I told them that my understanding was that God created us – all human beings – equally, and while our sex might dictate our reproductive capabilities, it didn't determine our abilities or talents when it came to what we accomplished inside or outside the home; that I believe we should embrace what God has given us and use it to benefit our family, friends, neighbors, and the world as much as possible. I also explained that I accept the scientific evidence that states the Universe and the world were made over a period of billions of years, and that I believe life evolved under the guidance of God's Great Hand. Then I said that I realized they wouldn't agree with me and that was okay. I also kindly stated there was really no need for them to share more magazines with me and I wished them a pleasant day. I looked the church's address up in the phone book, stuck the letter in an envelope, and sent it on its merry way.

The letter came back a week later. Seems this church has no mail receptacle on site. I put the unopened envelope into my desk drawer.

I forgot all about it until two months later on a sunny spring morning when I was out in my side yard digging patches to plant beans and watermelons. Up the gravel driveway came a dark sedan. It slowed and stopped beside me. It was the preacher from the Mennonite church and his wife. Very cheerful, very happy, waving. The two started to get out of the car to give me another magazine. I held up my hand and said, "Wait, please. I have a letter I tried to mail you. I'll go get it and be right back." The man continued to smile but the two remained in their car.

I found the letter, brought it outside, and handed it to the preacher through the driver's window. He took it and then held out the newest church magazine. I said, "No thank you. But please read the letter. It explains that I respect your religion but we have some differing views about God. You don't really need to bring me any more of your church literature."

His expression changed immediately, the smile falling away. His wife's face tensed. In a surprisingly forceful voice (the preacher in him rising up, maybe?), he said, "There are things in here that are important for everyone to know and follow."

I could feel the adrenalin stirring in my arms. I don't care for confrontation. I said, "We have some different understandings about God. I'm sorry, but I don't need to read your magazine." And yes, I know, I probably sounded a bit strained at that moment. Then I added, "My sister, who lives at the end of the driveway, feels the same way I do. We do respect your views but don't agree with all of them. So you don't need to go there, either."

The preacher ignored me. He and his wife drove up to my sister's house with their church magazines. A couple minutes later they came back down past our house. I was digging in the yard again but stopped to wave at them, to try to make a little peace. The preacher and his wife just stared at me in passing and kept on going. They haven't been back.

I hated feeling a sense of bad blood between believers. I honestly didn't want to create tension. But it was there. They felt it. I felt it.

Ugh.

And, of course, as I mentioned earlier, there are those online flare-ups between believers, those "You're wrong and will burn!" and those "Believe what you will at your own peril, moron!" And on and on and on.

Yet back during the time in which I was involved with those online religious discussions there appeared, in the midst of one heated, especially unpleasant, discourse on religion, a lone post: "I was accused of atheism on another thread because I don't consider myself Christian. This is not true at all. But no one is listening."

Oh, wow! Yes! Hi there! I recognize you, you likewise-anonymous poster, you! You might recognize me, too.

It was a relief. I felt an affirmation. I wasn't the only one looking up, loving God, yet standing outside the gates of the houses of worship. And while those of us beyond the gates may have various understandings on some of the particulars, many of us want to be reassured that it's all right and safe to express our beliefs openly, honestly, and joyfully. We need to know that God doesn't expect us to hide and keep silent. That doesn't mean we want or need to proselytize or hand out magazines.

Now, I'm not posturing for a debate. I'm not throwing down a gauntlet or drawing a line in the sand. I'm not goading anyone into an argument. (And I won't be taking part in any more online religious chats, that's for freakin' sure!) I am not asking anyone else to embrace my understandings of God. I'm writing this book to share my spiritual journey to this point, to explain how the Divine Creator has influenced my views and has instructed my life so far, and to reach out to other un-churched believers as well as those curious about us. Your journey may be similar to mine and it may be very different. That's fine. I want you to feel free enough about your own relationship with God – if you have one – to talk or write about it. I want people to know that we don't have to have a theological degree to have a theology, to have a church to have a religion, and we should be able to share openly.

And please – let's cool our spiritual and emotional jets. Let's find our commonness and stop focusing on the differences. To nonbelievers and believers alike I'm pleading: "We are brothers and sisters, we are of the same family on this beautiful, mysterious, terrifying, glorious world. Let's try to act like it."

A Prayer

Dearest God,

We lift in prayer all Your Beloved children. They are our dear brothers and sisters, placed upon this world with us to live, to learn, to grow, to love and be loved. There is not one who is without great value to You – the wealthy, the successful, the poor, the downtrodden, the lovable and those who seem unlovable. The woman hauling water, the child riding a bike. The boy forced to carry a gun, the politician struggling to decide what is right. The man left in the gutter as he clutches a bottle, the young actress on the screen. The old lady next door with all the pets. The old man fumbling with his wallet in the grocery store line. The addict selling drugs. The nurse comforting the dying. Every single person who lives, has lived, or will live, is Yours. Let us remember this. Help us treat them as You would have us treat them. Keep them in Your Care, Compassionate Lord. And help us do our part in sharing Your Amazing Love.

Amen.

2

Concepts of God

First of All – What We Can't Know

Ever been hanging out in a public area – coffee shop, park, library, bus – and overheard people's conversations about religion? I spend a good amount of time at our local Starbucks. My husband, Cortney, and I go there for what I call "mini vacations" so we can work and relax and look at something other than our own four walls. A coffee shop is a fascinating place, where people meet for first dates, to discuss business, to write or sketch, to have quick lunch-hour birthday parties, to work on something-or-other, and sometimes to have Bible study groups.

Not long ago, when we were at our local Starbucks (a quick aside: we love the people who work at our Starbucks!), I became aware of two men several tables away. They were backing and forthing about the tenets of Calvinism and Arminianism, both Christian theological belief systems with some ideas in common and others quite different. Both of these systems attempt to explain the relationship between God's Sovereignty and human responsibility or role in the matter of salvation. A very intense yet civil discussion between these two guys, one who looked to be in his mid-twenties and the other who was more likely in his late forties.

At another time, in this same Starbucks, I overheard portions of a solemn discussion between a young couple (soon to be married) and their minister. The minster was quietly yet clearly instructing the bride as to her upcoming responsibilities as a Christian wife.

And then there are the Bible study groups – sometimes teens, other times two or three adults pouring over scripture while sipping a coffee or tea.

When religious discussions are going on at Starbucks or elsewhere and I'm close enough to hear, I listen in as subtly as I can. I can't help myself. Okay, I can help myself but I don't want to. I want to hear what other people believe. I want to hear how they explain their beliefs to each other, how passionate they might be or not be about them. It could be that they relay a bit of timely wisdom that I need, and I don't want to miss that. It may be that they pose questions about God that I've never considered myself or they may say something that drives me crazy. And so I try to listen in. Some of these people speak with utter confidence and assurance regarding the Creator. Others speak as if they have many uncertainties regarding God and His Great Mysteries.

I've come to believe and remain convinced that at the core of the various monotheistic religions (with, sadly, a few such as Westboro Baptist Church excluded), is the belief that God created all there ever was, is, or will be, that He loves His creation, and it is His will for us to love, too. As mentioned earlier, I believe that is the Basic, Most Important Truth of God. It is the Foundation. And it is available to all of us. It's what we can know.

Yet there is much we can't know.

There may be some who claim to understand the whole of God and therefore feel competent to argue any religious or spiritual issue. If there are such people, bless them; I can imagine that such a sense of certainty would be a comfort. Yet such knowledge is impossible. None of us – *none* – have the full picture of God. None of us – *none* – have the capacity to hold and comprehend the entire Truth, Wisdom, and Power of God in our hearts, minds, and/or souls. We will seek and we will find. Absolutely. God will share with us what we need. Yet there is much about the Divine that is impossible to fathom, to comprehend.

Try this and you might understand what I mean:

Imagine a blade of grass. Any blade of grass in any yard, field, or crack in the pavement. You can see it. You can feel it, smell it, taste it (if you're into licking grass blades, not necessarily recommended), and listen to it rustle in the wind. You are aware of that grass. You can focus intently on that grass. But can you see its inner workings? Can you see the water moving through the xylem, water necessary for the grass blade's life? Can you see the process of photosynthesis that is going within the chlorophyll-containing cells; can you see the conversion of water and carbon dioxide and the sun's energy into food for that blade of grass? Perhaps you could witness this process, or part of it, if you could put a slice of the blade under a microscope.

Okay, now. Imagine a couple blades of grass beside the first one, three or four, maybe. Can you, at the same time, be completely aware of what is going on inside those blades at the same time?

Add, now, all the other blades of grass in a field or yard to the picture. Every single one of them. Can you see them all at one; can you be aware of each and every one, individually, at the same time? Can you witness and comprehend the inner workings of them all at the same time?

Next, bring in all the trees that surround the yard or field. Can you know the workings of all those trees and all those blades of grass at the same time? Can you be clearly and consciously aware of each and every one of those plants, what is happening to each and every one of them simultaneously? Can you know each leaf that is ready to fall and each bud that is preparing to open? Can you know which cells are damaged by insects, which plants are ready to die, and which seeds, underground, are preparing to sprout and burst through the soil?

Now include all the animals in that tree-surrounded field or yard. Each earthworm, each flea, each ladybug, each cricket, snake, chipmunk, squirrel, slug, ant, robin, chickadee, snail, mole, vole, mosquito, mouse, spider, centipede, millipede, tick, and groundhog that live there. Can you hold each and every animal in your mind at the same time? Can you have a conscious awareness of each hair on each mammal? Each and every scale on each reptile? And what of each claw, chitinous leg, or antennae, each mandible, thorax, abdomen, eye, or wing on each insect? Can you know all the experiences each one of those animals has had during its lifetime? And are you able to hold each and every animal as well as every plant in your mind at the same time, understanding the inner workings of them all at the same time, clearly, perfectly?

Next come the soil and rocks and minerals in that field or yard. Can you comprehend the existence of every molecule of humus, topsoil, and subsoil in your mind at the same time, in addition to the plants and animals, and all with perfect understanding? Can you know how long each pebble and rock has existed it its form and when it will break down and join the soil? Can you know each and every microbe in the soil, how long it has lived, how long it will live? Can you be consciously aware of every molecule of air that blankets the field and trees? And every molecule of water as it rains onto the ground, is absorbed, is used and released by the living things and then returns to the sky through evaporation?

And now expand that to every field, desert, mountain, forest, and ocean of the world, and every living and non-thing – each and every grain of sand on each and every ocean beach, every drop of water in every river, the mists in the rainforests and glaciers in the tundra, every parrot and penguin, crow and cardinal, gorilla and guinea pig, poison ivy plant and pansy flower, every mite, euglena, cedar spore, tumbleweed, bristlecone pine, redwood tree, giant panda, poodle, salamander, scorpion, man, woman, teen, child, infant. Can you hold each and every one of these things in your mind at the same time and be completely and consciously aware of them all in that same time? Not only be aware of them, but also understand their workings, their beginnings, their endings, and their transitions...all in the same moment? What of the atmosphere? Each breeze, rainstorm, cloud formation. Every snowfall, hail fall, tornado, and hurricane.

Now include all the planets of our solar system and our sun. Add all the planets and moons and suns and black holes and quasars and pulsars and other space matter of our spiral galaxy. Now include all the galaxies and all the space between the galaxies.

And now any other universes that might exist? Can you hold everything in your mind at the same time with perfect understanding of the workings of each and everything thing – minute and large, living and non?

Then can you know active consciousness of all sentient creatures in the Universe/Multiverse at any given moment, each and every one? Can you know the thoughts of each one, hear the cries and shouts of joy of each one? Do you hear and understand every prayer, those uttered aloud and those uttered in the heart?

Can you also know what has occurred during any and every moment of creation, everything that has come and gone, and everything that will come and go, from the beginning of time until eternity? Can you know, even, what was before time existed?

If you are able to do all of that then you are coming closer to understanding God's Mind and Power. But then there are several final and important questions.

Do you know without a doubt the truth behind the beginning of creation, every detail of the when, why, and how it occurred under God's Great Hand? Can you understand creation as God understands creation, exactly how He has formed and fashions all that is – all the matter and energy, all the non-living things and all the organisms of amazing variety and complexity? Do you know how to infuse evolving, living beings with a consciousness, inquisitiveness, individuality, and creative drive? Do you know how to create souls that will leave mortal bodies at death to join the Divine in the beauty of eternity?

Some naysayers see the concept of God as a crutch – petty, silly, and childish. Yet there is nothing more intellectually, emotionally, and spiritually profound than encountering God. For there is nothing more powerful, intelligent, wise, and profound than God. The most brilliant human being, should she encounter the Wonder of God, would be awed into silence. Pit the brightest human intellect against Him and that intellect is miniscule.

Since it's impossible for humans to comprehend the whole of God's Incredible, Mysterious Mind, arguments claiming to know it all are futile. Such arguments only drive people apart when we should be finding paths to each other. But come on, it's *okay* that we don't know it all. Really, truly okay. God reveals Truths to us in various ways. What He offers us is enough to fill us to overflowing, more than enough to inspire us, guide us, and encourage us. More than enough to amaze and startle and teach and trouble and comfort us in the most incredible of ways. The more we open to our Creator, the more we can know Him. In our lifetimes – or in a million lifetimes – we could never grasp all that God is. And that's all right. He's God. We're not. He is the Creator. We are His creation. He is the Glorious Holy. We are the beloved, creative, intelligent, talented, powerful, inquisitive, empathetic, determined, insightful chosen beings whom He Adores without reservation.

The Rainforest, the Tundra, and the Sunset

Flip through a phone book (there are still phone books, aren't there?) or browse online and you'll find listings for tons of different churches and houses of worship. God-lovers around the world (and around the Universe/Multiverse as well, since I have no doubt we Earthbound humans don't make up the whole of God's family) hold varied concepts of the Creator beyond the Basic, Most Important Truth of God. There are so many believers and so many understandings of the Divine. Even within certain religions, denominations, and individual churches, there are those whose ideas vary on one or more issues from what is preached to the flock.

So, how could so many concepts of God possibly be on a right path? How can people who truly love God and feel His Love for them not have the exact same religious views yet still be all right?

Imagine that long ago, before mass communication was the norm, there were two young boys. One lived in the steaming, lush rainforest, surrounded by dense and shimmering trees, fragrant flowers, cascading streams sparkling with sunlight, colorful fruits, and brilliantly-plumed birds perched in tall branches. The other boy lived in the snowy tundra, a region of breathtaking treeless stretches, of beautiful craggy mountain peaks, vast blue skies, tiny rugged plants emerging in the brief summer warmth, and thickly furred animals that migrated with the seasons. Neither boy had travelled from his homeland nor seen pictures of any places beyond his own.

One day, a woman, out on adventure, arrived in the rainforest. She asked the boy to write a letter she could take with her – a letter describing the world. The boy did as he was asked. The woman then traveled to the tundra. She met the boy who lived there and asked him to write a letter she could take with her – a letter describing the world. The boy did as he was asked.

Then the woman gave the letter written by the boy in the rainforest to the boy in the tundra. The boy of the tundra read the letter and scoffed. "This isn't the world at all!" he said. "The boy who wrote this made up something he wants the world to be, not as the world really is! Warm rains, tall trees, and large blooming flowers? There are no such things! Ridiculous!"

"But wait," said the woman. "Is there anything in the letter that you recognize?" The boy studied the letter carefully then said, "He states that the world is beautiful, mysterious, and good, and it provides what is needed to live. I know that is true."

The woman went back to the rainforest and gave the boy who lived there the letter written by the boy in the tundra. The boy read the letter and sneered. "What a fool, to pretend that is how the world is! He has invented an imaginary, fanciful world of drifting ice, treeless plains, and white-topped mountains. He is deluding himself!"

"Is there something in the letter that you recognize?" asked the woman. The boy studied the letter then said, "He states that the world is beautiful, mysterious, and good, and it provides what is needed to live. I know that is true."

The boy in the rainforest wasn't wrong. This is how he understood the world. And it was wonderful and familiar to him, comforting and right, and not at all fanciful. The boy in the tundra wasn't wrong. This is how he understood the world. And it was wonderful and familiar to him, comforting and right, and not at all fanciful.

Most importantly, both boys recognized a great, most important truth – that the world was beautiful, mysterious, and it provided what they needed to live.

Someday these boys may venture from their homes and gain new and wider understandings of the world, and will add that to what they already know. They will explore and experiment, observe, question, challenge, and accept, dismiss, and learn. No matter how much they discover on their travels, they will never know it all. Neither could completely comprehend the whole of the world, the whole of creation. But they will grow in wisdom and understanding.

Ever since the early prehistoric persons were struck by an awareness of the Divine, people have wondered and worshipped, prayed and petitioned, sought and sat in quiet contemplation of the Source of creation. Yet as similar as our seekings might be, it should be no surprise that we experience certain aspects of God differently from each other. It makes rational sense that there would be various concepts of God, keeping in mind the differences in our temperaments, personalities, sensibilities, intelligences, senses of curiosity and skepticism (He created us with such variations, right?) as well as our upbringings, education, experiences, cultures, and families. He reveals His Truth to us on our most intimate, most personal levels, reaching into the deepest fibers of our being. What an amazing, glorious realization. He does not speak to us in a foreign language or secret code. And God is available to every single soul, right here, right now. He offers a true, Divine Breath of Fresh Air to each as he is, as she is, who she is, who he is, where he is, where she is. The Reality of God is so Glorious that it sweeps us up in awe, wonder, and knocks us down in perplexity and astonishment.

Here is another way to look at how we perceive God.

Three women stood on a hillside to watch the sunset. One said, "How beautiful and peaceful it is! How powerful and inspiring! Such a beautiful shade of red!"

A second woman said, "How beautiful and peaceful it is! How powerful and inspiring! Such a beautiful shade of orange!"

The third woman said, "How beautiful and peaceful it is! How powerful and inspiring! Such a beautiful shade of yellow!"

For whatever reason, the women detected and understood the colors differently. Perhaps their unique vantage points, side by side on the hill, created a different view through the atmosphere, the shifting air. Perhaps the cones and rods in each woman's eyes detected colors differently. Yet in spite of this, they all agreed on the beauty and wonder of the sunset. Each identified and appreciated the sunset's most important, simple, powerful truth.

If God had wanted us all to be exactly the same, He would have made us exactly the same. We are all of one family, all equally valuable, equally loved, and equally important to our Creator. Yet we all have our differences, too – physically, emotionally, mentally, environmentally, and experientially. God is well aware of this. Why wouldn't He be?

Sincere believers the world over honor, love, and praise God. They do this in numerous ways, in various rituals or prayers or practices that speak most deeply and truly to their hearts and souls. The earnest faith and adulation offered God by adherents of the many religions, denominations, and spiritual traditions should not be ignored or discounted. Most of them, most of *us*, who love God agree on the Basic, Most Wonderful, Most Important Truth of God – the bottom line – and that is that He loves. He *loves*. Sharing love is the reason He created. And it is His will that we strive to love, too.

I'm not trying to form a new religion. I am not attempting to call anyone from his or her unique and personal relationship with God, but rather to affirm that God is God of *all*. God comes to us and we come to Him in ways we understand, ways that connect us to His Joy, His Comfort, His Challenges, His Love, His Forgiveness, His Peace, His Guidance, His Miracles, His Assurances, His Power, and His Glory.

The Church That Love Built

This may sound strange, but even though I don't attend one and haven't for many years, I love churches. I love houses of worship. I really, truly do. When I pass a church on the street, I feel a pull toward it. I feel an appreciation, a joy that God is loved, honored, and sought in such places. Some churches are visually awe-inspiring, with towers, stained glass windows, arched doorways, and steeples that speak to an artist's, architect's, or congregation's desire to glorify God through the beauty of the structure. Others are more plain, perhaps a small wooden structure, perhaps a storefront, with a dignified simplicity that echoes the love of those who gather there. Sensibilities and finances dictate a house of worship's exterior. It is the people who attend that make it what it really is. I love that people love God.

There are quite a few recognized monotheistic religions, sects, and denominations across the globe, enough to make you go, "Hey, wow!" They include:

- Judaism. In the United States, there are four main branches of Judaism - Orthodox, Conservative, Reform, and Reconstructionist.
- Islam. There are two main branches of Islam - Sunni and Shi'a.
- Sikhism.
- Yazidism.
- Christianity. There are many churches and denominations of Christians. A sampling follows:
- Adventist
- Anglican
- Baptist (Southern, Primitive, and Independent)
- Brethren
- Catholic
- Church of Christ
- Church of God
- Congregational
- Episcopalian
- Jehovah's Witness
- Latter Day Saint/Mormon
- Lutheran
- Mennonite
- Methodist (United and Free)
- Moravian
- Orthodox (Coptic, Greek, Georgian, Ethiopian, Romanian, Russian, Serbian, Latvian, Ukranian, and more)
- Pentecostal
- Presbyterian (Presbyterian Church USA, Evangelical Presbyterian, and Reformed)
- Quaker/Friends

Salvation Army
Swedenborgian
Wesleyan

Several reliable resources I've found have listed thousands of Christian denominations, many of which are independent breakaways from the larger, more readily recognized churches.

So would God, who made us and understands us to the deepest cores of our beings, look at the God-loving house of worship on one street corner with more favor and affection than he looks at the God-loving house of worship on the next street corner? Does He turn up His nose or condemn the sincerely offered, soul-deep songs or practices or prayers of one while loving and honoring the songs or practices or prayers of the other? No. God isn't a God of churches. He is not a God of families, cites, regions, or nations. He's the God of individual *people* first and foremost. He doesn't lump us together and then condemn or condone us in groups. Yes, God loves when we come together to offer our gratitude, to share our experiences of Him, and to encourage each other to follow Him by loving and caring for each other. But He does not embrace one house of worship over another.

I find it very sad that members of one house of worship will point their fingers at members of another house of worship – one that teaches the love of God and love for humankind – and swear that the others are sorely deceived, apostate, or Hell-bound. It seems that people are so in need of "others" to make ourselves feel "in-the-right," to give ourselves a sense of community with an enemy at the gates, that we miss the humanity of those we don't know well or know at all. I shake my head in despairing wonder as one group of people who love God turn their backs in anger, mistrust, offense, and even hatred when faced with another group who loves God but has varying understandings of Him.

I don't know all the details of these churches – the particulars of their worship services, their creeds, their interpretations of various scriptures or religious writings, or their ceremonies and rituals. But it seems that if time, effort, and finances went into building and maintaining these churches then there is a sincere desire and drive behind those efforts. There was or still remains a yearning to come together before God to honor Him and to then leave the building and share that experience with others through loving behaviors. And again, that is the bottom line.

I've no doubt that many church-going, God-loving people are truly inspired by the particular religions they embrace. As congregations and as individuals, they feel the pull toward the Divine and are awed by the experience. The variations don't threaten God. However, they seem to threaten some people. And so I asked members of people of various religions a simple question. It was my hope that the answers would reveal the deep, genuine reverence that can be felt by members of different religions. It was my hope that with these answers we can discover the common thread among us.

My question was: "What is one teaching, song, tradition, passage, prayer, or ritual in your faith that you, personally, find to be especially wonderful, inspiring, and uplifting?" Some who agreed to answer wanted to share more than one thing. Wonderful! Thank you! In some cases the responses were nearly entire chapters themselves, so I had to trim a bit, yet the passion and points remain intact. Here are the replies:

Giana, a member of the Church of Jesus Christ of Latter Day Saints, said: "I am certainly not perfect and fall short but I try really hard. Women are special in the eyes of God and his Son, Jesus Christ. We, the women, have a specific role on this earth. It can work with career women; it's harder for them but it can work. There are so many women today who must work or chose to work but both can be done together with lots of dedicated effort.

"I was taught a song in Jr. Sunday School. I sang it to my children and now to my grandchildren. At night when I have turned out the light I sing this song to help me go to sleep. 'I am a child of God and He has sent me here, has given me an earthly home with parents kind and dear. Lead me, Guide me, Walk beside me, Help me find the way. Teach me all that I must do to live with Him some day.' The message brings such peace to my soul and to my grandchildren."

Amira, an Egyptian member of the religion of Islam, said: "I love Islam because Allah forgives us for whatever we've done. We just have to pray for his forgiveness. Allah doesn't ask us for perfection! All kinds of people will be blessed if they obey Allah. Islam appreciates women and doesn't prefer men to women, for Allah has said, 'Paradise lies under the feet of mothers.' I love that we all are weak and our fates are determined by Allah but we must choose our ways, whether bad or good things. There are many things to tell you about Islam but I don't know the meaning in English."

Keith, a Baptist, replied: "One of the many Biblical passages that mean a great deal to me is Romans 8:28, penned by the Apostle Paul, which says: 'And we know that all things work together for good to them that love God, to them who are the called according to His purpose.' I find this portion of scripture to be especially encouraging, and use it as an anchor to steady my faith and feelings, particularly when the storms of life occur. It is here that I am reminded that my Heavenly Father – the God of Abraham, Isaac and Jacob – will take all circumstances and incidents, both good and bad, and use them for my ultimate good and development. I can know, through confidence in God's Word, that He never gives up on me and takes a personal interest in my life. He's forever molding me – slowly and surely – into what He wants me to be. Even when things are hard, or when I make missteps and poor decisions, God is here. That, for me, is comforting."

Janice Marie, a Lutheran minister, said: "Like you, I am appalled and saddened by the ways that 'Christians' judge or even attack others who believe in the same Lord and Savior, Jesus Christ. I've been a recipient of this condemnation more than once. In fact, I've told people that I've been 'damned to Hell' more times than I can count. I've been accused of being unchristian because I don't 'believe' that – fill in the blank (homosexuality, abortion, birth control, women as pastors, etc.) – is sin condemned by God and will lead to eternal damnation. I've been rebuked as apostate when I express my views about the authority of the scriptures (I don't interpret the scriptures literally) or about how only God has the authority to judge whether a person is 'saved' or not, and the God I believe in is more grace-full than any of us humans can imagine.

It's interesting that these condemnations have actually made my faith and sense of purpose stronger. When someone decides that I'm a lost cause, I smile and say, 'We may disagree on this, but I believe in a God of love and forgiveness. Regardless of how you feel about me, Jesus loves you and died for you. In Christ, you are my sister/brother, and I love you and will pray for you.'

"Now to your question: My favorite Bible passages are (key verses highlighted):

John 1:1-14

1 In the beginning was the Word, and the Word was with God, and the Word was God.
2 He was in the beginning with God.
3 All things came into being through him, and without him not one thing came into being. What has come into being
4 in him was life, and the life was the light of all people.
5 The light shines in the darkness, and the darkness did not overcome it.
6 There was a man sent from God, whose name was John.
7 He came as a witness to testify to the light, so that all might believe through him.
8 He himself was not the light, but he came to testify to the light.
9 The true light, which enlightens everyone, was coming into the world.
10 He was in the world, and the world came into being through him; yet the world did not know him.
11 He came to what was his own, and his own people did not accept him.
12 But to all who received him, who believed in his name, he gave power to become children of God,
13 who were born, not of blood or of the will of the flesh or of the will of man, but of God.
14 And the Word became flesh and lived among us, and we have seen his glory, the glory as of a father's only son, full of grace and truth.

Romans 3: 20-24
20 For 'no human being will be justified in his sight' by deeds prescribed by the law, for through the law comes the knowledge of sin.

21 But now, apart from law, the righteousness of God has been disclosed, and is attested by the law and the prophets,
22 the righteousness of God through faith in Jesus Christ for all who believe. **For there is no distinction,**
23 since all have sinned and fall short of the glory of God;
24 they are now justified by his grace as a gift, through the redemption that is in Christ Jesus.

Romans 8:31-39
31 What then are we to say about these things? If God is for us, who is against us?
32 He who did not withhold his own Son, but gave him up for all of us, will he not with him also give us everything else?
33 Who will bring any charge against God's elect? It is God who justifies.
34 Who is to condemn? It is Christ Jesus, who died, yes, who was raised, who is at the right hand of God, who indeed intercedes for us.
35 Who will separate us from the love of Christ? Will hardship, or distress, or persecution, or famine, or nakedness, or peril, or sword?
36 As it is written, "For your sake we are being killed all day long; we are accounted as sheep to be slaughtered."
37 No, in all these things we are more than conquerors through him who loved us.
38 For I am convinced that neither death, nor life, nor angels, nor rulers, nor things present, nor things to come, nor powers,
39 nor height, nor depth, nor anything else in all creation, will be able to separate us from the love of God in Christ Jesus our Lord."

Mary Jane, a life-long Catholic, said: "I had to sit back and think about it for a while because the feelings are so tender. Being a cradle Catholic I was brought up with a certain structure that didn't always make it easy to have questions. I really did love the faith I was in though there just were so many changes happening post Vatican II. I saw how my father struggled with changes from his childhood and it wasn't always easy for me to know what to think. I guess all of us growing up in any faith have these questions and it takes a lifetime to sort them out.

"I knew I wanted to remain in my Catholic faith because I saw what peace it brought my sweet grandmother. She didn't have a lot of education but found so much peace in her prayer life and her devotion to Mary. I wanted to have that. So, now years later I think what wraps me up safely in my faith is that I know wherever I might be what ever country whatever time of day if I happen to stop into a Catholic Church for Mass even if I don't know the language the Mass is always the same format. The Mass is the same everywhere. That gives me a very peaceful feeling. It makes me feel happy. It makes me feel refreshed and ready to live and love another day. I also feel that the priests I have sought out on my somewhat bumpy journey have filled me with the belief that God is the one who knows what is in our hearts, and our faith is a very personal part of our being. I find that continuing in the faith of so many generations of my family has been the very best path for me. And I find peace in the traditions and rituals of the Catholic Church too. They can be so lovely."

Jon, who is Jewish, said that one thing he found to be most inspiring is: "Mi Sheberach, the prayer for healing. Here you have a community of individuals praying for people they don't even know, which, to me, is touching and beautiful when experienced in a crowd of say 30 - 100 people. Here it is:
    Mi shebeirach avoteinu
    M'kor hab'racha l'imoteinu
    May the source of strength,
    Who blessed the ones before us,
    Help us find the courage to make our lives a blessing, and let
        us say, Amen.
    Mi shebeirach imoteinu
    M'kor habrachah l'avoteinu
    Bless those in need of healing with r'fuah sh'leimah,
    The renewal of body, the renewal of spirit,
    And let us say, Amen
"In thinking about it, I think another reason it resonates with me is that my high school best friend died of HIV when I was in graduate school in Texas. He died alone and unloved, ostracized by

his Evangelical Christian family. So to hear 50 or 100 people praying as a community for people they don't even know is uniquely moving. The actual reason why it effects me is ephemeral and, at least for me, the harder I try to describe the experience the more it's like trying to catch smoke.

"Generally, the Mi Shebeirach would only be heard in Reform and Reconstructionist synagogues. I don't believe I've mentioned that I fall somewhere between Reform and Reconstructionist."

Karen, a United Methodist, said: "First, a defining scripture for me is Micah 6:8, which says, 'Do justice, love kindness, walk humbly with your God. This is not a particularly Methodist verse, but it informs how I behave in the world.'

"Second, one teaching Wesley United Methodist Church talks about a lot is prevenient grace, which essentially says that God is always at work in us – all of us – even when we turn away or refuse to pay attention or are just not sure we believe. God is working. God is a verb. He's there even when we are not. Do you know what I mean? That's a particular Wesley teaching that I carry with me ALL of the time. So, when I feel particularly anxious about one of my kids – I know God is working in them, in spite of what they are doing, saying, etc.

"Third, many, many hymns drive me. I especially love old Wesley hymns. My very favorite is 'Come, Let Us Use This Grace Divine.' Utterly brilliant. Another hymn whose lyric sends me right over is 'Prayer is the Soul's Sincere Desire' (unuttered or expressed...prayer is the falling of a tear when none but God is near....prayer is a sigh... etc.). And I expect the people at my funeral to sing 'Abide with Me.'

"Fourth, I remain a United Methodist because after I studied the *Book of Discipline* before joining our current church, I realized just how closely aligned I am with most of the UM disciplines. As a body, the UM church has a way to go. We've been slow to allow for gay or lesbian pastors or weddings, for examples. But we are moving in the right direction. On the whole, though, the denomination is progressive, forward-thinking, and self-conscious. (I use self-conscious because I can't think of the word I want...the denomination evaluates and explores itself regularly and makes informed and thoughtful changes over time when it finds itself out of step…so conscious of itself…at least in my experience.)

"The liturgy is vital to me, also. I completely love Communion and especially love it when we go high church and use the full liturgy. To me, the liturgy roots me in the past and reminds me that for centuries, people have done this ritual and said those words. It reminds me that Christians all over the world worship in their way with the same liturgy. And the Lord's Prayer. It is the perfect prayer. One I use all of the time in all situations. (That is, when my prayer isn't, 'Oh God Oh God Oh God!')

"No denomination or church is perfect. Even in our church, which is pretty special, we tend to talk to each other instead of greet the stranger in our midst, but we work toward being that radically hospitable place Robert Schnase talks about in *5 Practices of Fruitful Living* ... we respond to God's love by loving others radically."

Mary, an Episcopal priest, said: "The practice I'd like to share for this chapter is the Eucharist, as it's most often known in the Episcopal Church, also called Mass, Holy Communion, or Lord's Supper in various traditions. 'Eucharist' comes from a Greek word for 'thanksgiving,' and it reminds me never to take God's gifts for granted. At Eucharist, the community gathers to hear stories of divine love and human efforts to respond (Scriptures), to offer God our shared concerns about one another and all God's creation (prayer), and to offer our lives as symbolized by money, bread, and wine. Candles, processions, liturgical colors, and songs all enrich the celebration.

"Finally, we partake of God's self-offering in the form of the bread and wine blessed and shared, which we receive as the body and blood of Christ. We go out 'rejoicing in the power of the Spirit, to love and serve.' Many other forms of prayer and meditation strengthen me at home and during paid and unpaid work, but none of these can replace this weekly gathering to hear, share, thank, feast, and be sent into God's world."

Kim, who currently attends the Church of the Brethren, though not regularly, answered: "Since Dad has passed, I have not been back very often. I still love those people and God with all my heart. I feel that I would like my children to listen to and follow God's will. My favorite rite of the Brethren Church is Maundy Thursday service that I have only humbled myself and my children to once. It is a celebration of the last supper and it is the washing of the feet of your brothers and sisters in memory of how Christ washed his disciples' feet."

Johnny, a Lutheran as well as a follower of *A Course in Miracles*, offered this heartfelt song he wrote, "We Must Remind"

1. The hand cannot say to the foot
"You are not a hand,
Therefore, you are not part of the body."
The eye cannot say to the ear,
"you are not an eye
Therefore you are not part of the body."
Likewise, we cannot say to each other
"You are not like me
Therefore, you have no place at the table of the Lord."
We must remind each other that we all are one,
We're all part of the body of Christ

2. The builders rejected a stone
But God had different plans
He made it the cornerstone
On which His whole church stands
Likewise we cannot say to each other
"You are not like me
Therefore, you have no place at the table of the Lord."
We must remind each other
That we all are one
we're all part of the body of Christ.

3. Our Lord Jesus spent His days
In the company of outcasts
Whom society turned away

But His love for them was steadfast.
Likewise we cannot say to each other,
"You are not like me
Therefore, you have no place at the table of the Lord."
We must remind each other
That we all are one
We're all part of the body of Christ
we're all part of the body of Christ.
- copyright 2008 Johnny Schaefer

    Each of these people has found a deep, sincere connection to and comfort from God through participation in their particular house of worship. So how could the Baptists say of the Catholics down the street, "You don't truly know or love God"? How could the Catholics say of the Methodists across town, "You can't possibly know or love God"? How could the Methodists say of the Mormons in the next town, "Your love for God is not real," or the Mormons say to the Pentecostals, "Your love for God is incorrect and so you don't truly know Him"? How could the Pentecostals say of the Muslims, "What you feel for and from Allah is not real," or the Muslims say of the Jews, "You cannot possibly love Allah or feel His Love"? How could the Jews say to the Jehovah's Witnesses, "Your relationship and love for God is false," the Witnesses say to the Episcopalians, "You are apostates who do not know God," or the Episcopalians say to the Sikhs, "You have no true connection to God"? How could anyone dare claim that others' music, prayers, traditions, or unique understandings are not Divinely-inspired, are not lifted up in true humility and worshipful openness, are not loved by the Creator?
    God alone knows the mind, the heart, the soul of any member of any church or mosque or temple or other house or worship. And if that church or mosque or temple or other house of worship teaches and emphasizes the Basic, Most Wonderful, Most Important Truth of God, it is teaching God's Will for us.
    So here is my offering to you as I stand on my religious path. Yes, it's a path beyond the gates of organized religion, but it's a path, it's a journey to and with God. It often meanders this way and

that, sometimes climbing rocky hills and descending into shadowy valleys, sometimes crossed with briars and sometimes clear and sunny, but it is a path instructed by the Basic, Most Wonderful, Most Important Truth of God. I see you there on your nearby paths. Hey there, fellow children of God! Here is my outstretched hand to you – believers, doubters, non-believers alike. I will never throw my beliefs in your face but am happy to share what I believe and why. I hope to be planting seeds of understanding, kindness, and peace.

A Note To Non-Believers...

Are you still here?
That's so cool. Thanks for hanging around for whatever reasons.
I believe with total conviction that even as God understands the many various ways people have of seeking and following Him, He also understands those who don't believe in Him. Why wouldn't He? He is God. He knows why everyone is as they are and why they believe or don't believe as they do. Believing or not isn't a deal breaker for God, 'cause He gets it. He really does.
Take, for example, Nate Phelps, son of the infamous Fred Phelps, founder of the Westboro Baptist Church (most infamous for it's less-than-charitable "God Hates Gays" campaign and protests at funerals of American military personnel and just about every famous person who dies, declaring they are all in Hell.) Nate was raised in what was claimed to be a Christian home, in what is called a Christian church. His father's primary message was that God hates most of His creation, inspired by a particularly cold and cruel version of Calvinism. Fred Phelps taught that from the beginning of the world God chose who would be saved and who would be tortured in Hell for eternity, and that nearly everyone (except members of the WBC) is destined to Hell because of God's hatred for them. The purpose of the church was (and is) to harass, torment, and condemn those outside the church, taunting them and loudly savoring the idea of billions of people burning forever in a lake of fire, and then profit monetarily by suing anyone who attempts to stop or silence them. Fred's son, Nate, was abused

mentally, physically, and spiritually by his father due to the hate-filled doctrine of the WBC. And so, when Nate was eighteen, he escaped, never to return. Since then, he has been "finally freed to embrace my innate secular humanism." No wonder. So be it. God understands completely. Nate might reconnect to God at some point in his life. Then again, he may never try to reconnect. And it's okay.

And I hope Nate wouldn't mind me saying, "God bless you, Nate, for escaping and reclaiming your life from such a twisted nightmare."

And then there are many people who have never had a belief in God whatsoever. I have friends who say they find no reason for there to be a God and no need for there to be a God. In spite of the heavy-handed "moral" of the story in the 2014 film *God's Not Dead* – which suggests that not only are atheists less-principled and more selfish than believers (in the movie, the believers are evangelical Christians), but that they (as exemplified by the character of Professor Radisson) come to atheism because God has disappointed or angered them – there are plenty who embrace atheism or agnosticism through observation, study, and consideration. Others have no interest in a concept of the Divine and never felt the need consider it. There is no question that atheists and agnostics are as likely to be well-principled, compassionate, and selfless as believers. Bless you, wonderful, loving and compassionate people, for who you are. Bless you as you go on your adventurous life journeys.

A Prayer

Dearest God,
 Sit with me, Lord, and let me sit with You. You are Greater and more Glorious than any soul can imagine, and in Your Perfect Wisdom You have created me as I am, and You love me as I am. Let me be silent with You. Let me be still. Hold me and keep me. Remind me that as Almighty and Perfect as You are, You have never lost thought of me. You have never lost thought of any of us. Thank You.
 Amen.

3

Why Believe?

Three Reasons We Believe

It seems to me there are three primary reasons we believe whatever it is we believe.
1. We've been taught during our earliest years or most vulnerable times that a certain something is true.

Imagine a family living on one side of a mountain and another family living on the other side. The first family tells their young children that the family on the other side of the mountain is cruel and hateful. In most cases the children will believe what their parents have taught them. They have no evidence to the contrary, and trusting in the authority figures in their lives, they accept the information as factual.

Or imagine people of one religion teaching its followers that those of another religion are apostates, deluded, and are going to burn in eternal fires of Hell. These lessons have been taught to the followers since their toddlerhood and they trust the authority of the leaders and the written materials that support the claim.

Or, imagine that during someone's lowest moment, during a time of deep depression or desperation, another person comes forward, offers a compassionate helping hand, and shares teachings about a loving Creator who inspires compassion and who loves all His people. These teachings speak to the person's great need and are joyously accepted.

2. We really want to believe something because we desire it or because we need to. We want to be accepted by others who believe and so we believe, too. Perhaps what we believe is terrifying and so we need to believe it to feel safe. Perhaps that something is so gloriously wonderful that we need it to be true and so we will ourselves to believe it.

Imagine young man who has met a young woman – on campus, at a bar, a gym, a church, it doesn't really matter. He sees her as his dream woman. The love he's been waiting for, his beloved, his soul mate. She's brilliant, endearing, and obviously enjoys her time with him. After a few weeks and a few dates, he believes she loves him as much as he loves her. At this point in time, whether she loves him or not, he believes it is true. It is so wonderful, this idea, that he believes it to his very core. Maybe she does. Maybe she doesn't. But he believes it.

Imagine little girl is driving her father crazy with her whining and tantrums. The father has tried every kind of reward, redirection, and punishment he can think of. Then the father sits down with the child and says, "Listen to me, and listen carefully. There is a bright red monster that hates nasty, whining children. It has yellow eyes and silver claws. It lives in our attic, and can hear everything you do. Every time you stomp your feet or scream or demand your way, the monster hears it. The last thing you want to do is make that monster angry." The father's presentation is so serious and so ominous that the child is terrified into believing it. Her fear creates the belief, and it stays with her.

3. We are compelled to believe something because of a personal, deep, and profound experience. This experience shows us that a particular something is true. It might be something that catches us completely by surprise. It might be something we suspected was true for a long time. But we experience it, and now we know it. Now it is part of us.

Imagine an elderly woman living on the streets. She has been alone for years, eating wherever food is doled out or whatever she can scrounge from bins. She sleeps in shelters at night when she can find a spot or under a bridge when there is no room. She wanders the sidewalks aimlessly during the day, avoiding conversations, staying away from others out of fear of being attacked. She has become numbed to life, managing to remain alive but with no sense of belonging or purpose. She believes that no one cares for her...why should they? She's old, she smells, and she is sure she has nothing to offer. Then a young couple finds her and invites her to their home to share a meal. She refuses. Certainly they want to taunt, hurt, or rob her of her meager possessions. The next day, they return, and bring her some warm clothing and another offer of a meal at their home. They tell her they care and just want to share with her. Again, she refuses. With time and persistence, the couple finally convinces the woman to come to their home. She finds it to be a warm, comfortable place. The couple is genuinely welcoming toward her. She is doubtful but hopeful that they care about her. Day after day, they invite her to their home, and she goes. She begins to be more open with them, telling about her life, her hopes, and her failures. They listen and they share their own stories. Over time, they invite her to move in with them, a surrogate grandmother, as they have no other family nearby. She accepts and comes to believe without a doubt that these people care for her. This profound, personal experience has shown her something she never would have expected. She is certain they love her. And she now believes she has something to offer – her love in return.

Believing

In any one person, there may be an intertwining of two or three reasons for belief – prior engrained teachings, wants/needs, and deep personal experiences. Because of this, there will be countless variations in how we perceive the world, our lives, the lives of others, and God, if we believe in God.

When members of a denomination or individual house of worship gather, they bring with them the teachings that are most deeply rooted, their wants and needs, and their intimate, personal experiences. All this will influence how they each perceive what is offered them by their leaders and their sacred texts. While those who gather may wholly embrace the basics of the religion, they likely will have some differing beliefs when it comes to some of the details.

In one pew of any particular Protestant church there may be a woman who, when hearing or speaking the word "Heaven," envisions what she believes – a place with pearly gates and a smiling St. Peter, welcoming those who have died into an eternal world of clouds, beauty, winged angels, and God on a glorious throne. Next to this woman is her husband who, when hearing or speaking the word "Heaven," envisions a realm not of sight but of pure emotion, an eternal state of bliss in which God's loving, comforting Presence is all that is needed and desired. Next to the husband is an elderly man, nearing the end of his life, who envisions Heaven as more earthly, a place of pure, cool rivers and fall-colored mountains, an Earth transformed but retaining the beauty of God's creation where an old man can still hike the mountains and drift on a crystalline lake in a boat with his favorite old dog; a place where God drifts along, too, a Perfect and Comforting Companion. A few folks down from the elderly man is a young college student who, when hearing or speaking the word "Heaven," sees in her mind the Universe as she has been studying it, incomprehensibly glorious in scope, wonder, swirling beauty, where conscious souls, once having left their physical bodies, join all other souls with God to see, to know, to understand, and to experience All That Is and to become One with God. None of these beliefs are wrong. These varying views should not be a point of contention. These people understand Heaven to be the best there can be, the most glorious that can be. And of course, that is what Heaven is. The Best to come. The Most Wonderful that awaits us. The Love that is Eternal.

What I now believe to my core regarding God is based in all three of the reasons, and most wonderfully and primarily in the third.

I was taught about God and Jesus (as both God and as the Son of God) as a young member of Main Street United Methodist Church in Waynesboro, Virginia. It was a lovely church with sweet people – and it still is. As a child I accepted the comforting idea that the Lord was always around, was aware of me and all of Creation, and truly cared. I liked the framed pictures on the wall and in the Bible that showed a gentle Jesus knocking on a door, carrying lambs, and holding children's hands. As a teen, however, I began to wrangle with certain teachings that didn't resonate (why were only Christians allowed to go to Heaven? Why would God allow a devil to screw up people's lives and their chance at eternal joy and peace?) After high school graduation, I attended the Methodist-affiliated Ferrum College. I got married the summer following my second year, and my husband, Roger, and I finished our bachelor's degrees at Madison College (now James Madison University), a public institution in Harrisonburg, Virginia. As a young couple, Roger and I didn't do much with church. Later, when we had two children, our family became members of a local Presbyterian church (we wanted our daughter and son to have a connection to a community of believers, and we were both believers). I didn't know much about Presbyterian doctrine, but the services seemed very much like those of my old Methodist church. Plus, I liked the minister a great deal. A super nice, truly caring, and friendly guy.

Several years later after that, however, the Protestant beliefs as a whole began to crumble in my mind. Then they fell away completely. Life was an enormous challenge. My marriage was coming apart. I had a job teaching in an elementary school where the principal was a sometimes scary, unpredictable man who harassed teachers who didn't flatter him. There seemed to be no evidence for God's existence and plenty of evidence against it. I was turned off by what religions had to offer and I found religious adherents to be, for the most part, clueless, desperate, arrogant, or sad. I accepted the idea that human beings created God in order to make sense of life and reality. People longed for an eternal parent figure, someone to turn to with their sorrows, someone to complain to when things were unfair, to question when they were confused, to comfort them when frightened. That made sense. Sure, lots of people might want there to be a God. But that didn't mean there was a God. I might need to be able to fly or read minds at times, but that didn't mean I would be able to. My reaction to people who talked about or preached about God was this: Really? Okay, prove it to me. Prove there is a God. You can't do it. So just be quiet.

At that point in time, I would have accepted writer James Lindsay's claim in his 2015 book *Everybody is Wrong About God* that those who confess their belief in God are actually admitting they have social and psychological needs that they don't know how to meet. I still loved my family; I still cared about the plight of humankind. But I had no interest in anything Divine and I quit thinking about it.

Then things shifted for me once again.

My first re-awareness of God came when I was newly separated and soon to be divorced. I had quit teaching a year before to write full time. My income as a freelancer was spotty and at times non-existent. I was no longer part of the income pool that my husband and I had together. Circumstances required us to sell our house in the country and I relocated to a modest apartment in town, an apartment I could barely afford along with groceries and gas. I cashed in my teaching retirement to help, which earned me criticism from other folks – "What about when you're older and need that retirement income?!" "What were you *thinking*?!" (Well, I was thinking I kinda really needed the money then and there, that's what I was thinking.) I got several credit cards and used them...running them up to their limits, hoping beyond hope that in the next month or so I would land that big writing gig that would make everything right again. But that didn't happen. The writing gigs were there, but they paid little. I took on substitute teaching jobs and presented creative writing workshops to bring in extra income, but I was treading water. Deep, dark, scary water.

I would lie awake at night, overwhelmed, paralyzed, depressed. Fear squeezed me dry of joy, energy, and hope. I'd stare for hours at a water spot on the ceiling above the bed or the bent Venetian blinds covering the bedroom window, wondering if I'd ever sleep again, if I'd ever be happy again. I couldn't imagine I would. During the day I would walk from one room to the next and then have no idea why I'd done that. I put car keys down then a minute later had no memory of where I'd put them. I was on the verge of crying at any given moment. My recurring mental mantra was, "What's the hell is the point?" Cheerful people made me even more depressed than I already was. Happy songs *really* pissed me off. At my slow, way-out-of-date computer I struggled to decide on a right word or sentence for the next story or book, only to feel fog rise up in my mind and drag the word or sentence away from view. I was so depressed I wasn't able to fathom seeking some other form of employment. I knew I wouldn't get a job, anyway, as stupid as I was. I had no skills. The employers would laugh in my face.

The divorce was as amicable as possible (my ex-husband is a wonderful, caring human being – we had just grown far apart in many ways and couldn't bridge the gap any more), but anyone who has gone through one can affirm that no matter how amicable a divorce is, there is still a great deal of pain. One beloved family member was very resentful and angry as he blamed me for the breakup. He avoided me; he wouldn't talk to me. That silence seethed for nearly two years, and it was a knife to my heart. I tried to communicate but he wanted nothing to do with me, so I had to accept it as his choice. My sister and best friend, Barb, was a great support, but even with her encouragement and great sense of humor, I frequently felt alone and unable to imagine how anything could possibly get better.

My first and only panic attack came during that time. I was scheduled to present a daylong creative writing workshop at a middle school on the other side of the county. The workshop was to begin at 9 a.m. It was nearly 8, and the school was a half-hour away. There I was, lying in bed in my pajamas, staring at the water spot, unable to move. Emotionally paralyzed. Tears dammed up inside me, refusing to be released. My heart pounded like a jackhammer and it was hard to breathe. I felt like I would blow up any minute. I wanted to get up and run somewhere, anywhere, to get away from myself as far as I could. I thought...no, I *knew*...I was going crazy. I don't know how I did it, but at some point I forced myself to roll off the bed, get dressed in something presentable (no showering, no time, though I didn't really care, anyway), to go, to put on the happy face, make it to the school with six minutes to spare, and present the activities to classrooms full of seventh grade students. It took so much out of me I came home afterwards and spent the next 15 hours in bed. Not sleeping much, though. Just numb, exhausted, dazed.

In 1979, Barbara Gordon published a memoir entitled *I'm Dancing As Fast As I Can*. I've not read the book and never saw the movie based on the book, but I felt I understood the title. I was scrambling as hard as I could. And when my workdays ended and I turned off the computer or got home from a school, I lay down on the bed, face to face with the specter of impending bills, a failing life, staring at the water spot on the ceiling.

It was then I realized I needed there to be a God. I wanted to pray, to know I was heard. I wanted to believe that even though I was embraced by despair, something greater than myself was embracing *me*. I wanted to know that in spite of my current suffering, there was something, a Power, beyond it all who knew me and loved me. I wanted that Divine Parent.

But I didn't pray. Prayer was nothing more than wishful thinking directed upward or outward into the void. Prayers were only desperate pleas with no destination, no recipient. Screw prayers. I forgot about God again.

And the months dragged on.

One Sunday morning in April I was feeling particularly defeated. Amazingly, there were a few gallons of gas in the tank, so I drove up Afton Mountain and turned north onto the Blue Ridge Parkway and into the Shenandoah National Park (again, amazingly, my pass was good for another two months). The mountain road was heavily fogged, coating my windshield with water droplets and shrouding the air with misty cotton, so much so I could only see three or four yards in front of the car. I drove very slowly. There was the sense of moving through an isolated dream world; turns in the road, overhanging tree branches, and roadside stone walls were revealed only as I got within several feet of them. On I went, certain there was tarmac ahead even when I couldn't see it, and on one level not really caring if there would be or not. I felt a deep, wandering dullness, an emptiness that was flat and complete. I had nothing left and I didn't care.

After a while I saw a sign for an overlook. I slowed and pulled in, turned off the car, and sat staring through the windshield. The white cocoon of fog mirrored my sense of thick, dulled defeat. I rolled down the window and let the fog settle on my arms and face. As far as I could tell, no one else was on the overlook. Maybe no one else on the Parkway. That was good. I didn't want to be near anyone.

And then the fog began to break apart.

It seemed to be happening only in front of the car, not to either side, as if someone had grasped the mist and was drawing it back like curtains on a stage. I sat. I watched. I still felt nothing. As the mist parted it thinned and dissipated. And there before me was a vast blue sky and rounded mountain ridges. Below were the mint-green foothills and pink flowering trees in the valley. Sunlight washed the entire scene, giving it a painfully bright glow. My sense of nothingness became a sense of tininess, a sense of pure and utter insignificance, and I began to cry. This was the most comforting feeling I'd ever experienced. It was insignificance with significance. Here before me was Creation, stunning, grand, impossible to absorb in its entirety. And I was part of it. I was as much a part of it as the sunlight, the overlook, the ridges, and the flowering trees in the valley. As I watched birds circling the air and cloud-shadows traveling across the landscape, I felt the Spirit of the Creator rise up and move down, encircling me, holding me. Knowing me.

Oh my God.

Immense, All-Powerful, All-Understanding. All-Loving.

Oh my God!

The frustration, anger, and depression that had kept me knotted up bled away. Incredible peace flowed in and took their place. Suddenly and quite involuntarily, my lungs gasped and I drew in a deep, profoundly cleansing breath. It was what I know now as literal, Divine "inspiration."

I was buoyant.

I was light.

I sat and just *existed* in that moment. I just *was*. And with all my being I knew this was God, surrounding me, sitting with me. I hadn't done anything special. I hadn't prayed for anything. I was banged up, tramped down. Yes, at one point I had wanted to believe; I had wanted God to be real, but I'd long since given up on that. I hadn't sought Him or reached for Him. I'd dismissed Him completely. And *He* had reached for *me*.

I had not believed and now I did. I believed completely in the Hand that created everything. In the Mind that conceived everything. In the Love that encompasses everything. Joy! Relief! My reawakening drove home the certainty that I wanted to open to

God in my life. Wholly. As best I possibly could. The moment on the mountain freed my heart and mind. My sense of God was back. That intimate, profound, genuine encounter made it impossible for me not to believe. And then came other experiences that confirmed the one on the foggy mountain.

My sister, Becky, died after a long bout with cancer. She spent her final weeks at home with her husband and with help from Hospice. Becky was just a year and a half older than me, and she and I had become closer in those last months than I ever thought we would. We had an especially touching time at the "jewelry party" Becky planned for Barb, my sister-in-law, and me, an intimate gathering during which she laid out all the jewelry she had collected over the years and let us divide it up among the three of us. We knew she only had very little time left, and yet this party was as uplifting and fun as it was sad. We told goofy stories. We laughed. We cried a little.

A week after the jewelry party, I got a call from my brother-in-law. It was early morning. Becky had passed away around 4 a.m. Her time had come to return to God. I cried a lot.

Around 7:30 that morning I was preparing to call my daughter, who lived in Northern Virginia, to let her know that Becky had died. But before I could dial, the phone rang. It was my daughter, asking how Becky was. She said was asking because around 4 a.m. she had a dream – or a vision – in which Becky came to her, looking peaceful and beautiful, and saying, "I'm all right now." I was instantly covered in goose bumps. Becky was gone, but her soul had stopped by on her way to God to reassure my daughter that she was all right.

That experience was so profound it made me even more certain of God. No other Power would have caused this beautiful outreach, this beautiful affirmation of the Divine Eternity that will be ours.

Still other experiences have reaffirmed to me the reality of God.

Several years ago, as I sat working on a story at my computer, focused on the screen, when I was caught up in a waking dream that I hadn't asked for nor expected. Right there, overlaying the solidness of my office – the desk, computer, bookshelves, walls – I saw a grove. Trees were illuminated in sunlight, flowers of myriad colors waves in a breeze, and there was soft grass beneath my bare feet. I looked around, watching, waiting for whatever was to happen.

Then I felt the Presence. It was enormous; it was perfect in Love and Understanding. The Presence enfolded me and I was overwhelmed. I knelt in the grass, sensing the Presence – whom I knew was God – kneel with me. I folded my hands in absolute awe of what was happening. And I prayed there in that sunny grove (in my office), kneeling barefoot in the grass, (sitting in my chair with my sandals on), thankful, aware of God in His infinite Power, stunned by the wonder of it all. My spirit was swept up in Perfect Beauty and Peace. I was with God. He was with me and always had been.

That waking dream has stayed with me. The transcendent rush has faded but I will never forget it. I will never stop being thankful for it.

God's connection to me, one lowly member of His universal family, has also been reaffirmed on occasion in quiet ways. Sometimes when I listen to certain music I've felt His Spirit. Other times, when my thoughts are elsewhere, a sense of Him will touch my heart. An awareness of God can happen when observing everyday events, things we often dismiss as mundane. Elderly people helping each other along a sidewalk. Children deep in whispered conversation. Watching chickadees splash in the birdbath, observing ants doggedly dragging chunks of food over rugged terrain to their anthill. God is not just the Lord of the spiritual but is Lord of the physical, too. Neither exists apart from the other. It is all His Creation.

A while back, as I was sitting in the car waiting for Barb, who was in the post office, I was thinking about God and feeling disconnected and sad. I scooched down in the seat and I looked out through the window into the clear sky. And there, written with white clouds against the blue, was the word "HI." Three small, thin clouds apart from all the other clouds, no contrails anywhere nearby, spelling out a greeting. It was the coolest, most awesome thing (and for those who might wonder, in and around the small town where I live there are never planes creating skywriting.) On seeing this "HI," I was caught again with that spontaneous, deep inhalation of air, that Divine inspiration, and I laughed out loud. I knew without a doubt this message was from God. He had put that there for me to see. A casual, sweet, and perfect greeting from my Creator. "Hi!" Yep, He's here. He loves us! He loves me!

What We Expect To Come With Our Belief

Our day-to-day connection to God and our expectations of Him come in many forms. They are shaped to a great degree by the teachings of the house of worship we choose to attend, if any. They can be influenced by friends with similar or dissimilar beliefs. They are inspired by our individual explorations and experiences. Those of us who believe in God will discover how He fits into our lives.

Some believers see God through deists' eyes. They determine that He created all there is then stepped back to let humans and the nature take complete control with no further involvement of His own. Some believers expect God to be a constant presence, an immediate source of peace and instruction in all circumstances. Others envision God as a frequently displeased parent who is ready to smite the believer for infractions both large and small. Still others think about Him only now and then, asking for direction or help, and then thoughts of Him fade into the background. There are those who believe He will sometimes make Himself heard and other times He will be silent. Believers bring to their vision of God their own hopes and fears. Regardless of how varied those hopes, expectations, and fears might be, God understands. He knows why we believe as we do.

The beautiful thing is this – however we envision God, regardless of how we fit Him into our lives, we (believers and nonbelievers alike) already fit into the Life of God. We are never out of His Thought and His Heart. We are never alone.

The Beauty of Belief

There are wonders and comfort in belief. When I become quiet and open to God, it's easier to stop fretting over things that have already happened and stop longing for things of the past, because He reminds me those things are behind me and cannot be changed.

When I become quiet and open to God, I am more able to be in the present and see more clearly those things that are worth my time and concern and those things that are not.

When I become quiet and open to God, I'm more able to face the future, because I trust that whatever comes, as difficult as it might be, God will be with me.

When I become quiet and open to God, I'm more able to deal with the jagged energy that sometimes arises out of nowhere to make me anxious, fearful, or frustrated. Mindfulness of Him makes it easier for me to slow my breathing, to let my soul drift to the center where the Divine resides most deeply. I can speak to Him and He can encourage me, allowing that ragged energy to fade away.

When I open to God and am aware of Him, I become less apprehensive of life in general because I know He is here. When I become less apprehensive I'm able to stop being so self-absorbed. When I am less self-absorbed I am able to give more of my attention, my care, and my understanding to others who might need me. I become less self-engaged become more us-engaged. I rediscover the beauty of our universal connectedness through the Creator. I am swept up, yet again, in the "peace that passes understanding."

The Age-Old Battle of Trying To Prove God To Those Who Don't Believe or Disprove God to Those Who Believe

We can't prove God exists. We can't prove that God doesn't exist. Either you believe, you don't believe, or you leave the possibility open but are not convinced.

There are those who believe creation proves God, and there are others who say that pain and suffering or certain scientific discoveries prove He doesn't. I'm not here to try to convince anyone that God is real. We aren't meant to try to prove Him but rather live a life guided by Love. Yet in the course of religious discussions, in particular those conversations between believers and non-believers, the issue of God's existence inevitably comes up.

Believers demand atheists provide irrefutable proof that God doesn't exist. Atheists demand believers provide irrefutable evidence that God does exist. In all honesty, I tend to lean with the atheists on this requirement...if the existence of something is to be discussed, the burden of proof lies at the doorstep of the believers. In any other discussion, the one who claims something exists that others cannot detect (Bigfoot? The Loch Ness monster? Ghosts?) is the one who must provide the evidence. That said...

God does not *have* to be proved. If God wanted believers to prove Him, He would have offered something so concretely evident, no living human being would be able to deny it except those who would deny the existence, say, of a tree or mountain or ocean or the stars. But the bottom line is this...He doesn't need to be proved.

I can't prove God exists any more than I can prove to you that I experienced a transcendent moment in the Shenandoah National Park. You can't prove He doesn't exist any more than you can't prove to me that there is no such thing as a transcendent moment. I can't prove God exists any more than I can convince you that the feeling I have for my husband is deep love. You can't prove what I feel for him isn't deep love, either. And no, belief in God is not inherently anti-intellectual. My acceptance of the existence of God has come from an opening of the mind and heart rather than a closing of them. This is true for others, as well.

And so the argument for or against God's existence is futile. Sure, it can be a fascinating debate for some. But I don't debate. I believe if I...if we...live by God's Simple Truth, and love and care for one another, we are doing His Will for us. And that's enough.

An Aside: Defending God

Another activity that I find to be a waste of energy and at times a destructive force is that of "defending God or God's honor." Strident anti-God trash talk might make me sad, not because it offends God or me but because of the scorn that seems to accompany it. I may tell whoever is speaking why I have another view on the matter. More often than not, though, I'll let it go. It's that person's opinion and he or she has the perfect right to it.

Yet there are some who feel it is their sacred duty to lash out at those who say, do, write, or draw anything that offends their personal or collective understanding of God. As if God is standing with hands on hips or is stomping His feet that someone has dissed Him. As if God is so small He can't handle or even fathom human criticism.

Some religions teach that criticizing, poking fun at, or just saying a "wrong thing" about the Creator is the ultimate no-no, that blasphemy is considered a sin. I understand that such an attack is emotionally and spiritually painful to some believers, and they imagine God is likewise hurt and angry. Yet I couldn't worship a deity who was so insecure He would want his children to shun, exile, torture, imprison, or kill His other children for actual or perceived criticism of Himself or for insulting or destroying writings that are attributed to Him. God's Greatness puts Him way beyond that. He understands everything. *Everything*. As there is no subject too dangerous to discuss, there is nothing so awful that can be said or done "against" God that He would require us to destroy each other because of it. Let's honor God by being equally compassionate and loving to those who love God, those who hate God, and those who have no sense of or belief in God at all.

A Favorite Song – "Be Thou my Vision" – Partial (Dallan Forgaill, 8th century; translated by Mary E Byrne, 1905, versed by Eleanor H. Hull, 1912.)

Be Thou my Vision, O Lord of my heart;
Naught be all else to me, save that Thou art.
Thou my best Thought, by day or by night,
Waking or sleeping, Thy presence my light.

Riches I heed not, nor man's empty praise,
Thou mine Inheritance, now and always:
Thou and Thou only, first in my heart,
High King of Heaven, my Treasure Thou art.

4

Here We Are: Often Silent, Un-Churched Believers Speak Out

When I knew I would write this book, I also knew I didn't want to be the only voice to introduce the topic. Yes, this is about my un-churched journey in particular. But while we have that un-churched believer dealio in common with each other, I by no means speak for every un-churched monotheistic believer when it comes to the issues I'll be discussing.

So let me present to you to some un-churched or otherwise un-house-of-worshipped (try to say that three times really fast) people, to let you hear from them regarding their personal experiences, why they are un-churched, and their feelings about God and about sharing their beliefs with others.

How did I find these folks, you ask? Or you don't ask, but I'll tell you, anyway. I started by posting a call out to my Facebook friends. Of the thousands of friends, I probably know, in person, about 200 of them, and know maybe thirty of them well. Some of those I don't know are people who read my books, some are friends of friends, and some, well, I have no clue how we got linked up on Facebook (and as long as they don't post creepy or hateful comments, they remain friends.) So anyway, in my post I asked if there were any un-churched monotheists who would be willing to answer five simple questions. I asked these people to let me know by way of a private message.

I got several responses right off the bat. Then Facebook friends began to share my call for respondents with *their* Facebook friends as well as some friends and family members who weren't on Facebook, and so on – kind of like that 1980's Faberge shampoo commercial. I received more replies.

And a varied bunch of respondents they were. They came from all over the United States. They are women and men of all ages. Most grew up in one organized religion or other while a few never attended a church at all. Some are employed while others attend school. Still others are unemployed and some are retired. I had hoped to get a few solid replies. I'd intended on including them as part of the second or third chapter. Yet when I saw what was offered by way of responses, I realized these people deserved a chapter all their own.

Here are the six questions I posed:

1. Were you ever a member of a church? If so, which one and for how long?

2. If you have been a church member, what made you decide to leave, and why do you remain un-churched?

3. As an un-churched believer, how would you define God? How do your beliefs instruct and influence your daily life?

4. Have you ever discussed your beliefs with churched persons? If so, do you feel your beliefs were understood and respected? If not, what was your experience?

5. Do you hesitate to discuss your beliefs with others? If so, why?

The replies were candid, varied, thoughtful, and heartfelt. There were answers given and even some new questions posed. Some of the responders embrace a more traditional, recognizable (to the Western mind) concept of God. Others express their struggles to understand who or what God is. Still others feel no need to define Him/Her. And most expressed a belief that God is good. God is love. God loves.

Many said they'd been hesitant to share their beliefs publicly and were glad to have a safe venue to do so. I could almost hear some let out long-held breaths. There were those who said they never hesitated to share their beliefs. Others said they didn't feel the need to do so but were willing to share for this project.

Some respondents wrote wonderfully extensive and detailed answers; due to space I had to do a bit of editing so I could include them. The points, however, remain unaffected.

And, surprising to me, some who responded to the call were not un-churched believers. Yet they came forward, wanting to share. Dan, from Massachusetts, said, "I don't think I believe in an almighty power such as God. Rather I think of God as a concept that defines morality." Garrett, from Virginia, is a spiritual young man who finds his deepest connection to the Celtic Pantheon; he said he suspected that he wasn't the demographic I was looking for, but was willing to discuss his beliefs if it would help the book. So even though I had to decline these folks' kind offers, I greatly appreciate the fact that they offered.

It seems people want a safe place where they can discuss their religious or spiritual beliefs or views, regardless of what they are. Fantastic!

Now let me introduce some fellow un-churched believers and share their answers. And I want to thank every one of them for their willingness and honesty.

Kim, Panama City, Florida

1. I was a member of the Assembly of God growing up and in my thirties, I converted to Catholicism.

2. We didn't leave the church insomuch as we just kind of stopped going. Both my husband and I lost our dads within a month apart and it seemed that each time we went to mass it was only about money.

3. I define God as the creator and all that. I pray and read the Bible usually daily.

4. I only discuss religion when it's a welcome conversation; otherwise it's too volatile to discuss with people whether they believe or not.

5. I have atheist friends and that's fine. I try to just discuss it if they want to. I'm not one of those people who shoves my beliefs down other people's throats.

Joseph, Grand Rapids, MI

1. I grew up First Congregational (Protestant). Went fairly regularly birth through early high school. Have I ever been a member as an adult? No, I guess not.

2. We went off and on when we had kids. Helping people live better lives has always appealed to me, to be a better person. But songs like "Our God is an Awesome God" always felt like "and yours isn't." There are big things I fundamentally find offensive and inconsistent. So I find myself drawn in then repulsed.

3. There is a force in the universe. Mankind has always sensed this and tried to describe it. Something beyond ourselves. Each person must sort this out and stitch this together for any true faith. Personally I pray daily, read the *Tao te Ching* and the *I Ching*. I'm always struck that the lessons I learn from these 4,000-year-old texts, when shared with a devout fundamental Baptist friend, have the same good message somewhere in the Bible, a 2,000-year-old text. Is Christ real? I'm inclined to say yes. But that's between whatever's out there and my prayers. And so far I've asked the question, opened up, but feel it's an incomplete conversation coming from the other end. So I define myself as a heathen monk, and whatever I am so far is between me and God.

4. Wow. Yes, I have. My first foray back into acting after a 27-year hiatus was at an ULTRA conservative, Christian theater. No drinking, no swearing, when they say Satan they mean it. They believe the earth is 6,000 years old, and homosexuality is a choice, a bad choice. BUT, they are the real deal. They accepted me no matter what. And I am a VERY accomplished heathen. They are truly loving, generous, un-judgmental people. Weird I know. One is now very much one of my dearest, sincerest, best friends. She is mid-thirties, unbelievably witty, intelligent, an unbelievable mind. AND, never had a drink, never been kissed, and yes a virgin. She and I have had numerous lengthy, respectful, intelligent conversations. We are both better for it. And both fundamentally in our same spot but broadened. There are many in this group who are just as devout, just as fundamental, but have accepted me fully. Again, I'm a heathen. Yet they ACTUALLY are living and acting as Christ taught. I don't feel there are many truly like them.

5. YES, I hesitate. I live in Grand Rapids. A Bible Belt and not any Bible Belt: Christian Reform, CRC. Conservative. More churches per capita then any place in the country. Socially what church you go to may be the first question, not what do you do for a living. And saying you're a Christian is a business asset. I won't say I'm something for gain; that is so important a question, and so fundamentally unanswered for me. If asked I won't shy away from the answer, "I pray and that question is still unanswered for me." But I won't seek to discuss it with those I don't know or don't trust.

I do have a fundamental guideline. Follow those that seek the truth. Beware those who say they've found it. True Believers, I find, still question and have humility about it all.

Dayne, Hickory, NC

1. I was a member of Friendly Baptist Church when I was a child until age nine when I went to live with my grandmother.

2. I never really was able to get much from it as a child and my grandmother was highly against going. I prefer to sleep late on Sundays now and every church service I've ever attended gave me the creeps. I just cannot feel that people know as much about God as they claim. I don't trust them and I find many "godly" people uneducated and intolerant of others.

3. I define God as the creator of the universe...not just humans but atoms, molecules, energy, everything. I find God more of a force. Our planet is in too perfect a position and our bodies work to well not to have something behind it. I feel that God prepared this planet for us by allowing us to evolve. I give everyone and everything its rightful respect in regards to its position in our universe.

4. I've discussed my beliefs with church people but not many. In my experience they all nodded their heads as if to say, "Poor fool. You cling too much to science and nature." I could tell they thought I was misguided and needed to read the Bible more.

5. I always hesitate and usually keep my beliefs to myself. I do not want to hear the same broken record about how my beliefs are wrong and theirs are right.

Holly, Portland, ME

1. I was born into a Protestant family and was an unchurched non-believer for a long time. Then, due to a personal crisis, I became a believer. I decided to choose a "formal" religion and converted to Judaism. I was a member of a synagogue for three years - one year of study for my conversion, and two years after that.

2. I decided to leave because the study of Torah and tradition (while fascinating) took more time than I chose to spend, and I didn't have a lot of use for the social aspects of attending synagogue. However, I still self-identify as Jewish, because I love the religion.

3. I define God as my "Higher Power," my better nature, a benevolent mystery. I see God as the Creator in terms of the mystery that ignited the Big Bang. I have kind of a dual concept of God that way - both as a personal guide and as a big remote force behind the universe. My better nature is an expression of God doing work through me. God works through people, in my world. So I definitely believe in one God, but with many aspects. I try to find gratitude every day for the goodness in my life, not take bad turns personally, and maintain faith that everything will work out - maybe not according to my desires, but how it's supposed to work out. I also work on patience and acceptance as I try to live in a more harmonious way with God and nature. It's very important to my mental and spiritual health to meditate on these topics daily.

4. I discussed these beliefs at some length with my Rabbi when I was converting. She saw no conflict with my understanding of God, but of course to live as a Jew involved adopting traditions and observances that I eventually found cumbersome. I live with a bunch of agnostics/atheists, and they respect my choice to believe as I respect their choice to not believe.

5. I do not hesitate to discuss my beliefs with anyone that I feel will respect my faith.

Jo-ann, Fiskeville, RI

1. I was baptized Catholic; later my family converted to Episcopalian and it was in that church that I was confirmed. I went to many churches and my Mom moved us around annually.

2. I left organized religion and churches because of man-made, ancient rules that did not allow for our evolution as human beings. Examples: homosexuality (even though it's found in all animal life on earth); the belief that children are born with the sins of their parents (I cannot abide by the belief that God would consider his most precious creations sinful – I think that is a man-made declaration.)

3. I follow the belief that God is a loving, nurturing, and giving creator who wants us to life, grow, and learn. I believe in treating others as I wish to be treated, in spreading love, joy, and help wherever and whenever I can. Mutual respect and love help us create the world that God wanted for us.

4. I mentioned them in passing on occasion but was immediately dismissed…losing all respect for organized religion.

5. Yes, I hesitate because most people get too defensive and argumentative. They refuse to or can't keep an open mind.

Natalie, Indianapolis, IN

1. I grew up Catholic from birth and had to go every Sunday for classes and then church. I was baptized and had first communion.

2. I left right before my confirmation (which happens at age thirteen or fourteen) because of what I learned in my religion classes. I didn't like the way men and women were treated differently and I didn't like the way I was treated when I asked questions. In class I learned confirmation was me choosing to take the Catholic faith, and I refused. I tried a very liberal United Methodist Church as an adult, but I found hypocrisy in the church leadership. I'm totally turned off by most churches and the so-called leadership they offer. The Christian bigotry is also not for me. I'm pro-choice, a feminist, and believe in LGBT rights and social programs. I don't think I'm going to hell for any of that.

3. It's hard for me to define God because that's in flux for me. I believe that there is something greater than ourselves, but I doubt it's a grey haired father figure. My beliefs led me to work for social justice, volunteer, and choose social work as a career. I live my faith by putting my beliefs into action and making an honest effort to make our society a better place to be.

4. I have discussed my beliefs with a few people from churches, and I don't believe that they were understood or respected. There was a lot of polite head nodding and smiling, and then an offer to join their church because "it's different." I have researched churches several times because I like the sense of community they can bring, but I can't be a part of something that goes against my own core beliefs.

5. I do hesitate to talk to others. I believe strongly in a separation of Church and State so I fight for that, but I often ignore pointed questions about my own religion. It's so personal for me. I pray all the time. It's a constant conversation in my head. God doesn't answer back but the right people tend to turn up in my life at the right time. I believe God speaks through people.

Katina, Stuarts Draft, VA

1. I was never a member of a church but I attended Central Baptist Church for about two years.

2. I left because I felt that I really didn't belong there. And to be honest, the pastor there is very old and a little monotonous. I have trouble really getting a message from him. I have been to a few other churches in the area but I just haven't gotten that feeling "this is where I belong".

3. God is the creator of everything. Most days I believe that God is everywhere and in charge. I try to live my life as if there is a heaven, someplace to go after death where I will be reunited with loved ones. I keep the commandments and know that Jesus died so that I might live forever.

4. I discuss my beliefs with churched persons frequently. My brother-in-law is a pastor. I always feel that my beliefs are understood. Even though he doesn't share some of my beliefs, they are definitely respected. There have been a few issues where we disagreed and he sent me articles to "prove" that he is right (mostly to do with gay marriage). I don't feel God has a problem with this. Although my brother-in-law doesn't have a problem with homosexuality, he does not feel that they should be able to marry.

5. Sometimes I am hesitant to discuss my beliefs because I am unsure that I know enough to accurately make my points. I also

do not like conflict so I keep my beliefs to myself with certain people.

Danni, Walpole, MA

1. I was a Roman Catholic from birth to around 1999.

2. This is a two-answer question, which preface by telling you that I was quite devout, especially when living in Greensboro, NC. The church there, Our Lady of Grace, was like no other I had been to because it was run by a specific order of priests (The Marian Brothers out of Stockbridge Massachusetts. I love them even though I no longer practice religion, I know that their doctrine to love and family and tolerance is a good way to live life.), whose way of looking at things was in sync with my own. Less about the bad, more about the good. Love, family, and tolerance for others was a big part of their practice. That church was more than a church. It was my home. I was in their very active choir and my daughter went to their school.

I reluctantly left Greensboro in 1998. Here in Massachusetts, I found the churches to be lacking in spirituality. They would rush through the Lord's Prayer to get it over with; devoid of any reverence whatsoever. I found nothing inspirational, no matter how many churches I went to. I missed my life in Greensboro, I missed my church, and my mother was dying. I found no comfort in the churches here. Only annoyance.

Answer: (a) I guess you could say that I didn't return to the church because I couldn't find one that I approved of. Going to mass here is more like a chore and that's not a very good reason to go. That depressed me even further. I didn't think God would hold it against me.

(b) Like many people, there were sections of the Bible that seemed ridiculous to me, even as child. The older I got, the less afraid I was to question it. My first thought was that since the Bible was written by man and man is, as we know, quite flawed, then the Bible had to be flawed. This wasn't helpful with regard to holding onto my religion. Did Moses really part the Red Sea? To me, it is much more believable that aliens leant a hand.

I remain "un-churched" because the older I get the more I see that religion has done more harm in the world than it has good, especially since the events of 9/11. Did I want to be a good sheep?

Did I want to keep my head in the sand? Did I want to be a part of something that perpetuates killing and division? No. More wars have been fought and more hatred sown because of religion than for any other reason, and it's getting crazier all the time. In this country, as you know, a small group of fundamentalist Christians have held our Congress hostage. More hate is spouted from these people than the love their religion dictates. I fear we are becoming a theocracy. And I have great sympathy for atheists. Can you imagine how they must feel having laws thrust upon them designed around a God they do not believe in? In this country, we're not only supposed to be free to practice whatever religion we want, but we're supposed to have freedom FROM religion as well.

But at the deepest core, my shunning of religion stems from the fact that men wrote the religions and they cling to them to justify their subjugation of women. This is true of all religions familiar to me.

3. This is a question I struggle with every day. I guess we have to go back to getting older. We question things we'd never dared or thought to question when we were younger. With age comes less tolerance for bullshit. That is why I put religion aside. But God is another thing altogether. When you separate God from the dogma and the bullshit, it comes down to two things: How superstitious you are and how deeply the old hooks have their barbs in your backside.

I have to ask myself if I believe in God because I'm afraid not to. And why would I be afraid to *not* believe? Simple: Because of death.

I often think God is for little old ladies and recovering alcoholics. Then I think not. Do I dare even think this? Do I dare question his existence when in the end he could turn out to be real and then I'm screwed? I believe in an afterlife. What sort? Whether it is the heaven we've been taught or another dimension, I do not know, but I now lean toward the latter. This has also come about since leaving religion behind. Perhaps we go on to join a combined or collective consciousness, or rather, a collective unconscious that becomes conscious when we die. I think this lofty state is available to us on this earthbound plain, but precious few are able to achieve it. Perhaps through evolution, when we're done spitting through our fingers and fighting over religion, we may evolve enough to achieve such a state of consciousness. Simplistic, maybe, but I'm still evolving.

And one cannot discuss God without discussing death. Death and God go hand in hand. Is it because we fear death that we cling to the belief in God? If you are superstitious, that's a definite yes...even if with reluctance. So, reluctantly, I cling. It's not just the existence of God, but also the existence of ghosts. And saints. I find it hard not to believe in saints. Why, if I no longer follow? Could saints be the very people who in their mortal lives ascended to that higher state of consciousness, or were they touched by the divine hand of God? I bring up saints because one saint in particular affects my daily life: St. Anthony. He is our Patron Saint of the lost. And sister, I lose stuff all the time. Whether it be keys or my wallet, you'll hear me chant: "St. Anthony, St. Anthony, please come around. Something is lost and cannot be found." And yes, you're allowed to laugh. Whether or not he is directing me, I do not know, but he's never let me down because I still have my keys and my wallet is on my desk. I once dropped my keys in the dark during a blizzard, and did not know I dropped them until I got to my car. My tracks were already covered. I prayed to St. Anthony. I walked the way I had come. I stopped, looked down, and in spite of the whipping wind, stinging snow, and darkness I saw the tiniest speck of something that did not belong with all that whiteness. I shoved my hand in the snow and brought up my keys. Some people would call that divine intervention. Maybe they're right. I do not know.

If you believe in God, must you believe in the devil? There are those who say that by the laws of the universe, if there's God, then there must be his opposite. Then again, evil could be a manifestation of the negative unconscious collective. Either way, I'm not taking any chances. Demons scare the living crap out of me.

So my answer is this: I struggle with these questions daily because I am inching ever closer to death and I'm too superstitious to let go for now. I would define God as a bystander who gave us free will, and what we do with it must both delight and sadden him. I also believe that God must be plenty pissed off at all the religious bullshit. Whether or not he created the universe, I do not know. Maybe *it* created *him*, and he used all the wonderful elements contained therein to begin earth, its animals, plants and us.

4/5. I have kept all of this to myself until you asked these questions. It has been my experience that even to hint at such questioning is quite unwelcome. As an example of how this has affected me, let me tell you this: After meeting my professor of this last year, I let a "Jesus Christ" slip under my breath, but she caught it. To one so deeply entrenched in Christianity, this sort of thing is akin to picking your nose, farting and burping all at the same time and while locked together in a tiny closet, not to mention blasphemy. "Don't say that!" Now and then in class she would make her belief evident by giving us hints about herself, such as her favorite music being Christian rock. In an email, I once got a Bible quote. Because I am ever-polite and did not want to get on her bad side, I wrote back that I had not heard that passage in ages, and added a "thank you."

And in this world of the Internet, I see posts from both sides: The accepted inspirational and the struggles of the atheists. We put up with their religious beliefs but there is no tolerance for ours, as you can see by the recent political climate. Also, I do not like to offend people and devout churchgoers would find my views offensive so I have said nothing. I know that it is easier to remain silent because I cannot change their minds, nor they, mine, so what would be the point? They believe that they are right and you must bow to their way of thinking. I find this to be foolish, unyielding blindness, considering that what they believe in has no basis in fact: "That's why it's called 'faith.'" They may be correct and I am 100% wrong, but I'd rather be judged by God. I think I'd suffer a lesser punishment. The churchers are into punishment. I'm hoping that you will write your book.

I'm hoping that you can change a few minds and the world changes for the better. It is worth exposing myself. I have not even told my daughter, who as I said, was raised in the Catholic Church and who is still faithful. I did not tell her out of any sort of fear, but because I am her mother and what I say has influence on her; I want my daughter to reach her own conclusions through her own processes, as I did mine.

Ryan, Grand Rapids, MI

1. I was never an officially member, but my parents were. It was called Berean Bible Church. I attended services there from the time I was a baby, until I was about 21 or 22.

2. Around 21 or 22 was when I stopped going to Berean Bible Church and began attending the church of a co-worker. I liked it a lot at first. However, at this time, I also began developing an interesting in Eastern religions. Especially Buddhism. I found many of the teachings to be the same between the two, and was dismayed at how dismissive the "Christian" faith was of this other faith, even though it was so similar. I'm talking about basic teachings here. Anyway, I stopped going to church period shortly thereafter and just made a decision to research all faiths on my own. Over the last few years, I have grown particularly attached to Gnosticism and Buddhism. I feel no shame or hypocrisy in calling myself a Christian Gnostic Buddhist.

3. God, to me, has become what I call a Creator. And that creator has many faces and teaches through many different teachers. I still pray every day. I still seek "god" in everything around me, all the people, places, events, dreams, etc.

4. My parents accept my beliefs, but don't like it, really. To them, church is the basis of faith. I believe the concept of "church" to be more emotional and mental than physical. I think I've been met with some who believe I am a heretic, and others who accept that I have found a mutable, ever-expanding path WITH God (as opposed to TO God, if that makes sense?)

5. I don't ever hesitate. It's one of my favorite topics and I discuss it and debate and explore it every chance I get.

Cookie, Groveland, FL

1. I was baptized Episcopalian, confirmed Methodist, grew up attending church with my family and was very involved in many church activities, went to a Methodist college where church and chapel were required, then got out of the habit when I started my first job, lived alone, and knew no one.

2. I moved to a new community and stopped going, was never invited by anyone to go to or join a church, married an un-

churched, and we never joined one after we were married.

3. I believe that God is a spirit that watches over us and gives us the "conscience" that helps us make the right decisions in our lives. These beliefs help me follow the teachings in the Bible about loving your fellow man, doing unto others what you would like done to you, treating others with respect, following the Ten Commandments, always trying to do the right things, and living a life that is considered "good" by common standards.

4. Most, if not all, my friends are churched people. We don't really discuss our beliefs, although we sometimes make little jokes about each of our denominations. The jokes are always accepted in good faith (pun intended) and laughed about. We are all very accepting of each other and our choices in all aspects of our lives. My friends accept that I am un-churched, but I think the fact that I live the kind of life I do lets them know that God and his teachings are a part of my life, whether I attend a formal church or not.

5. I don't feel the need to discuss my beliefs with others. I don't like people who try to force their beliefs on me, such as those who come to my door and want to discuss their religion and pray with me. That makes me uncomfortable and I don't want to make others uncomfortable. Religion, like politics, can be a hot button issue, and my friends and I don't feel the need to explain what we believe or why we believe as we do.

Elaine, Louisville KY

1. I was a Southern Baptist until I moved out of my parents' house in my mid-twenties.

2. Originally, I needed the extra sleep on Sunday mornings but then I stayed away because of all the hypocrisy I had seen and continued to see.

3. I think of god (no capital "G" for me) as a benevolent but usually disinterested being who pretty much put us here and turned us loose. How else to explain the horrors mankind has had to endure over the centuries? To be honest, I don't think of god unless I'm in a bad place in my life and need some guidance, which I may or may not receive.

4. I have never discussed my beliefs with a churched person as I'm not interested in getting into an argument. Most of the churched people I know are VERY narrow-minded and if you don't

follow their beliefs, woe be unto you.

5. See my answer for #4.

Loretta (hometown not given)

1. I attended the Brethren Church for 20 years then the Mormon Church.

2. I joined the Mormon Church because my husband was a member and I liked their teachings about family because I grew up in a large loving family. However, we left because we mixed business with church and it was a bad idea for us financially. Other members, not knowing the whole story, verbally abused us. It got harder to attend. We hold no hard feelings, but our beliefs have changed since we stopped attending. Now feel we have grown and expanded our beliefs. I use "we" because my husband feels the same way.

3. God is a loving parent who loves you unconditionally. When we do wrong he is disappointed but still loves us. He allows us to make our mistakes because he knows we will grow and learn from them and everyone has worth and you don't have to be inside a building every Sunday to be "Christ-like."

4. Yes, but to a select few and they are loving, non-judgmental friends. With others I feel like the ol' saying "Don't discuss politics or religion."

5. I feel that I am a good, kind, loving, non-judgmental person, and those who work, play with me are aware of my beliefs.

Paula, Dearborn, MI

1. I have never been a member of a church. Growing up my parents were not churchgoers. I would occasionally go with my grandmother and she attended Catholic churches. I would go with friends so I have been to many different kinds of churches.

2. I never stuck with one church; I never got much out of them.

3. I'm not sure I can define God, I had a dream once when I was in a very dark time in my life. It was sunny and beautiful out and all of a sudden a face filled the sky, a smiling masculine face. I suddenly felt very at peace. I don't know what or who God is but I believe we are closest to God when we are at peace and when we

are sharing peace and love with others. My belief teaches me that I should treat other people the way I want to be treated.

4 & 5. I have from time to time discussed my feelings about God with people who are involved in church and I have to say that most of the time I feel like we are talking about two different Gods. It really does make me hesitant to discuss it with people.

Beth, Poquoson VA

1. I was a member of Grove Avenue Baptist Church in Richmond when I was in high school. I was a member for about six years, but I only attended for three.

2. As I got older and learned to think more for myself and make my own choices (as opposed to letting my parents tell me what to think) I ultimately decided to stop going to church mostly because the other people who attended the church struck me as rude, mean and closed-minded most of the time. I was also turned off by the fact that our pastor harped on getting enough money coming in so he could buy the BMW he'd always wanted! He might have been joking, but it really bugged me when he finally DID get that BMW. Church, to me, also seemed to be elitist. Some people weren't "good enough" to come to that church.

3. I define God as the creator and caretaker of all life. I believe that in return for giving us life, we should strive to respect and treat with care all living things, and that's the primary "rule" I try to live by.

4. I don't think I've ever discussed my beliefs with churched persons. I've never had the opportunity to discuss it with anyone other than my parents, and I think I shied away from discussing it with them because I didn't think they'd "get it."

5. If the subject came up with people other than my parents, I don't think I would hesitate. Maybe ten years ago I would have, but not now. The older I get, the more I appreciate being able to debate things with other intelligent adults. I doubt I would say much to someone I felt was extremely closed-minded, however. I don't think there's any point in discussing things with people who refuse to listen to others with an open mind.

Cary, Las Cruces, NM

1. I joined the Southern Baptist Church when I was about

eleven. I attended services every Sunday and Wednesday for about two years.

    2. The only reason I went regularly was that we were living near my maternal grandmother. When we moved away, we stopped attending services.

    3. I think of God as a force that created the world and then, with the exception of Jesus, let us do our own thing. Kind of a Christian deist, which is a total contradiction in terms.

    4. Never tried to discuss with churched persons. Always felt they were usually too tied to their own beliefs.

    5. I don't discuss with my beliefs with anyone except my partner. I've never been good at debating, which is what I feel such a conversation often turns into. Plus I believe everyone is entitled to his or her own beliefs.

Michelle, Lake Station, IN

    1. As a child I was raised in a Catholic church from birth to confirmation age, around eleven. Soon after, I became an atheist until I was almost twenty. At that time I was "born-again" or "saved"; it was my own choice. On the beach. Just told God if He was really there, I'd be willing to give it a shot. Soon after, I joined an Independent Baptist church (not knowing how legalistic they were.) That lasted maybe five or six months. I stepped away from church until 2003, and then attended a Southern Baptist Church for three years.

    It was during this time that I read the Bible cover to cover several times and studied God's word (at home, on my own) intently. I feel like this was the biggest spiritual growth time in my life. It was also filled with traumatic and horrible situations. Looking back, I believe God was drawing me near to Him and teaching me His way rather than man's way. From 2006-late 2011 I was again un-churched. I've been attending a different Southern Baptist church, but that may change again as the pastor and youth pastor and their families are leaving.

    2. The first Southern Baptist Church that I attended was very dysfunctional. The pastor was power-hungry, a control freak, legalistic, and demeaning to women. As a strong, bold woman, I feel he and the leadership were threatened by me, by my ability to

learn, by my gifts of discernment and teaching. Oddly enough, they were VERY threatened by the excellent, honest, pure, and LOVING relationship I share with my husband. They did not approve of the way we doted on each other, did things for each other, and shared the workload of running our home. So much so, that in the end, the pastor staged what I call a "witch-hunt" to expel me from their congregation.

3. I'm not sure my answer will differ much from the church in this aspect. I do believe God is a Trinity: Father, Son, Holy Spirit. I believe God is ever-present. He wants an intimate relationship with us. But relationships take a LOT of time and hard work.

4. Many churched people (in my opinion) seem dumbed-down. They go to church on Sunday, listen to an hour sermon and think they have a relationship with God. In my marriage, if I were to put forth only an hour a week my so-called marriage would not be a marriage. Churched people don't seem to understand how much time and effort I put into my relationship with God. And no, my beliefs don't seem to be respected.

5. Me? Ha. No. I'm rather bold. LOL

Ty, Chapel Hill NC.

1. I was a member of Southland Christian Church in central Kentucky when I was about aged 9 to15. From ages 15 to 28 I attended a few other churches for no more than a year and never joined any of them.

2. I initially left Southland because my mother and stepfather divorced and my immediate family became a single-parent household. For financial reasons my mother had to work two full-time and one part-time job and I myself began working. We had not the time nor energy to attend church regularly. As I became older and life became more stable, I attempted to attend other churches, but while I felt there were a number of good people there, I was also disillusioned by what I construed as un-Christian attitudes.

3. I try not to define God other than I believe God exists and means for each of us to treat one another well. In my daily life, I try to follow what has almost become a cliché, the Golden Rule. I try to give others the benefit of the doubt, at least at first.

4. Over the years I have discussed my personal beliefs with a number of ministers and a couple of rabbis, though I am very careful about the individuals with whom I am speaking. Some people are open to listening about the beliefs of others while some are not. In general, I felt I was understood and respected, but then I try to broach such subjects only with individuals who I believe will offer me that respect, if not also the understanding.

5. In general, yes. I do care to discuss my beliefs with others but I hesitate. Why? Because many people are not respectful of others, and are often downright rude and even hateful. And in no way am I referring only to those who claim to be Christians. A growing number of atheists are just as disrespectful, from my experience.

Suzanne, Paso Robles, CA

1. In 2003, I was baptized and became a member of the Plymouth Congregational Church. I left the church in 2008 and I hope to return someday but not while the current pastor is there.

2. Our simply wonderful pastor retired. The new pastor is a sham as far as I am concerned. When my marriage fell apart and I ended up in the hospital, I had to call my retired pastor in Ohio; the new pastor could not be troubled with giving support or counsel.

3. God is un-definable. Male and female. Creator. Love. Speaks directly through conscience. Does not judge but asks that we examine ourselves and our motives.

4. Since I am a Christian-Pagan, I am very careful with whom I share. I have studied ministry and found an accepting fellowship there. My former pastor understood and helped me to understand the validity of my beliefs.

5. I am Christian by geography and upbringing. I see value in most all belief systems and have discovered that my beliefs are both Christian and pagan in nature. It is very difficult for me to make others uncomfortable around me so I usually keep mum. I can let others see the good in me that they can handle and then I keep the rest hidden.

Michelle, Brevard, NC

1. I was a member of the Hillsborough United Church of Christ for about two years.

2. We moved. I haven't yet been able to find a church that was so all-inclusive. I don't think I ever will.

3. To me, faith and religion are much simpler than most churches make them out to be. I believe God created the universe and is the force of good in the world. I also believe Jesus Christ was sent by God to instruct us to love and be good to one another. As such, I try to live my life this way. It doesn't always work, but I do believe I can talk to God and ask for guidance when I'm having a hard time with it.

4. I try not to discuss my beliefs, but sometimes my family and I will get into it. And sometimes I just have to blurt something out. I do think in some cases that I am listened to by the churched people I discuss things with, but sometimes I can almost see them shaking their heads sadly as they walk away.

5. Yes. I think it has something to do with the way I was brought up. My family was sort of withdrawn. Good people, but not very expressive about important things. Part of being brought up in the South, I expect.

Teresa, Centreville VA

1. I was a member of Main Street Methodist Church from 1960-1976. I rarely went during the college years as I was away, and my family didn't go every Sunday anyway. I became a Lutheran when I moved to Fairfax. That lasted a few years. I went occasionally, but not consistently.

When my son was born, around 1992, I started going to New Life Christian Church (a non-denominational church that had modern music, bands, casual dress, and was just full of cool, younger people.) Everyone was "nice."

2. I left the last church because it got way too big and I didn't feel like I belonged. But the final straw was when the minister's wife and another female church leader became so vocal about Obama when he first took office. They predicted all kinds of gloom and doom. Not only that, they stated, "I don't want my tax dollars going to pay for abortion." And other such garbage related to whatever propaganda they were reading. Also, a number of them who home-schooled were constantly putting down the quality of education of public schools. I was a public elementary teacher at

that time. Another male assistant minister posted a lot of pro-Republican and anti-Democrat rhetoric on Facebook, or just argued and debated. Another female continued to post anti-gay Bible verses and took it upon herself to "pray" for me due to my political beliefs. Actually, Facebook had a lot to do with my leaving because so many of them were commenting against things that I valued. In the church itself, it was actually the same old goody two shoes stuff, but no direct political preaching that occurred while I was there.

I visited my brother's Catholic Church once, and the priest came right out and said the Catholics needed to unite and stop supporting both parties. They needed to always vote for the candidate (or party) that was 100% against abortion. Period.

3. As an un-churched believer, I would say that I go back and forth on whether or not God is real and exists, mostly because of the rhetoric from those I think are extremists, including my extreme right wing holier than thou sister, whom I've crowned the "Bible Bully." There is still that question in the back of my mind that wonders if she is right, but it has more to do with my lack of confidence than with religious doctrine. I feel that God cannot possibly be so mean and that he must love everyone, including gay people. I have very dear friends who are gay, so I will defend them to the death. I do not feel God is the dictator some of the other churches, especially those down south, seem to push. I do not like that FEAR is such an important part of the fundamentalist movement. So, it is my hope that I am not completely wrong in my perception. I also believe the Bible was written by humans and that it was written to go with the culture of that time in history. This has been a relatively recent discovery I have made. It has many good guidelines, but is not absolute. As for why the fundamentalists choose a few verses to justify their bigotry is beyond me. But, you absolutely cannot argue with one of them. They always have a comeback and refuse to budge.

My beliefs probably do influence my life, although I am not overtly aware of it. I am basically honest, kind, and compassionate. And then there is that feeling of GUILT that hovers over me if I do anything even remotely "wrong." Guilt and fear are two aspects of religious teachings I would rather not have, but they are always there.

4. When I was going to New Life, I went to a few Bible studies. I would ask a few questions about what if or why something was the way it was. Everyone was always "nice" but I felt that the self-appointed elders were a tad self-righteous and got more out of their position of superiority than being non-judgmental. I would agree with them or say nothing, so I never truly revealed my own thoughts. I definitely felt that I was lacking something that they all had. It was probably a complete commitment to faith. I have always questioned everything, I guess. The worst parts were the surprising comments they made on Facebook. It really took me by surprise. I "un-friended" most of them and then decided not to go back there.

5. I have no problem discussing my beliefs with people I consider to be friends who have like beliefs, but I cannot hold my own when up against someone (like my sister) who eats, sleeps, and breathes their church. I never have the words to come back. So I just back down and go away feeling crushed and angry. My sister probably makes me angrier than anyone, but she is also the reason I so vehemently reject what I perceive as the "church." And, I think of the other people from New Life to be just like her.

I visited an Episcopal church a short while ago. The original parishioners had been kicked out by the right-wing group that took over about five years earlier. A group of them split from the diocese because they did not like that they were allowing gay people to be priests. They confiscated the building. Finally the Supreme Court of Virginia said the group that split had to return the property to the diocese. It was great. The minister was a woman! And there were several gay people there who finally found a church to welcome them. If I did decide to go back to a building for church, I might go there. At least I know they are not against gay people or women. After not going for quite a while, I have gotten just lazy about getting up on Sunday morning, so that would be another issue for me to deal with at this point.

Jacquie, Staunton, VA

1. I attended church for most of my growing up years. I was a part of Staunton Alliance, a non-denominational church. Most of the churches I attended were non-denominational. But I was

always fascinated by churches with more rituals, though those churches had more strict beliefs than I did.

2. I stopped being churched when I was pregnant and unmarried. They made me feel like I was the ultimate sinner. I'd rather believe in a God of acceptance and love. It was too fear based. All fire and brimstone. Too much of how we are all going to hell.

3. I define God as a God of love. God sees the good in people, the best in people. And loves them no matter what their flaws are. My God loves everyone no matter who they are and who they love.

4. I have discussed my views. A roommate of mine's sister was all about conversion. I told her I can't believe in a God who hates so readily.

5. I don't hesitate to discuss my beliefs. But to be honest, it very rarely comes up.

Elizabeth, Philadelphia, PA

1. I was raised in a moderate Southern Baptist church in Danville, VA, going to Sunday school and church pretty much every Sunday. My mom did not pressure us to be baptized on a certain schedule, and I was a free thinker, so I did not decide to get baptized until I was an adult. I did so in my childhood church. In some ways, I still consider myself a moderate Baptist, because I appreciate the fact the denomination allows for individuals to commune with God and interpret the Bible themselves.

2. My reasons for being un-churched are somewhat complicated. When I moved to NYC, then to Philly, there weren't many Baptist churches similar to the one I was raised in. While I did occasionally attend the services of other denominations, I never found one whose basic tenet appealed to me as much as the Baptist faith. While Southern Baptists have evolved into an ultra-conservative sect, the basic tenets of the Baptist faith, including priesthood of all believers, recognizing the right of Christians to interpret the Bible as God directs them to, religious freedom and separation of church and state, and being old enough to consciously make the decision to be baptized, always seemed more logical and meaningful than those of other denominations.

I still occasionally enjoy going to church services of various denominations, but I do not believe that my relationship with God is controlled or determined by my presence there; to me it is simply a place where I can commune with others who believe in God and celebrate those beliefs in a public setting. The formality of the rituals and music associated with worship also appeal to me at times, though I feel closest to God when I'm speaking directly to him in my everyday life. I should also note that I'm married to a Catholic, and while many of my Catholic friends believe it's okay to differ from the church's teachings on certain things, I could never convert because I have issues with committing to a church that says I have to follow their priests' instructions in how I commune with God. That contradicts my Baptist-raised belief that I can understand God just as easily and be guided by my own conscience.

3. I am constantly considering and questioning my beliefs about God, which I feel is a healthy exercise. At its most basic level, I believe that most single-deity religions worship the same God, and that men have created the differences in the specific traditions and ways in which we worship him. I do not feel the exact ritual or methods one uses to worship God makes a tremendous difference, and it amazes me that such things have started wars—it seems to me that God is way too busy to be paying attention to every little thing a person does before praying to him. I also feel strongly that the Bible was written by men and is a piece of literature that should not be taken literally at all times. Thus, I do not see a conflict between evolution and religion; I see no reason that God's perception of the six days it took him to create the universe would be the same as mankind's. I also don't find any conflict in believing that God could create evolution to change species over time, in the same way He gave humans free choice. My personal beliefs make me sensitive to the religious beliefs of other people. I believe they have a right to worship as they choose, since I was raised to believe they each can commune directly with God and interpret the Bible themselves. After all, Baptists were once persecuted for their religion, even by other Christians.

4. I only discuss my religious beliefs occasionally with others, since my relationship to God is very personal to me. Even as

a child, I often studied Bible stories and read passages in the privacy of my room. I got a lot more out of those sessions than from the Sunday school lessons. Most of my close friends who are churched understand that I am in many ways personally devout despite not embracing a specific church. They do not seem to have an issue with my faith. I'm not sure my in-laws, who are Filipino and thus very Catholic, understand my views on religion or anything else, but I'm an enigma to them in many ways! I think they appreciate that I usually attend Mass when I'm visiting, and I find that I enjoy the ritual of the service (except for the fire and brimstone homily that frequently touches on political topics.) In general, when I have gotten into a conversation with people about religion and have mentioned my views such as the creation being compatible with evolution, I have found most people agree and have similar moderate views. Of course, I live in the Northeast....

5. I don't generally bring up religion in conversation, since my relationship with God is very personal to me. However, I find myself more hesitant/defensive about talking of being raised a Southern Baptist than my un-churched views. Most people I encounter do not realize that the SBC was once considered a fairly liberal Christian denomination. Now that it has been overtaken by fundamentalists, my childhood church and many others have diverted their mission money to other, more moderate groups. Most people also don't realize that the very nature of Baptists means that the SBC can't direct their members how to believe the way the Pope can to Catholics. Our churches and constituents are decentralized and those pronouncements are statements rather than directives. Yet it's difficult to explain that the Baptist religion actually says I can interpret the Bible on my own and commune directly with God and that separation of state and church is good, since the SBC are the main face of Baptists in many ways.

Laura, Anaheim, California

1. I was a member all my life, even went to Catholic School at St. John the Baptist in Long Island, NY. The last church I was a parishioner was at St Pius X in Conyers GA.

2. Around 2000 I was only attending once in awhile and holidays. I was going through a divorce and I had some personal loss on 9/11/2001. I was depressed and isolated myself a lot. I felt even more depressed after going to mass. I can't explain why but around 2005 was the year I lost my children. It really made very little sense to go anymore after that.

3. I believe God is Love. That's the best way to explain it, whatever umbrella that covers. Our desire to do the right thing, care about the welfare of others etc., it all falls under that power.

4. At first, I tried but I'm not into arguing and that is what it would turn into. I don't want to be on the defensive. So I would bow out and leave it with "let's agree to disagree".

5. Yes, I don't even like religious discussions any more.

Pam (hometown not given)

1. I was Catholic from birth until my parents allowed me to stop attending church at fifteen or sixteen. There were always things that I couldn't reconcile about church teachings. I joined the local Unitarian Universalist church about eight years ago, but I virtually never attend services, only a few social functions each year. Their beliefs are compatible with mine and not exclusive of other traditions, although they tend to be more agnostic/atheistic/humanistic than I am.

2. There were questions I had early on about things in the Bible and things taught by the Catholic Church, including unequal roles for women and men and the fact that dogma and rules always seemed to be dwelt on more than the very prolific teachings of love. I don't know if Jesus was the son of God any more than any of us are, or even if he intended to be taken that way, but he was certainly a person worth emulating. Too many "Christian" sects like the God of the Old Testament more than they like or follow Jesus.

I have the rather radical belief that the God of the Old Testament was not a God that I would follow at all, and that Jesus was much more of what is admirable in a God. Probably my biggest problem was that the God of the Old Testament was jealous, angry, petty and mean. Why would I worship him/it? Not worthy of anyone's worship. Additionally, the letters of Paul pissed me off many times. I feel quite sure that the Bible was written and assembled by humans with their own agendas, but somewhere in there, the very good person of Jesus has a kernel of truth that I can believe in as a child of God, and an example of ONE of the offspring of a God who is worth worshipping. Also, as another radical belief, I find reincarnation a very plausible life sequence, if such things are designed by a compassionate God. Much better to say, "Hey, you didn't get it quite right this time, let's give it another go and maybe you'll get it the next time."

3. It would be presumptuous for me to define God. That being said, what I believe about God is that s/he is incomprehensible, perfect, bigger than any of the definitions we can put to him/her. Bigger than gender, bigger than sect or religion, bigger than Muslim or Christian or Hindu or Jewish. Bigger and better...love and compassion and ultimately unselfish...the antithesis, in many ways, of that Old Testament "God." The only thing I know for sure is that love and compassion are more important than everything else, which is maybe why I define God the way I do.

4. Yes, I've discussed my beliefs with a few churched people. But usually not in any depth, because they seem to feel that my differing beliefs are a reason to convince me of the rightness of their beliefs, which are almost always more rigid and less loving than what I believe. Recently a very conservative churched friend responded to a post of mine on Facebook. "That sounds apocalyptic, have you made your peace with God?" My response may have sounded flip, but wasn't meant that way. I said, "Yeah, we're cool."

5. I hesitate in most circumstances to discuss my beliefs with others because of the above sort of response. I am fine with my beliefs and fine with what may befall me if I am wrong. I have no interest in being converted or in converting anyone else, but I usually find that others are much more interested in converting me because they are so convinced of the singular, exclusive "rightness" of their own path. I like the saying that there are many paths to the top of the mountain. I don't think mine is the only one.

Martha, Stuarts Draft, VA

1. I grew up in a church called Fredericksburg Baptist

Church. We went every Sunday for Sunday School and church and every Wednesday for choir practice and dinner. Even when we moved 20-30 minutes away, we still went faithfully twice a week. In my later years of high school, I started to bow out more on the Wednesday nights for other commitments and I tried to get out of church whenever my Dad would let me. When I went to college, there was no more church for me except when I was home visiting my parents. A few years ago, my husband and I explored the idea of going back to church and started going to Greenmonte Fellowship and attended services there for a little less than a year.

2. Oddly enough, there have been two times I have left churches and three times I decided to remain un-churched. As a high school senior, I simply wanted to do other things with my time. I didn't want to get up early, get dressed up, and sit through services. Lots of times, I worked Sunday mornings and never felt as though I was missing anything. So my decision to leave the church then was one of convenience. But as I progressed through my college years, I began to have more and more conflict with my very Baptist family. My grandfather was a Southern Baptist minister. My father, in my opinion, is not a deeply spiritual man, but he has always dutifully attended church, though often from the safety of the children's nursery where he helped out. My cousins are all deeply religious and spiritual and would never miss a church service. For my siblings and me, there never seemed to be that strong of a connection. But my brother, like my father before him, was dutiful. He attended church and did not have alcohol at his wedding reception even though he is a regular drinker. My sister seemed more connected to the church and also rejected alcohol at her wedding, due to fear of angering my grandparents and because her husband-to-be had family members that struggled with addiction. Both lived "in sin" with their significant others long before marriage but kept that a secret from my grandparents to maintain appearances.

Then there's me. I'm not a wild child at all. I've never smoked marijuana, for example, or experimented with any drug past two cigarettes and alcohol. But in my family, I am the black sheep. I struggled with the idea of lying about who I was since I saw nothing wrong with it. I had been dating someone for over a year and wanted him to come to my family reunion with me, and of course sharing a room since we had been living together. I told my grandfather that that was my plan and he more or less flipped. He drove from Richmond to Williamsburg to tell me how much of a sinner I was. He even asked to pray for me right then and there and proceeded to tell God that he hoped I could change my life before I went straight to hell. He wanted to know the extent of the relationship and when I told him that it was none of his business, he grew angrier. I also told him that I had not been attending church and mentioned something about having issues with the ways my gay friends were treated. You can imagine how that went over. From that day until his death, the relationship between us was very strained. I dutifully asked him to say a prayer at my wedding since I had asked my stepfather to perform the ceremony. He did so but the prayer was loaded with references to wishing some of us knew what real love really was and how real love could not exist without God. He also sent me a scathing letter after I informed him that there would be alcohol at the reception and told me that he wished I had the personal strength to avoid it.

    I realize that this is a lot of family background, but it really is pivotal to understanding why I have such a hesitancy to return to any church. I spend 99.9% of my waking time giving to others --- financially, emotionally, anything I possibly can. And yet, because I don't sit in a room and daydream for one hour a week, there are people that say I'm going to hell. I used to say that I believe in Kindergarten religion - love one another, do unto others, etc. - and that that clearly doesn't exist in churches and religions where they scream about the sinners amongst us. I have absolutely no problems with homosexuality or gay marriage and could truly care less if someone is gay or straight. I don't think any of us has a right to judge anyone else since we all have backstories that make us who we are. And yet thoughts like those seem to be rebellious in churches where there's often an expectation to lie about who you really are and be the perfect Christian for that hour each Sunday. I have no desire to lie about who I am so I'm probably just not a good fit for most churches.

    3. I wish I could define God but that's something I struggle with. Some days, I'd tell you that God is some sort of higher power

within the universe, kind of a marriage of fate, karma, & positive energy. Other days I'll tell you that God is the embodiment of all of the positivity on Earth: love, kindness, empathy. There are even days when I look at my atheist cousin and can completely understand his beliefs. It just varies. The truth is that I don't know how to define God except for some sort of higher power within the universe. That belief doesn't specifically instruct my day-to-day life but the basic tenets that I learned in my early church days certainly shape who I am today. I really honestly believe that we should treat everyone with kindness and patience. And I often fail at that but I try. I think we should resist the temptation to judge someone and instead spend our energy trying to understand them (not agree with them necessarily). I guess I see God as the ultimate supervisor of the Golden Rule. If people would simply treat others as they want to be treated, the world could be amazing. I can't control anyone but myself so I try to do that each day and to pass that lesson on to my students.

    4. Yes, I have. Ugh. Rarely do churched believers hear anything other than "I don't belong to a church." I've been prayed for, invited to attend numerous churches, etc, etc. And not because of my lack of faith or belief but because of my lack of membership. Occasionally, there are exceptions. One reason that my husband and I started going to Greenmonte is that the people we knew there were genuine, accepting, and seemingly nonjudgmental. They didn't seem to be concerned about the fate of our souls if we didn't come to church but instead thought we could enrich their church and enjoy it. A small difference but to me, an important one. These people are also some of the most kindhearted, loving families we know. While it's still a church and we struggle with them not agreeing with our more open-minded views of things, we did enjoy our time there and stopped going not because of any theological issues but because our toddler son made it logistically difficult. But I will admit that I have a hesitancy to return. I guess I'm still waiting to feel that "holier than thou" judgment that I associate with most churches and haven't yet been convinced that it's not forthcoming. I have no interest in hellfire and brimstone. None. And I don't need to spend an hour a week being told that I'm essentially a horrible person. I'd rather spend that time figuring out

ways to help my fellow man.

    5. The only times I hesitate to discuss my beliefs are in my classes. And it's for very different reasons. First, I have no time or interest to deal with parent phone calls telling me I need to change or reprimanding me for discussing faith in school. But mostly, I want these kids to make their own conclusions and not to take on mine like they often take on their parents. So if I don't put mine out there, they still have to think things through. As for adults, I sadly spend so much time with teenagers that I don't have a lot of adult conversation that works its way to church and faith.

Beth (hometown not given)

    1. I was never a member of a church.

    2. I remain un-churched because I haven't found a need in my life that would require me to attend a group to worship.

    3. There are a mixture of things that I believe in when it come to God. I believe in reincarnation. I also believe that there is a heaven and a hell. Part of me believes that my child should be baptized just in the off chance that whenever we all do get up to heaven, if getting baptized was the ticket in, I don't want to him to miss out and not get to see all his loved ones again. I believe that God fits in as a figure who watches. I think that things kind of move and change under their own power and He is there to make sure that things are running smoothly like they always do. I don't see Him as a creator but just a watcher. I was a biology major when I first started college, so I can't ignore evidence of evolution. God might have started some things but I think other living things adapted to match their environments or needs over time.

    4. I have discussed my beliefs with the pastor who officiated my wedding. He is a Presbyterian pastor and very laid back. I know that I was understood and respected for the fact that I felt that it was the right thing to do to get married in a church.

    5. I live in a very diverse community with many religions and races. I am open about what I feel. I have never been made to feel wrong for what I believe in. However, I had a very Southern Baptist grandmother who didn't understand where my point of view was coming from. I remember talking with her about it and she defended herself by saying, "Look outside. You don't think that

God made all of this for you? Look how beautiful it is." At the time I lived on a farm with rolling green hills and woods on the edge. She was the only one who felt sad, I guess, about me not having the same kind of faith that she did.

Chris, Kenosha, WI

1. I grew up in a white, middle-class suburban Presbyterian church, which is about as all-American as you can get. Then later, I joined an evangelical super church. My wife and I were married in the Evangelical Covenant church and later re-baptized. It wasn't until after our two sons were born that I left the church, and they followed soon thereafter.

2. I divorced myself from the church when I did some rigorous study on the evolution of the Bible, beginning with *The Complete Gospels*. The Bible is quality literature, and it does contain some very powerful spiritual truths, but the likelihood that Jesus is divine is far less likely than him being a Robin Hood/King Arthur-type folk hero/figure.

3. I don't know how I would define God. My cultural background leads me to believe God is an omniscient, omnipotent, personal (as in, he is a person) deity, but I'll readily admit that most of why I believe that is preference, not logic. I will say that if there is a God who created us, he/she created us to love, and therefore must also love. That seems logical.

4. Discussing religion is a bad idea unless you're sure you're in a safe place with a person who respects you, regardless of what you believe. My parents, who are still believers, now give me that respect, but for a long time, they treated me like I was going through a phase. To a certain extent, they still do. I find that agnostics are probably the most respecting bunch. Christians, by and large, are not. (And when I was one, I was no exception.) As far as being understood, I feel like I am by people who are ready to let go of their team colors and let truth guide them. But don't most people think the same thing?

5. I hesitate to discuss my beliefs with others. No one wants to understand you, they just want you to be on their team. Doesn't make sense. It just is.

Laura, Las Vegas, NV

1/2. My family joined a Presbyterian Church when I was about fourteen. We moved about a year and half later and never rejoined a church. My Mom joined one within the last five years but doesn't go much anymore. My Dad was raised in the church and he hated it so never pushed us.

3. I believe in God as something/someone out there who helps us as humans, but who still lets us make our own choices. I do pray to "him/her" but it's usually is more of a "please get me through X,Y,Z and I'll be good."

4. It really depends on who the person is. I lived in New Orleans a while and many people there were really religious. In the high school I attended, students would shove their views on anybody who did not believe what they did. As I got older, I've found more people willing to discuss and have conversations about God, religion, etc. Conversations about God are usually different from conversations about religion. My Mother and I both believe that God is out there and helps us find peace and make peace with things that have happened in our lives, but again, he/she lets us make our own choices.

5. YES! Many people I have met want you to believe in "their religion" more than "their God." I'd rather discuss God over religion any day.

Lisa, Beattyville, KY

1. I have been a member of four different churches. The first one was Belmont Baptist Church in Ashland, KY. I was a member from the time I was nine until I married at seventeen. The second church I joined was in England. As far as I can recall, it was nondenominational. I attended for about two years until I returned to the United States. The third church was Beattyville Christian Center where I taught in the church's school. The fourth church was Abundant Light, also located in Beattyville, KY.

2. I was basically thrown out of Beattyville Christian Center. This was hard to deal with because I really loved the church and its school. During the time I taught there, I was in a car wreck. It is miraculous that I survived. The pastor and my husband stayed with me almost around the clock while I was in the hospital. They

watched over me and prayed for me. I went from being brain damaged and paralyzed from the waist down to walking out of the hospital with my mind intact in just under six weeks. Yet I left because the lady who ran the church's school thought I was going to try and take over. I have no clue how she thought I was going to do this. She proceeded to kick me out of the school. I left and took my kids with me. The pastor did not even contact us to see why we left. That kind of hurt.

From there I went to Abundant Light for eighteen years. The church was a huge part of my life. The pastor and his wife were great friends of ours. I experienced things there that I will never forget – people were healed right in front of my eyes. I saw demons cast out of people. I saw relationships healed. Life was great. Then the pastor entire theology began to change. He started preaching universalism, although never admitted that he was. Then, when my daughter was molested by our neighbor, he preached that we must love the guy who did it and that we weren't to feel harshly towards him. He became distant and began preaching things that weren't even in the Bible. So we left. He didn't bother to ask why we quit attending.

After staying out of church for about a year, I again met up with the lady I had taught with at Beattyville Christian Center. She told me how wrong she had been and how much she missed me. I went back to church there, and for a while, things were great. But things started to unravel once more. The pastor was on drugs. He began making passes at my daughter, and his wife defended him. I could not handle that. I left.

Why do I remain un-churched? I always heard this as an excuse from people about why they wouldn't go to church, but never really understood it until it happened to me time and time again. I refuse to go back to church because of the two-faced actions of those preaching and those attending.

3. I would define God as the Creator. He is the one who healed me after my horrific car wreck. He is the reason I am able to walk, and the reason I am not brain damaged. I truly am thankful for that. I'm not so sure my beliefs influence my life much at all anymore. Sometimes I pray, sometimes I read my Bible, but not that often. Most of my time is spent reading, editing, and writing.

4. Most of the people who live in my town know exactly why we don't go to church, and this includes the ones who still attend those churches. No one seems to be brave enough to tell me I need to come back to church.

5. I'll discuss my beliefs with anyone who asks about them.

Diane, Lafayette, IN

1. I grew up in a very small town in Indiana and attended a Methodist church with my mother. We went most Sundays when my mother wasn't working (she worked swing shift in a glass factory). I have mostly good memories of singing the old hymns and the traditional Methodist service but I wouldn't say I was particularly religious. I believed generally in God but had a lot of questions when I got to college. I've struggled with depression most of my life so while at Indiana University I took a class on Death and Dying and began to question in earnest. I had a general belief in God but I hadn't really embraced the whole "Jesus" thing. In fact, I was rather put off by "Jesus" as my experience of Him had mostly been through overzealous Southern Baptists and a next-door Nazarene lady, all of whom I'm sure had good intentions of wanting to save my soul but were poor at public relations. The Jesus they presented required dressing badly, wearing no make up, and turning into a complete weirdo.

Anyway, I had a spiritual experience while at IU (1979) that was life changing. For the sake of brevity I won't go into it here but I was NOT going to church, not hanging out with church people, and this experience was completely outside of religious organization. Like the Apostle Paul wrote about his experience, it occurred suddenly, through revelation and not through any man. It completely convinced me over night that Jesus was indeed the Son of God, although a much different and vastly more powerful version than any Jesus that had ever been presented to me. Since I had absolutely no framework for what had occurred and didn't know what else to do, I went back to the only church I knew, the Methodist church in my hometown. I stayed for a while but found more questions than answers. I had a hard time lining up my personal experience with much of the traditional trappings.

Eventually I drifted away from church and religion again although I never stopped believing in Jesus. The experience had been real. I just wasn't sure how it all fit in with everything else. For the next ten years I avoided church and religion. I got married, divorced, had a daughter, and started a career as a psychologist. The depression returned and I remembered the experience I'd had in college. I was seriously contemplating suicide and pretty much gave God an ultimatum – if He were real then He needed to show up and let me know because if I'd just imagined that whole thing then I reasoned that there was no spiritual consequence to suicide.

Well, looong story short: He showed up. Again, suddenly, completely apart from any human influence, and within literally a few seconds completely changed my life, my thinking, my spiritual perceptions and once again reaffirmed that Jesus was indeed exactly who HE claimed He was (as opposed to much of who religion claims He is). Once again, I had no framework for what I experienced and didn't know where to look. Somehow I ended up meeting with a Lutheran pastor. He was very kind and spent a lot of time going through theology and the Bible with me, but I just couldn't line up his traditional belief system with either of my experiences. He and his church pretty much denied spiritual experience – that all ended with the apostles, he said, but that was not what my encounter led me to believe at all.

About that time the Vineyard with John Wimber was emerging and I "happened" upon a book that seemed to validate what I'd experienced. I found out there was a Vineyard starting up in Lafayette. I attended for several years. It was a good fit and a good learning experience for a long time. The church was mostly made up of escapees from the Faith Movement and so they came with a lot of baggage. They really WANTED to embrace freedom but they were constantly fighting their previous religious programming. They WANTED to be different but they just couldn't shake the traditional political and authority structures. They also began to develop an attitude of "spiritual superiority" that ran rampant among the Charismatics. It was a spiritual pride that was begging for a fall. The church shut down after the pastor's wife had an affair with the worship leader. I had already pretty much detached from the whole thing but there were a lot of wounded people.

I bought a house in my hometown where we spent weekends. I started attending another small Vineyard near there. The pastor had actually been a Baptist preacher who "saw the light" of spiritual freedom and resigned from his Baptist church. At Vineyard, he refused payment as a pastor and the authority trappings. He was a great guy and still a good friend. The end to this church however, still came from the same basic problems with traditional authority structure. In this case it wasn't the pastor but the people who couldn't let go of the idea that they had to have someone rule over them. Eventually the pastor left because he refused to take that role. They replaced him with one of their own who took on that traditional role.

I was about done with "church" by that time. However, I had gotten to know some people from another church in Lafayette called Maple Ridge. It was sort of traditional (came from the Missionary Alliance background) in that it was trying to be kind of charismatic but mostly failing - lol. I had made several friends there, including the pastor who seemed to be really interested in my experiences and who kind of courted me as someone who could help the church move in a more spiritual direction. I did end up joining the church - mainly because it was important to THEM that I do so. I had to take a fairly lengthy class that I thought was mostly indoctrination. My thinking was that they knew who I was, what I believed, and they wanted me there to move them in the direction of more spiritual freedom. That did not turn out to be the case.

2. Maple Ridge was the end of "church as we know it" for me. At first I was really courted and embraced by Maple Ridge because I had certain "spiritual gifts" that were highly sought after at the time. However, it didn't take long for that to become problematic because my gift involved being able to see the truth rather clearly and I wasn't easily intimidated or willing to bring my gift into submission. The pastor tried to "bring me under authority" and I felt like that was complete bullshit. I tried for awhile to toe the party line but it became clear he was rather obsessed with authority. The reason he had wanted me to join his church was to control my gifting rather than use it to lead the people into more spiritual freedom. It also was becoming more and more obvious

that he used that authority to control and manipulate the people in his church. The need to control and manipulate through fear is rampant in institutional Christianity. I read theology and researched the early Church (actually called the *Ecclessia* – church was a word added by King James with the idea of helping to keep the *Ecclessia* under control). I had also read the entire Bible from cover to cover (which most Christians haven't - they only really know what their pastors have told them it says), did word studies, and investigated the Hebraic roots and the cultural meaning behind scriptures. I found that most of the Bible is routinely misused and abused and used more as a weapon than a source of inspiration and solace.

I have always had this problem of thinking for myself, which incredibly pisses off people who are threatened by that quality. Nevertheless, I was still pretty "churched" and tried to hang in there and do the right thing until the pastor staged an intervention for me because of my unwillingness to submit to authority. I know how that sounds. We are not talking about some stereotypical cultish Pentecostal church here. We are talking pretty much mainstream and well-respected church in the community. It was eye-opening! That was it for me, and then God intervened again - supernaturally. I had a vision. In the vision it was very clear that I was released from the Institutional Church (IC). I had learned what I was supposed to learn there and thank God, I was no longer required to stay there. So I left, and unlike Lot's wife, I have never looked back even though several of my "friends" came to visit because they were worried about my soul. I lost many friends and it was a painful process, but I never regretted it for a minute. I've actually reconciled with several of the friends who caused me the deepest pain because in the years following they had their own eyes opened and their own experiences that brought them out of "Babylon." They sought me out to apologize and ask forgiveness. They are all on different paths regarding their de-programming but all have moved into greater spiritual freedom since leaving the IC.

3 .I have a very definite belief in God the Father, God the Son, and God the Holy Spirit. I have a very personal and revelatory relationship with each person of the Trinity. However, I have not found, in my personal knowing of this God, that He/She/They

(however you want to look at it) has much resemblance to the God that is portrayed by much of Christianity – especially the religious right, which I think actually may be more demonically inspired than anything else. I don't think most Christians intentionally try to misrepresent God but are so influenced by their religious programming and the fear that is inspired by the IC's authority structure that they are afraid to think for themselves or to question what they've been taught. I actually think that this is the "Babylon" the Scriptures command them to flee from. But until they realize they are enslaved by fear and that the only thing really imprisoning them is their own mindsets, it's not likely they will change. How does it influence my daily life? I just try to live as authentically as I can and to be sincere and honest in my relationships and my failings. I guess I feel a certain responsibility to try and challenge people to think and question what they believe and how they arrived at those beliefs. It doesn't matter to me what people believe as much as that they arrived at those beliefs by their own free will. I believe free will and freedom to think and choose are among the highest ideals of the God that I believe in. I think God wants to be KNOWN and how can anyone know Him if they are afraid to question him?

Here is the crux of my belief: I believe that God the Father cared more about OUR freedom to choose than He cared about the life of His own Son. To me that is the message of the cross. It was about OUR freedom. It was God's way of saying, "HERE is an incredible public statement that all debts have been paid for, all sins cancelled, all fears relieved. I'm willing to let my own son die so that NO ONE has to ever be afraid of me again." And yet, the IC has completely lost this message.

4. LOL Well, I think I sort of already answered that. Oh yes, I've tried to discuss this with churched persons and it has generally not been well received. People seem to like their mental/spiritual prisons. I have a few friends who have the same perspective as I do and we have mostly given up on trying to talk to churched people. I used to try but pretty much regretted it every time. I have basically come to the conclusion that apart from divine revelation it is not likely that you can argue or debate anyone into departing from their belief system.

5. Absolutely, I hesitate. I didn't discuss any of this for years and only recently have re-joined the discussion a little bit. I'm not sure I have even talked with anyone about the things I wrote above for many, many years and then only with a few who went through similar experiences. For about the last six years I completely excused myself from all spiritual/religious discussion and involvement. I didn't feel comfortable with most "churched" people because I have such a different perspective on most issues. I don't talk to unbelievers about it much because first of all I would have to try and hack through all the barriers imposed by the stereotypes perpetuated by centuries of organized religion, the media and the recent big mouths in the IC (for example, idiots like Pat Robertson, "Christian Conservatives," et al) who have given a completely false impression of Jesus. I don't blame anyone for wanting nothing to do with Church-ianity but I do get angry when I feel like Jesus is being falsely presented. That is the only reason I have re-joined the discussion at all.

Jenny, Grand Rapids, MI

1. I was baptized in a Southern Baptist church in West Virginia, the church where my cousins went. I attended that church during the three summers before high school. During the school year I was involved in two local churches in Michigan where I lived - Spencer Mills Presbyterian and First United Methodist. I was with the local churches for about three years, as well.

2. I quit FUMC when I asked them about what they do to help the hungry, homeless and those in need, and how they know if they are truly reaching them. They had the approach that people needed to come to them. It seemed offensive and unethical to dangle food and shelter on a stick until people cared to seek God. Maybe it was perceived wrong.

The second falling out was when they started asking members to tithe more for the building expansion. I could have understood the expansion to take in more people, but I didn't understand the necessity of a projection system, sound booth, recording studio, etc., especially when we were still failing to outreach. I'd been working with youth members of other churches to coordinate community-wide activities, but ran into issues of even being able to print flyers for such events using their printers.

I had an epiphany while attending a church lock-in at Spencer Mills. I'd started getting depressed...like suicide depressed, with the multiple failed attempts to do the good things I thought God designed me for. None of my efforts were selfish...like trying to get a skate park put in town, since there were so many people skating. That was COMPLETELY out of the question according to the church. I had heard that the church had done the same to others who were holding Christian rock events; they were shunning people for being "goth" even though one specific person was the most devout I had ever met, and the most inspirational. I was reading the Bible and noticed that three different people who had witnessed an event with Jesus had all quoted him differently. I asked the youth leader, and others, how I was supposed to take everything so seriously if the written work had so many blatant errors. They passed over my concerns.

I also took great offense to the lack of women leadership in the Bible and the church. It didn't make sense that our roles were to be defined through the men we support and that we couldn't lead a congregation in thoughts and perspective, but were still expected to drum up a following to get people "in there." The idea of trying to "be like Christ" wasn't correct. I am a woman and Christ is a man. If he is perfect and my sins prevent me from coming close then the church was telling me to chase not only one, but two goals I would never achieve:

* Being like a man.
* Perfection. (This I can understand slightly better, in that forgiveness closes the gaps, but I still don't feel like I need to make a public service announcement to God and the church of my wrongs...but better correct them with those that I have wronged.)

3. Ethics and Empathy. Mostly Empathy. That is all God, or a higher power, has given me. Straying from my instincts, intuition, and empathy kills me. Literally begins to suck any ambition of life out of me. I can recall every feeling I have ever had from walking past something or someone in need and not acting. So daily, it is my responsibility to stay aware, in tune, and acting on the needs of others... and not pass any judgment. I always give money to pan handlers in place of "tithing." I always share my resources with

pretty much everyone. And it always comes back in surplus. That is where I believe in the higher power that most people call God. And in these convictions, I know I can stand firmly even faced with death.

    4. Given the chance I have. And in most cases, they remain silent. I like to think it's because they don't understand or that they realized my system is a little more clear and logical. Perhaps it is the confidence in my voice and they are uncertain they could speak to such great assertion in their own faith?

    5. Absolutely not!!!! I am VERY open about this...as I have had many people thank me, or become inspired to want to be a "better person" and learn about how I live this way. That is a much better success rate that I had as a teenager in the church.

Miranda, Booneville, MS

    1. I have tried to write my response to these questions several times, and each time I chicken out! I have been having a crisis of the soul since I told you I would share my un-churched lifestyle. I have really been examining how I truly believe, and why I feel like I do. Forgive me if this is an overlong response. I went to a Baptist church as a child. My sister and I always rode the church bus. My mother went for a brief while but I barely remember her going. My strongest memory of my young church years, even before I was six years old, is of not feeling saved and wanting to be saved. I did not feel saved! I was baptized in Florida when I was eight or nine. Then we moved to Mississippi and I went to a Baptist church there. Then the people we rode with changed churches so we started going to another Baptist church. I don't know if I was ever a member there.

    2. I stopped going to church as a teenager because there was a family problem with the people we rode with. We lived in a very rural country part of Mississippi, and we were without transportation after that. By the time I started driving, church just wasn't somewhere I wanted to be. I was kinda bad, and I was uncomfortable going to church and acting like a good girl. I knew I was sinning and couldn't make myself want to stop so I felt like a hypocrite going to church.

    3. My belief in God is complicated and ever changing.

Common sense makes me question all I learned about God and the Bible. Also, my father's mother was somewhat of a church shopper, and read books on the occult. She never adopted one belief system, but wanted to learn about all of them. She had more of an impact on my spiritual development than just about anything else. I started wondering if God has dominion on every soul on earth, why are there countries who don't curl their hair and wear nice shoes to church three times a week like I was taught to do? Why are we right as Southern Baptists in our perceptions about what God wants us to do? I wondered about Chinese people, Jews, Catholics, cannibals, and atheists. It hit me one day that each area of the world has a set of beliefs that have been passed on for generations, but many have a common thread. I sort of pick the things that make sense to me and apply them to daily life. Kindness towards others, goodwill, basically trying to train myself to feel these things automatically instead of telling myself it's what I'm supposed to feel, like God has a checklist and audits my every thought and action.

4. I seldom discuss my beliefs with anyone. I have had more of a sense of disapproval than actual cutting remarks. Most people don't say outright that I am going to hell because I don't go to church. It's more of a "good luck if you are going to go it alone" sort of attitude, with a touch of "you are going to need it."

5. I hesitate because my personal doctrine is fluid and based on my own assumptions. I feel like there is a compass inside of me and I know when I am doing right or wrong. How to connect with God is something I struggle with. There are times when I am devout and pray without fail, then I doubt it does any good and there is no point.

Anna, Lubbock, TX

1. I guess I was a member of my parents' church. I was baptized there. It was my childhood church and was evangelical Baptist. I attended there until I turned 18, then I haven't been a member in a church since then.

2. I left the church because the one thing they had going for them was our youth minister at the time and they had a 'difference of opinion' and he and his family moved away. I felt the church

was hypocritical as well. They always said to make a joyful sound, but when I said I wanted to be a part of the choir, they wanted me to audition. They didn't like people questioning them, and I did constantly. And my parents always got "a talking to'" about my bad attitude. I remain un-churched because all the congregations that I have visited with Jon over the years seem to consist of very judgmental people that cannot or will not think outside the box.

3. I would describe the God of my understanding as a loving being who is a teacher. I believe that God gave us life, which includes choices, and steps back after this to make our own world and heaven through our choices. I use my belief system everyday in using compassion to guide my life and trying to do the right thing. This is really why I was drawn to social work and examining the human condition in a community setting. I think my belief system is pretty basic and simple about God....it just is and I don't feel a need to examine or scrutinize scripture or others' belief systems.

4. I have discussed my beliefs on many occasions with people in different religious walks, from the zealot to the casual churchgoer. When I talk about how simplistic my views are, most people look at me and say something like, "oh" and attempt to find a way to mold me into the way they compartmentalize their beliefs. They don't take the time to understand why organized religion doesn't work for me.

5. No, I don't hesitate to discuss and even debate the need for organized religion. I debate with my husband all the time about his need to belong.

Rob (hometown not given):

1. As a boy, my mother and I attended Kingdom Hall with the Jehovah's Witnesses. My mother wasn't allowed to attend services of any sort when she was growing up, so when she got older, and having a young child, she actively sought some kind of connection with God and some "church" to fellowship with. After having been witnessed to by a neighbor, we started our time with the Witnesses. Being young, I've not many memories of that period of time, but with the ones I do have, they're quite vivid. I remember watching door-to-door rehearsals on the Hall's stage, various

sermons, and, of course, since my mother was a smoker and a non-member, memories of us having to pass on partaking of communion.

Finally, there came a day when Mom sat me down and explained that the people we'd been "worshipping" with were wonderful but she'd decided it time for us to find another outfit to congregate with. Flipping through the phone book, she found a local Mormon church, but upon calling, no one answered the phone. Next came Temple Baptist Church. A young woman answered, a person not even an employee, but one just stopping by to say "hi" to a friend. This lady, Lynda, said she'd be glad to pick us up the following Sunday for services. My mother and I attended this church for the next eight years.

When I turned 18, I entered active-duty as an infantryman with the U.S. Army. Stationed at Fort Ord, California, I continued my personal quest to find God, and to know more of His word, attending/auditing numerous churches, from mainstream outfits, to many home-based Bible study groups. But it wasn't till I got out of the Army and came back to my hometown of Portland, Oregon, that my prayers to find a solid group to fellowship with were answered. I was 22. This group was The Way International, a fringe Christian, Bible-based outfit, considered by mainstream organizations as a cult. Here, I met my second wife, learned more than I ever could've thought possible (as well as having learned more of what I really didn't know), and eventually had my heart broken. My wife and I fellowshipped with The Way for the better part of the next nine years. Since this time, I've remained un-churched, and find it hard to even imagine ever being churched again.

2. With the JW's, the Baptists, The Way International, and, I imagine, with nigh everyone else who may answer these questions, I'd say it came down to two things: evil, and people. Fast approaching 45, I'm amazed at how much, more and more, I'm appreciative of simple mommy-wisdom, especially from my own mother. There was no question as to why we left the Witnesses. We left because Mom said we were leaving. I do, however, recall her explaining something to me, something which I've grown to appreciate throughout the years. She said, "Rob, I don't know a lot

of the truth, I'm searching, believe there's a God…but I know what wrong is, and this place, at least for us, is wrong."

Later, essentially growing up within the Baptist church, there was any number of both good and bad experiences. On the plus, I met some wonderful individuals, adults, men and women, many of whom were laymen, but who ministered by their sincere and honest walk, people who I still recall with great fondness. But then there was also what one might expect, the kinds of things you'd find if someone made a soap opera based in a church environment – social and economic cliques inside the church. Though my mother and I were members (and later, my younger brother), we were on the outside of things. We didn't have money. Over time, people became aware that my stepfather, my mother's husband, wasn't going to attend. No, we weren't shunned, but we were on the periphery of things church-related.

Around 17-years-of-age, a crossroads came about. My stepfather was given a choice by a judge, either suffer a major spanking, or endure lesser…but only IF he completed an alcohol-rehab program. My mother (with me alongside) talked to the assistant pastor, asking if he might minister/counsel or otherwise just show that the church was supporting her husband's decision to go through rehab, a 30-day in-house affair. The pastor declined. Not that my stepfather was unrepentant, or a non-member, but rather that the pastor didn't think he was qualified – with him never having had a drinking problem – to make a profitable visit.

Mom was incensed, and so was I. Though this "minister" wasn't driving a Rolls, he nonetheless drove a decent car, and lived in a nice house, and wore nice clothes, all at the laity's expense. After all, he was a full-time minister. Just not for my stepdad. Not too long after this event, I split for military service.

With The Way Ministry I thought I'd finally found a home. And for quite a long time I had, with people I could grow with, minister with, be ministered by, and so on. I at least learned the basics on how to study the Bible in its original Hebrew and Greek, learned much about Biblical numerology, astronomy (not astrology), and other wonderful subjects. But over time, again because of people, I experienced the dark side. For years, this outer-

edge Christian organization had endured charges of wife swapping, brain washing, sleep deprivation, and monetary abuse, charges of which I'd never seen any evidence. (And, to prop up my ego, let me say woe to the man trying to brainwash me. Having been raised in martial arts and being a veteran soldier, I was more than prepared to pull out a can of whoop-ass should a situation require.) Towards the end of my involvement, though, things in the ministry started to change. Ministers began micro-managing peoples' lives, wanting to view and approve individual household budgets, wanting to be consulted and to be asked for "their blessing" if a member wanted to witness to someone, move to another apartment, sell their home, buy a home, or otherwise make any major adjustment in their lives. It became onerous, oppressive, and a burden to the believer. Ultimately, my wife and I wrote to the ministry's headquarters, sure as could be that once leadership was informed, the bullshit would stop. That didn't happen. Instead, we were given an ultimatum: Play ball or scoot. We got outta there.
Eventually – and this is a matter of public record, not hearsay – it was found out that during this period of time, the president of this outfit was busy with his hand in the cookie jar, not only enjoying a ritzy lifestyle, but also – and how original is this? – an affair or two.

Five or so years later my wife and I divorced. The dissolution of our marriage, though our business, and our failure, still owed much to the hurt inflicted from a ministry gone bad. Since my Way Ministry days, I've considered myself a Bible believer still, a son of God, born again – all that, but a man who refuses to ever again be under a ministry's thumb. Religion, in all its various forms, has become quite repugnant, and I'd just rather fly alone. Or almost alone.

In the Bible, the word "church," is the Greek word: *Ekklesia*, and means a called-out group of people, or a group of people who're gathered for a singular purpose. This is a simplistic definition, and contextually-speaking, there are other more contemporary definitions. Still, a bowling club or a book club could be called an *ekklesia*, i.e., a church. Now, my church, my called out people with whom I can enjoy good food, good fun, and good fellowship, is made up of my five children and other dear friends and family I've had throughout the years. The number's not great, but the people have earned my trust through thick and thin.

3. Still a Biblical-zealot, I define God as a singular spiritual personality, without form or comeliness, the Creator of the heavens and earth, and father of His only begotten son, Jesus Christ. His word, as referenced by Peter, contains all things pertaining unto life and godliness. It, the Word of God, serves as my only rule of faith and practice, or almost. There are things I don't get, don't understand, and when those moments/subjects arise, I default to common sense, confident that when I stand before my God one day, I'll be able to say I did my best with what I had to work with. This is far better than wrongly-dividing or interpreting the Word and making horrible and irrevocable mistakes. All too often, one reads or sees things on the tube about some sexual peccadillo and then some crazy religious rationalization. Same, too, with medical situations, where children or other even adults, come to harm because of a supposed religious precept.

These situations, when they do happen, give God and His Word a black eye, and often lead people to throw the baby out with the bath water. If God's real, he gave us a brain to do more than just keep our ears apart.

4. Wow, tough question. I've talked to some thousands of people over the past couple of decades, in person, door to door, in malls, conventions, religious and secular events and gatherings, and certainly amongst those in my sphere of influence: friends, family, co-workers, fellow artists/writers. And I've endured, been hit with, or blessed by these encounters.

Being passionate about what I care about, I enjoy opportunities to speak about my writing, my interest in martial arts, and yes, my God, and what I consider to be holy writ, the Bible. With that, mistakes can be made. And I've made them: turning people off, giving the impression that I didn't respect another person's beliefs, giving the impression that I was judgmental or ready-to-condemn. I've pushed too hard, or simply just pushed when I shouldn't have. I've also kept my mouth shut when I shouldn't have.

Experience, often, is something one gets after they need it. Whether the subject is one's religious beliefs or something else, most people over the course of their lives can expect to step in it at one time or another. Still, when it comes to numbers, and increasingly so as I've gotten older and matured, more often than not I've experienced good outcomes when talking about God, the things of God, His Word, or...of religion in general, or of *that* church, specifically. And again, to give credit to where credit is due, mommy-wisdom is often the key: be more willing to listen than to speak, give an open ear, respect the other person's time. This lesson's also in scripture, where it says: Let every man be swift to hear, slow to speak, slow to wrath. But who pays attention to that?

It is a shame, though, when taking a stand has cost me a friend. In one case, a high school friend through all four years, upon us getting together after my military time, he had had a major change of worldview and had become a white supremacist. Eek! Under any circumstance, I can't imagine tolerating this particular view, but certainly, with having an interracial marriage that fostered two children, an ultimatum was put down: you're going to have to change, or we're done. Unfortunately, our friendship ended immediately.

Other occasions, it's been sad to be discriminated against because of being a white male Christian. With people (some people) presuming that because of that, I must be a bigot, a homophobe and/or a misogynist. Other times, it's discrimination from my fellow believers, because I write spooky and speculative fiction.

Many times, people get offended at the thought that someone actually believes in definitive truth, and a truth that's different. The atheist thinking that Christians are morons, or Christians saying that fags are damned or atheists are god-rejecters who should be punished. With more than 40,000 denominations in the U.S. alone, the term "Christian" or "believer" is not-so-wonderfully vague. The reality is, there's any number of different outfits, large to small, fringe to cultish, that span the spectrum: from those seeking to live a quiet and peaceable life, to be a blessing to not only their God but to their fellow humans, to those seeking something or someone to condemn.

I love the novel and even the movie *Needful Things*, and personally believe that the Devil is an equal opportunity master of exploitation, willing to work with anyone of any race, any sex, living in any land, going to any church, or NOT, any political party, any social level/class/or caste. I've met Christians who were despicable people, and atheists who'd give the shirts off their backs. Anyone who can't say the same has lived too sheltered an existence.

5. Yes, but not always, and not always for long. And it's simple. A person needs to take into account such things as opportunity, timing and occasion, and whether or not there might be a profit. I've been involved in martial arts for 30-years, and for about 20, those arts dealing with blades. I'm passionate about this field and when appropriate, I bring it up. The reality, however, is that many people aren't that interested.

With friends and associates, inevitably, at some point, things do come up, and when they do, I profess what I believe. I may or may not cite a verse, a book or an epistle, but I make a statement. Sometimes even if it's a hill that I'm going to die on. But generally, things work out, especially when I remind myself to give a fair hearing and be respectful if not of the other person's doctrine, then certainly of their right to have it and to have the choice.

In many ways, it's correct to say that a cult is the other guy's church. As an American, as an infantry veteran, a man who's brother is still serving in uniform, I confess to a certain degree of bias when it comes to the Islamic religion. I've wrestled internally with the thought of, say, having a mosque built on or near ground zero. Some of the questions I have are easy to answer: It's wrong to strap a bomb on a kid. Other times, not so much. At Ft. Bragg, my brother introduced me to one of the language instructors, a man from Afghanistan, one who's been in more than 135 firefights alongside our special forces teams. The man's married, has two children, and lives in the States. He's also a Muslim. Sitting down to eat a meal, he brought up: "Rob, your brother's told me that you're also a Christian. If you'd care to, please, bless this meal with a Christian prayer." I wasn't stunned – can't say that, but, well, it gave me pause. Since this experience I've gotten to know this man even better, and I he has nothing but my respect.

A cult's the other guy's church, remember? To hesitate about one's worldview, religious view, belief system, hobbies, kids, whatever, to give a knee-jerk response, is wrong. Censorship is wrong. To oppress, or to be a victim of oppression is wrong.

But there are situations, aren't there? On Facebook, a writer working an administrative position, talked about taking some heat from the school principal when the man found out about her dark fiction writing. When involved in these kinds of things, there's no one answer. Each case needs to be weighed on its own merit. Perhaps a lawsuit needs to be considered. Other times, writing under a pseudonym might be the answer. There are many factors that can be involved, and it's nigh impossible to give a specific answer to a hypothetical.

Kathy, Leland, NC

1. As a child I attended a Presbyterian church in California. It was fairly progressive. We were also welcomed as part of a large Catholic Italian & Portuguese family. By the time I was eleven, church was seldom a part of our lives anymore. I kept my belief in God that is taught and experienced by a child... that God is love. One summer vacation my friend and I went to visit her sister's family. They were Mormon and spent much of our vacation trying to indoctrinate us. I studied Conservative Judaism in my twenties in an attempt to please my boyfriend's family. They threatened to disown him if we married and he chose them.

Eventually I married into a Hindu family. My husband had also attended a Catholic school in Fiji. In my late 20's I decided to try to search out a closer relationship with God. I became a member of a Four Square Church for around four years. I also began an in depth study of the Bible, devoted to prayer, and living what I read. The church was made up almost entirely of non-churched people and grew in leaps while we attended. The music was fun & uplifting, and the message was down to earth, and practical application of Biblical principles and also good psychology. We also lived next to and were friends with a Jehovah Witness family. Then we moved to NC. We tried many churches in NC but did not find one that taught in a manner that we were comfortable. After about eight years a dear gay friend started talking about his church. I could tell her felt both loved and supported. I began attending his Unity church for around three years. They try to be a place where people of all faiths who want to come together are welcomed. Eventually there became a greater undercurrent of Buddhism and New Age beliefs and monotheism began being shunned. There were a lot of people there who had experienced a lot of pain in the Protestant and Catholic churches they had attended in the South and there pain had not been worked through. They eventually hired a Buddhist pastor.

2. When I was 18 and away from home, I attended a Presbyterian church. While seated in the pews and ragged man walked in. The women in front of me made hushed unkind remarks about him. That is the only thing I remember about the church...not the music, the message, etc. I never returned. We had various experiences while looking for a church in NC. One church the pastor sold the church property and ran off with all the money. One church the pastor was having an affair. In another we had problems with racism. A few were very bizarre. Several taught very hate filled messages. We eventually gave up.

When I attended the Unity church, I was part of a group studying Science and Spirituality. I was the only non-scientist or psychiatrist/psychologist in the group. It was great. If I found another group like that, I would be back right away. Obligations eventually dissolved the group. I can't participate in a group that doesn't respect and love others and seriously apply the verse "God is Love" and that we are to love and forgive all. I have enough trouble following that and beliefs that I am to be kind, gentle, etc. I need support in living a life true to God. Most of my beliefs are founded on words that ring true to me that I find in the Bible but they must also agree with the fundamental truth that God is love... and I believe we know what that is in our inner most being whether we acknowledge it or not. The reason that my beliefs are founded on things I have studied in the Bible is because that is what I am most familiar with. It is the book available to us in the US that is easiest for me to understand. I have tried to read other "Sacred" writings but don't get very far. I would rather someone tell me the things that they have read that are true for them. I also find truth in songs, quotes, other books, etc. One of my favorite verses in the Bible is "You shall know the truth and the truth shall set you free." If it doesn't set me free... there is a truth I am missing. I value and protect my faith in a wonderful, loving, present, monotheistic God. When I am around others who don't seem to believe the same, I am pained.

3. I have experienced lots of "signs and wonders" and they have cemented my belief in God. Some were seemingly small, some larger. God is Love... available to each of us, always and forever. God is omnipresent, the ultimate power, the One True Source of all that is good. God is Spirit. To me, the experience of God is Heaven... the separation experience is Hell. Whatever is afterlife, I trust that God has a good plan that includes each of us and I am not qualified to understand or know. It is difficult to admit the totality of my need but God is my daily life. There is no part of my life that isn't influenced by that need. When I am amazed at the world... it is God, the Creator and Planner I consider and am amazed at. When I trip up, it is God I ask to help. When I start my day and end my day and live my days, it is about becoming this person that God has planned for me to become, and I'm far from that person.

4/5. I talk guardedly with churched persons. I'm so rigid in my beliefs about so many things that I've come to a point of near isolation except for my family. My beliefs are neither understood nor respected by others. When I venture out for long, I am usually stung by an unkind, unloving remark and make a fast retreat. I am at a loss for words.

And so there they are, friends. Here *we* are. A sampling of un-churched believers, each following a path that is wholly personal, sincere, and God-inspired and God-challenged. We are your neighbors, sisters, brothers, friends, co-workers, parents, children, and fellow citizens. We believe as we do and God knows exactly why we do. We aren't deluded. We aren't lost. We are exploring along our lives' pathways, sometimes stumbling, sometimes upright, seeking and loving God in our own ways as He knows and loves us. And it is good.

A Favorite Saying:

God be in my head and in my understanding, God be in my eyes and in my looking, God be in my mouth and in my speaking, God be in my heart and in my thinking, God be at my end and in my departing. –
   Sarum Primer, originally published in 1514.

5

Religious Writings and Human Beings

The Hebrew Bible. The New Testament. The Quran. The Sri Guru Granth Sahib. The Book of Mormon. The Kitáb-i-Aqda. Some of the sacred texts that are the foundations of the most recognized monotheistic religions. Many were written several millennia ago while others were composed within the last few centuries. Most are held by their religion's followers as Holy with a capital "H," official Words and Laws of God. There are those who accept the writings in these texts to be inerrant: without error or contradiction. Not only are these writings held up as revealing the nature of God, but they also offer moral and behavioral systems by which to live.

Religious writings offer answers to a variety of questions. How did the world begin? Who are God's prophets? What personal actions or thoughts are right or wrong in the sight of God? How should one properly worship and obey the Creator? How should someone pray? Do men and women have different responsibilities or restrictions? How should those of the body of believers handle members who go against the teachings? What about those outside the body? How should they be viewed or treated? What of the afterlife – who deserves Heaven or Paradise? Is there a Hell and if so, what condemns a soul to eternal torment?

I love that there are spiritual books and writings. Like churches, I love that men and women throughout the ages have shared their religious experiences, their quests, their hopes and questions about God through oral tradition and then the written word. These religious writings have staying power.

I will admit I'm not very familiar with the Quran. I will also admit I am not very familiar with the Book of Mormon, the Guru Granth Sahib, or the Kitáb-i-Aqdas. However, in sampling each, I've found beautifully loving and inspiring passages.

From the Quran, the sacred book of Islam: "The true servants of the Most Merciful are those who behave gently and with humility on Earth, and whenever the foolish quarrel with them, they reply with [words of] peace." (al-Furqan 25: 63)

From The Book of Mormon, the revered book of the Church of Jesus Christ of Latter Day Saints: "Behold, hath the Lord commanded any that they should not partake of his goodness? Behold I say unto you, Nay; but all men are privileged the one like unto the other, and none are forbidden." (2 Nephi 26:28).

From the Sri Guru Granth Sahib, the sacred text of the Sikhs: "Give up your selfishness, and you shall find peace; like water mingling with water, you shall merge in absorption."

From the Kitáb-i-Aqdas, the revered book of the Baha'i faith: "O ye peoples of the world! Know assuredly that My commandments are the lamps of My loving providence among My servants, and the keys of My mercy for My creatures. Thus hath it been sent down from the heaven of the Will of your Lord, the Lord of Revelation. Were any man to taste the sweetness of the words which the lips of the All-Merciful have willed to utter, he would, though the treasures of the earth be in his possession, renounce them one and all, that he might vindicate the truth of even one of His commandments, shining above the Dayspring of His bountiful care and loving-kindness."

Certainly there are other sacred books for religions that I've not heard of before, smaller sects across our great, wide world. Apologies to those whom I've left out.

Based on my upbringing, I am more familiar with the Bible, both the Hebrew Bible (called the Old Testament by most Christians) and the New Testament. The Bible was the spiritual book of my family's religion. And my family owned quite a few copies – big, massive black volumes in which Jesus' words were highlighted in red, smaller white volumes, and little pocket testaments that were meant to be kept on hand at all times. I still own the white Bible from my confirmation at age twelve in the Methodist Church and it stands on a shelf with my collection of books on religion, spirituality, and the sacred. There are beautiful, loving passages in the Bible.

From the Hebrew Bible, the revered book of the Hebrew faith: "But I will sing of your strength, in the morning I will sing of your love; for you are my fortress, my refuge in times of trouble." (Psalms 59:16)

From the New Testament, the second half of the revered book of the Christian faith: "Beloved, let us love one another, for love is from God, and whoever loves has been born of God and knows God. Anyone who does not love does not know God, because God is love." (1 John 4:7-8)

Love and compassion seem to be an important if not the most important teachings of the major monotheistic religions. God's love for us and our and love for God. Our love for one another and our love for the gifts of God's creation. I've found powerful passages about love in all the revered religious books I've explored.

Yet there is more in those writings than passages about love.

Some Thoughts on the Bible

The Bible is many things. It's a collection of stories of ancient tribes and their cultures. These were a resilient people trying to survive a very harsh land during violent times, attempting to maintain a cohesive group, keep order, and find meaning in their lives. It offers genealogical lists, instructions for building tabernacles, how to grow crops and how to handle other daily activities, and accounts of battles with enemies. It is also a collection of writings that long for the Divine, seek the Divine, struggle with the Divine, and connect with the Divine. Written by different authors, some whose identities we can't know for certain, I find the Bible to be an intriguing, worthwhile look into the past of a people and their evolving relationships with God, each other, and the world around them. There are passages that speak across the ages. There are passages that draw me closer to God when I'm feeling distant.

This chapter isn't meant to tell anyone how to respond to her or his religion's scriptures nor it is meant to disparage those scriptures. However, I can't write a book about being an un-churched believer without also sharing my thoughts on certain aspects of the Bible. Other un-churched people might find they have similar thoughts. Others might not. And of course, that's okay. Your understanding of scriptures and your relationship with the Creator is personal, between you and God.

First of all, I believe God is greater than anything anyone has written, declared, or attributed to Him. Having read the Bible I've found things that seem genuinely, Divinely-inspired. I've been moved to my soul by some of the passages. I've also found passages that make it clear to me that the Bible was written by human beings. Humans who interpret, embellish, or even create stories to make a point they feel compelled to make. Humans who may be completely earnest but who make mistakes, because we're human and that's what human do. We never met the Bible's authors in person. We weren't there to get all the additional information surrounding the writings.

The origin, validity, and accuracy of the translations of the Bible (and the religious books of other religions, as well, though it's said the Quran has not been altered since its writing) is constantly in dispute. Who wrote what and when? How can we be sure, if we can be sure? Are some of the stories based on more ancient religious (some would call pagan) tales of the region? In the case of the New Testament, was there really a Jesus? If so, did Jesus really say all the things attributed to him or were some word put into his mouth to help develop a religion based on him? Did all the miracles credited to Jesus happen, or did someone create them to bolster the idea of him as Divine, as God incarnate, or at least as a powerful prophet? How have the various translations over the centuries altered what was originally written? And shouldn't we be free to question these things?

For example, there have been challengers and apologists regarding questions of Jesus:

A self-proclaimed Biblical scholar by the name of Joseph Atwill claimed in 2013 that the New Testament was not written by inspired men and apostles of Jesus, but rather by scholarly Romans who sought to quell the anger of Jews by offering them a peaceful prophet. Atwill maintains the pacifist Jesus was created out of whole cloth in to calm the subjects of the Roman Empire, to teach them not to rebel, for a heavenly reward awaited them, a reward that would remove the sting of their oppression.

A fragment of papyrus, claimed to be dated to the fourth century, was discovered and unveiled at a Coptic conference in Rome in 2012. This fragment contained words that were translated to read, "Jesus said to them, 'My wife.'" So perhaps, this suggests, Jesus was married. This papyrus has been claimed forgery by many but is still being investigated. Seems some of the jury is still out.

Thomas Jefferson, inspired by his personal understandings of God and Christ, cut apart a New Testament and restructured what is now called the Jefferson Bible. The Jefferson Bible leaves out the miracles attributed to Jesus as well as suggestions that Jesus was divine. Though there are United States citizens who point to the Founding Fathers as traditional Christians, it seems some aren't aware of Jefferson's particular form of Christianity. Jefferson wrote, "Jesus did not mean to impose himself on mankind as the son of God." He also accused the Apostle Paul as being the "first corrupter of the doctrines of Jesus." Jefferson accepted on principal the morality and ethics taught by Jesus, but he did not accept a religion based in a strict interpretations of the Bible. I would go so far as to say this is what some who embrace the Bible do, not by actually taking a razor and cutting out bits and pieces, but by focusing on certain portions of the book and skimming over or skipping other portions all together. And no, this isn't a criticism. I am merely reflecting human nature as we are.

On the other hand, C.S. Lewis, popular author and Christian theologist of the early to mid-twentieth century published in his book, *Mere Christianity*, what some believe is an unshakable argument as to the divinity of Jesus. He wrote: "I am trying here to prevent anyone saying the really foolish thing that people often say about Him: I'm ready to accept Jesus as a great moral teacher, but I don't accept his claim to be God. That is the one thing we must not say. A man who was merely a man and said the sort of things Jesus said would not be a great moral teacher. He would either be a lunatic – on the level with the man who says he is a poached egg – or else he would be the Devil of Hell. You must make your choice. Either this man was, and is, the Son of God or else a madman or something worse…Now it seems to me obvious that He was neither a lunatic nor a fiend: and consequently, however strange or terrifying or unlikely it may seem, I have to accept the view that He was and is God." As for me, I tend to raise an eyebrow at "either this or that" ultimatums. Lewis was a devout, loving, gentle Christian. I absolutely honor and respect his faith. Yet I can think of other descriptions that fall in that huge gap between "lunatic/devil of hell" or "Son of God" which could make sense to many of us.

There are plenty of other topics besides Jesus' divinity that Biblical scholars have wrangled with and even fought each other over. And they continue to wrangle, discuss, and fight over them today and likely will on into the future years of humankind, just as people of various religions will continue to wrangle, discuss, and fight over passages in their own sacred writings. Our upbringings, teachings, understandings, and longings will help us interpret the Bible. Or the Quran. Or The Book of Mormon. Or the Kitáb-i-Aqdas. If we appeal to God as we read or study, we may learn important lessons that can guide us to live our best possible lives. Yet what we take from those lessons may be different from what others take.

"You can't pick and choose," I've heard conservative Christians say when it comes to the Bible. "You must accept it all, or accept none of it." These Christians believe the Bible to be the whole and perfect Word of God, written without human interference or contradiction, purely inspired. I don't believe the same. I'm not chiding those who accept the Bible as inerrant, however. Just as I won't debate the existence of God, I'm not going to debate the Bible. Lord knows there are enough people around to do that.

Here is how I understand it…Human beings pick and choose; it's what we do. Most of us are born with a sense of reason.

Most of us have an ability and a desire to weigh our experiences then to sift out and avoid things that seem untrue, off-kilter, or even dangerous. We also choose and embrace those things that seem true or are pleasant, helpful, and good. We make simpler choices such as what clothing to wear, how to style our hair (if we have hair), how to spend any extra money we might have (if we have any extra money), how to decorate our homes (if we have homes), what to do with our spare time (if we have any.) We make more serious choices such as how to raise our children, if we should smoke or not, whether we are safe texting while driving just this once. If we find a food that makes us ill, we no longer eat it. If we select a fabric that gives us rashes, we no longer wear it. If a food sits well and improves our health, we will continue to eat it. If we find a fabric that is comfortable on our bodies, we will continue to wear it.

I'm not comparing God to a hairstyle, a well-cooked meal, or soft piece of cloth. I'm talking choices. We all make them. Without choices, we'd just lie in a ball in the corner. We were created by God with the need to make decisions, to hopefully make good choices with all the options and information we discover.

Some believers in the inerrancy of the Bible have said, basically, "God wanted us to have a set of writings that is perfect in its content. He spoke the words to the authors who wrote them exactly as they were dictated. Then God protected the manuscripts throughout time and during the many various translations so that nothing incorrect could be included and nothing correct could be excluded." This, they concur, leaves us with Biblical text that is without error.

Yet I wonder. Would God want us to have one perfect text that has no contradictions, challenges, or aspects to question? Or are we, created as thinking, curious, intelligent children of God, meant to explore and learn from inspired writings as well as our own experiences? Did God perhaps inspire those who wrote the books of the Bible but also allowed imperfect human speculations to show through? Does God expect us to believe without question stories such as Noah's Ark – that two of every animal species (including microscopic creatures such as water bears and rotifers) fit into a large ship in order to live and reproduce after the catastrophe of a flood – or is God cool with the fact that some of us believe it's true while others accept it as a fable that explores the darkness of human wrongdoing and God's unmatched power while still others see it merely as a dramatic *pour quoi* tale that explains rainbows?

We have to be free to ask these questions. God knows we will think and wonder because He created us to think and wonder. It's one of the reasons we have a brain.

The Basic, Most Wonderful, Most Important Truth of God and How God is Sometimes Portrayed in the Bible

I believe in the Basic, Most Wonderful, Most Important Truth of God. He is God the Almighty, the Eternal, the Creator of all that ever was, is and ever will be. He loves His creation with a Profound, Unconditional, Unfathomable Love and it is His will that we love and care for each other.

Because of my belief in that Basic, Most Wonderful Truth, I wholeheartedly embrace and celebrate passages of the Bible that speak of His Love, Wisdom, and Perfect Power. These words nourish the soul, send our spirits Heavenward, and draw us closer to the Glory that is God and the Beauty that is our inheritance as His own. They sing His praises and share moments of Divine Immersion. They offer true hope and comfort.

Because of my belief in the Basic, Most Wonderful Truth, I cannot embrace passages that attempt to attribute to God some of the pettiest and most unpleasant human traits. There are passages in the Bible that, if taken literally, promote the Creator as jealous, angry, hateful, and one who acts with a cruel, shallow concept of justice.

I believe that if those harsh claims about God are illuminated by the Light of the Basic, Most Wonderful Truth, we can see through and beyond them to know that:

1. God is not jealous. What would He be jealous of, and of whom? He knows why we believe as we do, why we feel the way we do, because He created us. He's known us since our beginnings, has been with us through our entire lives. He is aware of our wounds, our fears, our personalities, our likes and dislikes, our

peculiarities. He knows us better than we know ourselves. Because of this, it doesn't confuse or threaten Him that some people are compelled to seek what some people would interpret as "different gods." He is not resentful of those who seek multiple gods or no god at all. Jealousy is born of insecurity, a lack of understanding, and an egocentric view of matters. For people, jealousy is undesirable, but at times it is understandable. For God, it's not.

If you've seen the movie *Life of Pi*, you'll remember the moment when, adrift on the vast sea and ill equipped for this dire circumstance, Pi, a devotee of Christianity, Hinduism, and Islam, is terrified, devastated by the loss of his family and suffering from hunger and thirst. When he suddenly finds a fish caught up in his small float, he cries out, "Thank you Lord Vishnu! Thank you for coming in the form of a fish and saving our lives!" The utter humbleness, emotional devotion, and gratefulness in Pi's prayer is startlingly pure and perfect. Humbleness, devotion, and gratitude are qualities we feel when touched by the Hand of God. In that moment, Pi saw God as his Hindu faith had taught him, and his prayer of thanksgiving was no less perfect than the prayer of someone raised a Christian, Jew, or Muslim. I felt God in that moment, too. It took my breath away.

God is not jealous as to how we see the Divine, because it is He who gives us the desire and ability to connect to the Divine, and though we will never understand the entire Nature of God, He knows why we see and seek Him as we do.

I've read several defenses of the use of the word "jealousy" when it comes to the nature of God. These defenses say that God's jealousy isn't human jealousy but instead it is a "holy zeal." They differentiate between ordinary jealousy and God's zealous protection of certain people, His standing as God, and His Name. They state that jealousy is the perfect regard God holds for His own Honor and Supremacy and that He has a holy indignation toward any who might, according to one website, "violate his laws, offend his majesty, or impeach his character." Yet I believe this explanation still boils down to God having a less than perfect awareness of how His children will think and act then feeling insecure or upset when they head off in directions that are not straight and narrow. It reveals how the human authors of the Bible wanted to protect God from anything they determined was not holy or proper in God's Eyes. If the Almighty is thought of as "jealous," whatever variety that jealousy might take, then the faithful will be more careful to worship and obey Him in a prescribed manner.

Everything that is Divine – wholly loving, compassionate, almighty, and all-knowing, rooted in the Basic, Most Wonderful Truth – is God. And everything that exists belongs to God. He is not ignorant of the most intimate, personal, deepest facts about His children. He is not insecure. Perfect Understanding and Perfect Love cannot coexist with jealousy or even with "holy indignation."

2. God is not angry. Anger is a reaction that can occur in the face of things that frighten us, surprise us in a negative way, hurt us, make us feel weak, frustrated, annoyed, sad, threatened, lonely, or out of control. Anger can cause the person experiencing it to act irrationally or violently.

If someone hurts us, or hurts our friends or family, or hurts people we don't know but care about due to our sense of humanity, we may become angry. If we feel threatened by another person or persons or by a government or agency, we might become enraged. We sense that our safety or freedom is at stake. If we are made fun of or have our feelings hurt, we could become angry, and if not angry, then at least irritated or annoyed.

Human anger is understandable and natural. It's a powerful emotion with the beneficial potential to help us correct bad situations. Yet it is not an emotion we should savor, for its benefits are temporary. When we feel anger, we should acknowledge it and determine the root of the anger. Is it based in something imagined or something real? If imagined, we should address our insecurities and find a way to let the anger go. If real, and there is something constructive we can do to correct the situation that has made us angry, we should do it then let the anger go. If there is absolutely nothing we can do to correct the situation, then we should still seek a way to let the anger go. Allowing anger to consume us, letting it spin circles in our spirits, is destructive to ourselves as well as to those around us.

Emotions have a function just like everything else. God created and understands our emotions. He understands anger in

His children though has no anger Himself. Why would He? He is never frightened, unpleasantly surprised, hurt, insecure, weak, frustrated, annoyed, sad, threatened, lonely, or out of control. Even "blasphemy," which some religions see as any number of actions, words, or thoughts against Him, would not throw Him into a Divine Tailspin. He understands why we do what we do, whether we do it out of fear, greed, desperation, or even mental illness. He is not shocked or enraged by anything we do.

Before anyone goes into his or her own tailspin, let me make clear that I don't believe God couldn't care less what we do. In no way do I believe He accepts every awful behavior as hunky-dory. Read my lips (okay, read the following sentences): I am in no way claiming God is pleased or unmoved when His children murder, maim, torture, abuse, take advantage of, ignore, bully, and/or turn a blind eye to one another's suffering. Such actions are the worst of human behaviors, however they are initiated, whatever drives them. However, I hesitate to give a name to what it is God feels toward those actions. I don't know if there is a word for it. He knows why we did what we did. He knows what mental, emotional, and/or physical conditions have driven us to act in selfish, angry, or cruel ways. He understands what has made some of us seemingly filled to overflowing with anger. He is well aware of – more aware than we could possibly fathom – the emptiness, desperation, confusion, sorrow, fear, anxiety, sense of detachment, frustration, or illnesses that cause some of us to do dreadful things. Because He has perfect understanding, He is not angry. It could be that there isn't a human term for what God experiences when we act like brutes. What I do believe is that intentional, unloving actions against one another and against our environment are against God's Will because it His Will that we love and care for one another and the Earth. It is His Will that we help heal one another with our love and turn away wrath with kind and courageous actions. If we seek His help, He will strengthen us and guide us through love. This is part of our life's journey; these are our lessons to learn. God has Unfathomable and Profound Compassion for those who are so hurt and damaged that they lash out, and He has Unfathomable and Profound Compassion toward those who are wounded by the actions. We, His children, are here on Earth to offer compassion and understanding to those who are angry. We are here to help calm and heal the anger in each other.

Helping heal anger is not easy. It seems like an endless or even impossible task. But think for a moment about Keisha Thomas, a young African American woman who in 1996 shielded the body of a white supremacist during a KKK rally in Ann Arbor, Michigan, to protect him from the beatings of the anti-Klan crowd. She was courageous enough to pit love against anger even when it put her own life in danger. Think of the 14th Dalai Lama, the spiritual leader of Tibetan Buddhism, who was exiled to India from his native Tibet in 1959. He has seen the destruction of Tibetan land and culture by the Chinese government, who claimed the land and sent thousands of Chinese to live in and tightly control what goes on in Tibet. Tibetan monks living in Tibet have been arrested, imprisoned, and tortured. Tibetan Buddhists are forbidden to practice Buddhism and it is a crime to have a photo of the Dalai Lama or to even speak his name. Tibetans are relegated to second-class citizenship in their own land. Yet the Dalai Lama has consistently taught that love is the strongest power of all. He has consistently offered to talk to Chinese leaders in hopes of each side hearing each other and then truly understanding each other, with the goal of a peaceful and compassionate solution to the terrible situation in Tibet. Violence, he declares, is no solution but only ramps up anger and hatred and creates more violence. The Dalai Lama may not believe in God as I do. As you might. Or as people in various religions might. But the Dalai Lama is doing God's work, regardless, living God's Will in his compassionate response to others with the aim of reducing suffering. I have no doubt God smiles warmly on the Dalai Lama.

Bold, loving actions that counter anger as exemplified by Keisha Thomas, the Dalai Lama, and others are likely the ultimate challenge for humankind. But it is a task well worthy of our energies, thoughtfulness, and compassion. It is the great charge given to us by our Great Creator.

3. God is not hateful. Hatred is a deep feeling of dislike toward a certain target entity. Hatred, like jealousy and anger, is rooted in fear or insecurity. People hate when they feel betrayed, rejected, abused, or otherwise wronged. Hatred can occur face-to-

face, one-to-one, or can occur on a less personal level through conditioning, training, or brainwashing.

Hatred, like anger, can be a temporarily productive emotion. I hate how garbage and toxic materials are frequently and carelessly being tossed out or leaked out into the environment by individuals and industries who either don't give a crap or who are out to make a huge profit. I hate that some people wield cruelty and greed against others. I hate that there are people who are starving and struggling to survive while others with more than enough resources to help turn blind eyes to the pain and suffering. And so to counter my anger, I don't throw trash out the car window and when I have the chance, I pick trash up and dispose of it properly. I write letters to government officials, religious leaders, industry CEOs, and others in positions of power to insist they make positive changes. (And many thanks to everyone who takes productive actions!) In January 2011, I started an online Facebook-based project called Hand to Hand Vision which ran for 3 ½ years. Through this project, people donated beautiful, quality hand-made items that I then auctioned. One hundred percent of the money raised was given away in increments of $100, $120, or $140 to people for things like a bag of groceries, tank of gas, help paying an electric bill, medical bill, or car repair bill. It wasn't a large project but it was something concrete we could do to counter the despair we feel when witnessing people who don't have enough money for food, or who live in vermin-infested rental units because they can't afford anything better, or who must forego medical care because it's beyond their reach while others waste what they have with no thought to sharing. It is my plan to revive Hand to Hand Vision when I'm able, in order to auction more items.

"It is natural for men to hate those whom they have wronged," wrote Charles Carleton Coffin in 1872 in his book, *Building the Nation: Events in the History of the United States*. A cringe-worthy yet true statement. Having others angry with us for wrongs we have committed against them makes us defensive and defensiveness can devolve into hatred. But God has wronged no one. It is also human nature to feel hatred toward those we fear or distrust, or those who have wronged, hurt, or deceived us. But God fears and distrusts no one. He cannot be wronged, hurt, or deceived.

I try my best not to hate other people. I try to give the benefit of the doubt. As much as I possibly can, I want to see others with an eye of compassion. I remind myself of the words of Buddhist teacher Thich Naht Hanh: "When another person makes you suffer, it is because he suffers deeply within himself and his suffering is spilling over. He does not need punishment; he needs help." I believe that is true. I want to embrace this more fully and more completely.

But I'm human. I readily admit that I have hated and I hate, even though I don't want to. It's my issue to overcome. I've felt hatred for Osama bin Laden for the single-minded terror, obedience, and destruction he espoused and orchestrated. I've felt hatred toward Kim Jong-un, the "supreme leader" and "Eternal President of the Republic" of North Korea. His use of fear and power to create terror, obedience, and devastation (look up North Korean prison camps and executions if you don't know what I'm talking about – ghastly) is beyond comprehension. I've felt hatred toward the members of Daesh (ISIS/ISIL) who are butchering men, women, and children in an attempt to gain power. At times I've felt hated for the adult members of the Phelps family, whose Westboro Baptist Church (I even hesitate to ascribe the word "church" to them and their destructive attitudes and behaviors) seems to find intense pleasure and an addictive-like rush from bullying, tormenting, and damning others (you name it, they condemn them) by means of vitriol-spewing protests. I've felt hatred for Warren Jeffs, the so-called "prophet" of the Fundamentalist Church of Jesus Christ of Latter-Day Saints, whose arrogance and perverted concept of God's will allows men, such as himself, to take girls as young as twelve to be one of their many wives, and the men savor the sexual "initiation" of those poor children. Not only is there sexual abuse within the FLDS but also "lower" members often go without food while the "higher ups" dine in style. Jeffs is currently in prison serving a life sentence, but those who follow him continue to do so without question. Yes, there are deep-rooted reasons why bin Laden did what he did and why his followers continue to emulate him, why the emotionally-stunted Jong-un does what he does and why his heirs will likely emulate him, why Daesh is so hell-bent on wreaking terror and cruelty, why the women and men of the Westboro Baptist Church boil over with such seemingly joyful hatred, and why Jeffs and his followers believe and act in such a manner. There are reasons for everything that we feel and do, and in cases such as those I mentioned, the reasons can be feelings of disenfranchisement and desire for revenge, oppression, systematic physical, mental and/or emotional abuse, hard-wired and distorted mental issues including a sense of superiority and pathological narcissism, and/or conditioning from a young age to believe one has the right kill or abuse others to some sort of personal or political end. These men and women, and others who behave like them, were once innocent babies whose minds became twisted by abuse, greed, a need for revenge or power, mental illness, a sense of profound entitlement, or some other conditioning, shaping them into the people they were and are.

Knowing all this, I've also felt deep sorrow for those mentioned above. As best we can we must find ways to counter their horrific behaviors, to calm their raging minds. Sometimes I've fantasized that if I could get any of them away from their home bases for a year – to a mountaintop cabin, maybe, or a beautiful island – perhaps they could begin to learn something new. There they could meet courageous, patient, caring people of different cultures, ethnicities, and religions (a few at a time; best to take it slow!). They would have the chance to commune with nature and eat nutritious foods. They would have no responsibilities beyond basic personal chores and would have ample opportunities to listen to music, create art, read books about compassion, feel love surrounding them, and just be in the moment. With new information, new input, I believe some of their minds and hearts would begin to open and soften regarding their own circumstance and the humanity of all. In other words, I believe there would be hope for healing. Would this "year on a mountain / on a beautiful island" idea of mine border on brainwashing? I don't know. I don't think so. I see it as an intervention of the gentlest kind. But again, this is fantasy, a pipe dream. It's not going to happen in my lifetime, if ever. Yet I still love the idea. And there are still things we *can* do.

Bin Laden. Jong-un. Members of Daesh. The Phelps clan. Jeffs and his followers. I don't know the deepest, inner workings of these human beings. But God knows.

God *knows*.

He knows with perfect Understanding why these people are as they are; He has a pure Understanding that brilliantly outshines any knowledge that we, His human children, have pieced together. God does not hate bin Laden or Jong-un or Daesh or the Phelps followers. He doesn't hate Hitler or Stalin or any of the others who are pretty much the poster kids for hate, human beings for whom no one should shed a tear. These are people who have killed, maimed, tortured, harassed, bullied, and/or have taken advantage of others in some of the most cold-hearted of ways. There are those who will adamantly disagree with me when I say God doesn't hate them. They base this on passages in the Bible. "God hates all who do iniquity!" says a Christian apologetics website. "He is not simply an infinitely loving God. He is also infinitely just. He must deal with sin. He must punish the sinner!" Yet I cannot reconcile "infinitely loving" with hatred. I will never believe God has a limited comprehension of the reasons behind the awful actions of His children to the point that he would *hate* them, would cast them – His creations – aside like garbage, and perhaps even condemn them to eternal torture with no hope of redemption and rescue.

4. God does not impose cruel and inhumane punishments upon His children and validate it as Divine Justice. Human beings are all about seeking justice, and understandably so. But punishment and revenge get tangled up with justice, and to some they become the very same thing.

Kids taunt others who were caught in the act of doing something wrong – stealing, hitting a friend, cheating at school – and face punishment. Nothing new, we've all seen it or been part of it. The kids know the offender deserves to be corrected, and they savor the idea. The may grin or laugh or cheer, knowing what Justin or Cassie may have to face. Some hope that Justin or Cassie will endure harsh punishments at the hands of their parents or teachers. After the fact, they might even relish stories of those punishments. Is this righteous, justified (which is based in the same word as "justice") anger, seeking satisfaction? Or is it something else?

Adults do the same thing. Ever stand outside a state prison's death house on the evening that an execution is scheduled? I have. At the Greensville Correctional Center in Jarratt, Virginia, along with other members of our Amnesty International group. It was quite chilling, and I'm not talking cold night air. There was a party atmosphere; people celebrating with beer and crudely-drawn posters, laughing, cheering, savoring the idea that someone was being put to death as they waited. Is this righteous, justified anger, seeking satisfaction? Or something else?

Now I can hear some saying, "God has a right to be jealous. He has a right to be angry or filled with hatred. After all, He is God and He can do and be exactly as He chooses. Read Psalm 37:13. It says, 'But the Lord laughs at the wicked, for he knows their day is coming!'" On the one hand, the people are absolutely right. God can do exactly as He chooses. He has the right to be jealous, angry, or hateful. On the other hand, the author of this Psalm seems to be applying his human desires to God. Passages in scriptures or other religious writings that claim God is jealous, hateful, angry, spiteful, or cruel seem to fly, and fly hard, in the face of God's Perfect Understanding and Love.

Religious writings should inspire us to love God and each other, to be courageously, actively compassionate and aware. When I read religious texts that is what I seek. It's what draws me to them in the first place. It's what I believe our Creator wants of us. It is the most important message scriptures offer, for it is what is true and good.

An Aside: My Thoughts on the Word "Holy"

I believe the only Holy thing that exists is God.

I don't consider religious writings or scriptures to be Holy. They may be inspired and sacred. They may help us come closer to God, but they aren't God, so they aren't Holy.

I don't consider any person to be Holy. All people are wonderfully precious and sacred, because God has willed them to be. But I wouldn't call a leader of a religion "Holy Father" or "Her Holiness," because they aren't God.

I don't believe any land is Holy. Rather, I believe that all land is sacred, as all land is God's. Every single inch of Earth, from a path through a forest to a small bit of sandy beach by the ocean, from a square of sidewalk in a big city to a manure-covered, weedy patch of farmland, from a tiny backyard with an overturned tricycle to the well-manicured lawn of the most wealthy citizen is sacred. Yes, some revered events have happened in specific places around the world, events that have birthed religions or have hosted important, sacred events in a religion's history. These places have important meanings to religion's followers. Yes, land comes from God and is sacred. But land is not God so land is not Holy.

Feel free to disagree, of course. I understand why you might. For many it's just a matter of semantics. Barbara Brown Taylor, whose works I have very much enjoyed, says everything is holy as everything comes from God, who is Holy. I can appreciate that.

Follow that Scripture (Back to Keeping Our Minds, Hearts, Etc., Open...)

If someone willingly embraces a particular style of clothing based on the teachings in a religious text, and if that action is deeply meaningful to him or her and gives this person a closer sense of God and leads them to be loving and compassionate, wonderful! If someone willingly embraces a particular type of diet based on the teachings in a religious text, and it is meaningful to her or him and gives this person a closer sense of God and leads him or her to be loving and compassionate, wonderful! If someone embraces a particular style of worship – ways to sing or dance, ways to bow or pray, passages to recite or customs in which to take part – and it is meaningful to him or her and gives this person a closer sense of God and it leads them to be loving and compassionate, wonderful!

There has never been a consensus regarding sacred writings and teachings. I doubt there ever will be. People have interpreted scriptures in different ways ever since there have been scriptures to interpret. Some take all the writings to be literal. Some believe some of the writings to be figurative. Some claim the writings offer actual, accurate recorded history dictated to the authors by God while others see the writings as inspirational mythology. Still others believe they are a combination of both.

I have to continually remind myself that even if I can't understand why some people would embrace certain passages in a religious text, they do just that. Perhaps they were raised up with that belief from childhood or were frightened into acceptance. On the other hand, they may just as easily have been drawn to that understanding because it spoke to the core of their souls. I want to honor each others' ways of worship, based in religious texts or not, when those ways of bring them closer to God and His Basic, Most Wonderful, Most Important Truth about living and acting with love.

Regarding different understandings of the Bible, I've had my share of uncomfortable encounters, sadly. Other un-churched believers, such as several who responded in Chapter Four, have also had uncomfortable experiences. Here is one of mine –

I know a lovely Christian lady via Facebook. She is caring and sweet, though I've never met her in person. For a while she and I posted messages to one another, discussing life in general and my Hand to Hand Vision project more specifically, the charity to which she kindly donated. We'd often end our communications with "God bless you." When I first threw out a request for un-churched believers to answer questions for *On the Outside Looking Up*, she messaged that she was un-churched and wanted to know more about my proposed book. After I gave her a more complete summary of the project, she replied:

"After reading your email there are things I want to share with you but first, I'm compelled to ask you two very personal questions and although I'll always love and share with you whether you answer them or not, I do hope you will answer them. First, are you a born again Christian (have you confessed Jesus Christ as your personal Lord and Savior)? Second, what is your main goal, what do you hope to accomplish by writing *On the Outside, Looking Up?*"

I responded:

"No, I'm not a born again Christian. I do believe Jesus shared profound, God-inspired truths about the nature of our Creator and we have much to learn from his teachings. However, I honor and respect the beliefs of compassionate, merciful Christians who see in Jesus either a personification of God or a Son of God and the Divine Love he represents. Many of my friends are devout Christians. I also have friends and family who are Jewish. I also have some friends who are Muslim and others who are agnostics and atheists.

"The purpose of the book is to explain to (hopefully) the world at large, a world so often at odds with each other due to misunderstandings or intolerance of one another's religions – that there are sincere, God-loving people who don't identify with the specific teachings, theologies, rules, and/or regulations of one particular religion or other enough to join one. Many of us who are 'out here' hesitate to even discuss God or mention God's name, knowing all too well that when you don't identify clearly with a particular religion, or denomination, or sect, you are often dismissed, considered 'New Age,' deluded, or possibly even condemned. I can handle that, of course. I even understand it. I just find it sad. I have loved God and tried my best to follow His Guidance for years now, but fellowship with our brothers and sisters is such a wonderful gift. I would love to reach out to others who have found themselves in the same situation as I have – loving God deeply and simply, but not connecting with a particular church, denomination, or sect. Letting those often-silent believers know they aren't alone and they should not be hesitant to speak of God and talk about God. However, the greater goal of writing the book is to find fellowship among God's children....to let the churched people know more about un-churched believers such as myself (and others I've come to know), and to let un-churched people find a fellowship connection they may have been missing.

"You are an amazing Christian woman. I hope we can remain good friends, even though some of our understandings about God vary. The basic Truth of God as I understand it is this: God is the Creator of everything that ever was, is, or shall be, and He Loves His Creation and it is His Will that we love each other and love Him."

Following that message, my friend wrote to me of her encounter with Jesus, which was deep, personal, and touching. She said she'd had a terrible disease from which she was not expected to recover and God had cured her through her faith in Jesus. I told her I celebrated her love of God through Christianity, and that I knew it spoke to her on the deepest level. I have no doubt whatsoever that God healed her, that He blessed her with a miracle.

A short while later I received a Bible in the mail, one she'd sent me as a gift, inscribed sweetly with the statement that it was the best gift one friend could give another. Also included in the package was a small booklet by Gloria Copeland that stated, among other things, that Bible-believing Christians of faith could ask God to cure any illness and He would do so with no hesitation or question. It also stated that to pray for help with the phrase "if it is Your Will" is un-Biblical because it suggests that God doesn't want to heal us, when it is His Will to *always* heal those who are Christians and who ask for healing with perfect faith. Anytime faithful Christians are not healed when they pray for it, it is because of a shortcoming on their end.

This is where I sat back in my chair and said to myself, "Wow. I definitely don't agree here…"

Let me reiterate that I think my friend's faith is wonderful. Through her faith in Jesus and his teachings, and with God's Love, she was healed. How marvelous! She loves God and serves Him. Yet we'd found a specific point where our understandings of God differ. I rolled this around in my head for a short bit before replying:

"I received your card and gift. What a sweet and loving gift to send! There is much in the Bible that I adore and find truly inspirational and Divine. While you and I might not have the same understanding regarding the source of every passage in the Bible and we may differ in our views on the personhood or divinity of Jesus, I love some of the Psalms and know them by heart. I also love many of the teachings of Jesus that are found in the Bible. He truly was touched and guided by our Divine, Omnipotent, and Loving Heavenly Creator, and was willing to die rather than deny or denounce what he knew of God and what he knew he must share with others.

"I celebrate your Christianity; I know it speaks to you on the deepest level and I know without doubt that is how God has come to you. It's beautiful! And I thank you for your caring gift. I hold it and your kindness close to my heart."

I shouldn't have felt a little surprised when I never heard back from her that she also celebrated my relationship with God. I suppose she really couldn't reciprocate, considering the fact that she likely believes my relationship is incorrect or lacking. Maybe she believes I'll go to Hell. Maybe not. I don't know. I'm speculating. No doubt she prayed that I'd accept Jesus as my personal Lord and Savior.

Like I said, I shouldn't have been surprised. This is how it goes more often than not. Differing beliefs regarding God, salvation, inclusion, and eternity will likely determine how someone will judge – if they are going to judge – another's relationship with God. I wish it weren't so. But that's the reality. If people are sure they are 100% right, how can someone else also be right? If they believe they have the only way to salvation, then to them any other way is misguided at the very least and heading down the fiery path to damnation at the very worst.

Made In God's Image?

The Bible states that people were "made in God's image." If that's true, what does it mean? There are various thoughts on that. It can't mean we understand things completely as God does, because we don't. It also can't mean we have the same powers God has, because we don't. And I don't believe it means we *are* God or gods (unlike some spiritual traditions teach). Only God is God.

I think the passage attempts to explain our connection to the Divine. God Loves. We were created to love. God Shares. We were created to share. God Creates. We were created to create – to build, to imagine, to paint, to write, to devise and invent and develop wonderful things to help make our world better for us all. We came from God, our bodies from the elements He fashioned, our souls from the Spirit of God, Himself. We share His Glorious inheritance, an indestructible Divine element that connects us perfectly and eternally to Him. We are truly His children.

Now, while we're at it, let's take it a bit further – what of other animals, as in other sentient creatures? Are they so much "lower" as to not be connected in a special way to the Divine Heart that formed them? The Bible says God gave man dominion over all the other animals, but what does that mean? Or should it mean something? Does the passage speak to humans' belief in or desire for superiority, therefore giving us permission to do whatever we want to other animals? Or does it suggest that we are to care for the other animals?

Think about it. Chimps, bonobos, and humans are very close to one another, DNA-wise. A 2010 *National Geographic* report puts the chimp-human DNA connection at 96%; a Max Planck Institute for Evolutionary Anthropology put the bonobo-human DNA connection at about 99%. That's damned close, and if you ever watch chimps or bonobos with their families and friends, it's hard not to feel a sense of wonder at how much we have in common regarding behaviors and apparent emotions. What then, of dogs, who exhibit what many believe to be love, affection, and loyalty to those with whom they live? Or dolphins or pigs or elephants? They seem to play, care for each other, and have a sense of humor. And what about cats, hamsters, lizards, or turtles? Or slugs or stinkbugs or centipedes? What can we, as human beings, know of their value to our Creator? And if God created all creatures great and small – throughout the course of evolution or, as some might believe, over a period of a six calendar days – wouldn't He have done so out of love? And isn't love the most intimate connection of all? And if out of love, would He love them less than He loves his human children? What can we really be certain about the minds or…dare I say it?....the spirit or soul of animals? Are they aware of God and His love, if even on a simple level?

Speaking of which, I saw a short musical video by "Listener Kids" on YouTube a while ago (it might still be on there). An animated turtle, bird, rabbit, spider, and squirrel float down a river singing "Jesus Love Me." Very sweet. But doesn't that suggest that these animals, these "lower creatures," are not just put on earth by God and forgotten? Doesn't it suggest that they know that God, through Jesus, loves them; that they are joyful because they know their spirits are treasured enough that they want to sing praises to their Creator? Now, I have a feeling that's not what the maker of the video meant (most likely the animals were meant to represent human children) but that's what I took from it. When a dog or cat dies, people may comfort the bereaved owners by sharing the poem, "The Rainbow Bridge." We feel connected to our beloved pets and we hope the connection might continue. And so might they be connected to God in a beautiful, special way? Might they be created in His image, too? It shouldn't scare us, offend us, nor make us squeamish to consider that other living beings might have souls. We lose nothing in opening up to that possibility. We gain nothing by swearing against it. Just some things to ponder.

An Aside: A Scripture-Less Religion

I've been moved by writings of others regarding God. When I was a young teen, two of my favorite spiritual novels were *Christy* by Catherine Marshall and *Dear and Glorious Physician* by Taylor Caldwell. Some more recent nonfiction works that have moved me include Mirabai Star's *God of Love* and *Contemplation in Action* by Richard Rohr and friends. But as for my religion of one, I've no singular guide, no one recognized book of Divine Illumination. Other non-churched believers have said the same.

Several years ago, during one of those online religious discussions I've since sworn off, I was asked by an anonymous poster, "How can you claim to know God's Will without the Bible?" I replied that I follow God's Will as best I can through my personal relationship with Him. That God's Law is Love, Compassion, Mercy, and Forgiveness. I stated that people can and do encounter God without the Bible and that God isn't restricted to or confined to one religious text. Oh, you bet – my response set off a reply-firestorm:

"You are the devil's mouthpiece, for he hates God's Word!"
"You can't know God without the Bible!"
"Go to Hell, you heretic!" and so on.
Happy happy. Joy joy.

Disproving God or Proving God using Scripture

Earlier I talked about the futileness of trying to prove or disprove God. Often, this debate centers around the Bible's account of God.

When non-believers attempt to disprove the possibility of God, they often refer to the Bible. When they do that, they are actually trying to disprove God as described in the Bible rather than God Himself. They rail and rant, pointing out sections in the Bible that make God a pouty, mean-spirited, jealous, cruel, immortal jerk who flooded the entire Earth to destroy everybody except the Noah clan, killed all the first-born of the Egyptians because the Pharaoh was being stubborn, sent bears to maul children for teasing a prophet, burned people alive to prove He was God, let Satan torment a guy on a bet to see if he'd remain faithful, and so on. They also decry the sections of the Bible that paint God as a sleight of hand magician with no appreciation or knowledge of His own natural law; a deity who rains bread-like stuff from the sky, makes a donkey talk to his master, allows Jesus to walk on water, stops the rotation of the earth so Joshua can fight his enemy in proper lighting, makes a serpent talk in order to lure two people into doing what they know they shouldn't do, and keeps three men from roasting inside a fiery furnace (after burning other people up in another story).

If you are a Bible-believer, please realize that I'm approaching this as God-disprovers often do. And I can see their points. You investigate the passages of the Bible's God through non-believing eyes and all sorts of horrific and unscientific things leap off the page at you. And yes, even some believers see all sorts of horrific and unscientific things jump off the pages of the Bible.

On the other hand, when God-believers try to prove God using the Bible, they sometimes end up in a whirlwind of circular reasoning, also known as circular logic. Circular reasoning is a logical fallacy in which the person making the argument begins with what he or she is attempting to end up with. Circular reasoning is providing evidence for the validity of an assertion that assumes the validity of the assertion. Such as, "I am correct because I am not wrong." In other words, "God is real because the Bible is His inerrant Word, and that inerrant Word says that God is real."

The Bible discusses God, tussles with ideas of God, offers stories of encounters with God, and tries to explain the Divine through myths and legends and in some cases I believe, true stories. But the Bible isn't God.

As I said earlier, I won't debate the existence of God. I have more important things to do with my time.

Religious Writings and Reason

In Chapter One I shared Galileo Galilei's saying, "I do not feel obliged to believe that the same God who has endowed us with senses, reason, and intellect has intended us to forgo their use and by some other means to give us knowledge which we can attain by them." Through our honest, open, and rightful questioning, through exploring, wondering, and examining, we will find the path that is best suited to who we are. And these paths, if they are steered by Love and Compassion, will lead to the same place. They lead to our Beloved Creator. As we travel on our paths yet side by side, He will walk with us along the way.

God, the Gloriously Divine Heart and Mind, is not a present offered only to those who adhere to and follow a particular set of religious writings. He is not contained in any one book. He is not a prize won by one denomination or other, one church or other, one faith or other. God is God of all. No matter what, with absolutely no exceptions.

A Little Story Many of You Know

There was a terrible rainstorm. A man climbed to the top of the highest hill to escape the rising floodwaters. There, he lifted his hands and prayed, "Dear God! I beseech You to save me! I have perfect faith that You will! Thank You, and Amen."

The waters rose higher, and soon a canoe came by. The man in the canoe said, "Sir! Hop into this canoe so you don't drown when the water rises above the top of the hill."

But the man said, "No. I prayed to God to save me. I have perfect faith that He will do just that." So the man paddled off in his canoe.

The waters rose even higher, and soon a sailboat came by. The woman at the helm called, "Sir! Climb into this sailboat so you don't drown when the water rises above the top of the hill."

But the man said, "No. I prayed to God to save me. I have perfect faith that He will do just that." So the woman headed off in her sailboat.

The water rose even higher, and lapped at the summit in dark, heavy waves. Soon a helicopter came near and hovered over the man. The pilot of the helicopter shouted down, "Sir! I will lower a ladder for you to climb into my craft. This way you won't drown when the water rises above the top of the hill."

But the man said, "No. I prayed to God to save me. I have perfect faith that He will do just that." So the pilot in the helicopter flew away.

At last the waters rose so high they engulfed the hilltop and the man, who could not swim, drowned. His soul rose to meet God in Heaven, and the man was upset.

"My God!" he said. "I had faith that you would rescue me from the flood and yet I drowned! Why didn't you help me?"

God smiled kindly. He replied, "My child, I sent a canoe, a sailboat, and a helicopter to rescue you, but you refused the help."

6

Free Will and God's Will

Free Will.
Two simple words. One simple term. And much like the words "God" and "religion," this term has stirred both positive and negative reactions as well as endless debates.

Free will is defined by the Oxford dictionary as "the power of acting without the constraint of necessity or fate; the ability to act at one's own discretion." It is also defined in relationship to God or Providence, such as in the second Miriam Webster definition: "the ability to make choices that are not controlled by fate or God."

Some non-believers have claimed that the concept of an omnipotent, all-knowing God runs completely counter to the concept of free will. The idea is that if there is a God, if He is who many claim He is, and if He knows everything that is and will be from the beginning of Creation (or even before) to now and into the future, there can be no conscious choice for humans. In that case, humans would merely be playing a part prescribed for them. We would be helpless puppets. These people agree that we have free will, but it only exists because there is no God. I can see their reasoning.

There are non-believers who say that free will is an illusion. That human nature, genetics, and the elements of whatever nurturing we have received and continue to receive condition us to be as we are and to act as we will. We will be as we will be ("it is what it is") because we are hard-wired and react to circumstances as we are destined to react due to our biology and psychological makeup. I can see their reasoning, too.

When it comes to monotheists, there is no consensus on how free will – if it exists – plays out in the lives of human beings here on Earth.

There are theists who believe everything we do is our choice and that we come to God (or give in to Satan or the "dark side") of our own volition; that God is "hands off" regarding our behaviors. Deists, in particular, tend to believe strongly in human free will.

Then there are theists who interpret free will to mean the Creator knows what we are going to do, but does not control our actions. This would be similar to a parent understanding a child well enough to know with certainty how she or he will behave in a given circumstance (Let's put on music and Joey will dance. There's a puppy; watch Sara run over to pet him.) but the parent isn't forcing the child to behave in that way.

And then there are theists who claim there is no free will at all. They attribute everything that occurs as God's Intent and under His Direct Control – the death of thousands of men, women, and children due to hurricanes or tsunamis, the coming to power of people like Stalin, the kidnapping of school girls by Boko Haram militants or grisly executions of innocents by the terrorists of Daesh, the destruction of the environment by careless or money-grubbing factory owners, some people being desperately poor while others spend their millions on huge houses in which they could get lost. If God had not willed these things, the reasoning is, they would not have happened. One extreme example of the belief that everything that occurs is God's Divine Will came from John Hagee, a preacher who once claimed that Hitler's rise to power and the Holocaust was God's plan. Hagee preached, "Theodore Herzl is the father of Zionism. He was a Jew who at the turn of the 19th century said, this land is our land, God wants us to live there. So he went to the Jews of Europe and said 'I want you to come and join me in the land of Israel.' So few went that Hertzel went into depression. Those who came founded Israel; those who did not went through the hell of the Holocaust....God sent a hunter. A hunter is someone with a gun and he forces you. Hitler was a hunter. And the Bible says -- Jeremiah writing -- '*They shall hunt them from every mountain and from every hill and from the holes of the rocks*,' meaning there's no place to hide. And that might be offensive to some people but don't let your heart be offended. I didn't write it, Jeremiah wrote it. It was the truth and it is the truth. How did it happen? Because God allowed it to happen. Why did it happen? Because God said my top priority for the Jewish people is to get them to come back to the land of Israel." So, okay, if I'm understanding Mr. Hagee's train of thought, he was saying God willed Hitler to have Jews tortured and killed because they didn't go to Israel as they were supposed to, and to scare those who escaped the Nazis into heading south to their God-given homeland. Wow. That is so outside my idea of God that it boggles my mind. Hagee has since apologized for his comments, but he's not the only one to accept such human-created horrors as the Will of God.

Over time, I've come to believe that our lives are a combination of our wills and God's Will at work together. We experience, are affected by, and take part in both. I believe we can see evidence of God's Will prevailing on Earth. I also see evidence of human's will prevailing on Earth. Maybe this is a goofy, outdated pop culture example of how it seems to me, but in the film *Forrest Gump*, the title character says, "I don't know if Momma was right or if, if it's Lieutenant Dan. I don't know if we each have a destiny, or if we're all just floating around accidental-like on a breeze, but I think maybe it's both. Maybe both are happening at the same time."

Some of us are familiar with Jesus's beautiful prayer, in which he implores the Creator, "Our Father Who art in Heaven, hallowed be Thy Name. Thy Kingdom come, Thy Will be done..." I've thought a great deal about the phrase, "Thy Will be Done." Why would we pray to our Creator for His Will to be done, if everything that occurs is already His Will? It seems to me that Jesus was praying that people seek out, learn, and obey God's Will. And

His Will is that we strive to understand each other, love each other, and act compassionately.

What of God's Will When Bad Stuff Happens?

Terrible things happen to people and to our natural environment. Unfathomable, unexpected, and heartbreaking things happen. Some are natural disasters or accidents. Yet many others occur because of human greed, thoughtlessness, or arrogance. So where is God, then?

He is present. He is always present. There is nowhere God is not. He is as close as our heartbeats and as far as the reaches of eternity. He is always God, always above us, beneath us, beside us, around us, within us, there to inspire or direct or comfort and, sometimes, to wait. Even when we aren't aware of Him or refuse to consider Him, He is there. He is here. At times He reaches out with miracles that change the event. Other times He touches the hearts and minds of those involved, inspiring them to act in order to change the event. And then there are the times that He remains silent.

Just as God is aware of every proton, every atom, every cell, leaf, flower, every field, forest and everything within them, every ocean and beach and desert and mountain and everything that comprises those environments as well as every nonliving and living thing in its entirety, He is perfectly aware of everything every person thinks, knows, fears, experiences, hopes. And His awareness is an awareness rooted in Perfect Love and Wisdom.

So then here is the Big, perhaps the most Difficult Question: Why does God often allow our wills to prevail, even if temporarily, when those wills can set in motion some the most horrific situations? Why does He allow babies to die in automobile accidents or at the hands of abusers, allow people to be sold into slavery, allow dictators to torture or kill on a whim, allow heads of corporations to take advantage of their employees to the point that the employees must struggle just to feed their families as the corporate heads live extravagant, lavish lives?

Here's my answer: I'm not sure.

I've prayed earnestly, fervently in search of the answer. I have no doubt that most sincere believers have likewise prayed earnestly and fervently for the answer. At times I've sensed God's whisper, at the periphery of my heart, and I've felt partial answers but haven't been able to grasp the whole Message. We cannot know the whole of God's Mind. He sees things in a context of Eternity, a context of Wholeness and Completeness, a context much greater than we could ever fathom.

God does not bring down a plague, a tornado, a wildfire, or an earthquake to smite us for one infraction or other or to frighten us into submission with His terrible, unmatched power. God does not bring cruel people to power to make us suffer. It was not God's Will that Hitler become Chancellor of Germany in 1933 and then proceed to wreak some of the most inhuman havoc ever witnessed in history. It was not God's Will that members of Daesh capture and burn alive Jordanian pilot Lt. Muath al-Kaseasbeh or behead Christians, Shia Muslims, and Yazidis to rid the world of "apostates." It was not God's Will that American soldiers butcher nearly all the citizens of the South Vietnam hamlet My Lai in 1968 or torture prisoners in Abu Ghraib. God doesn't will us to pollute our skies and rivers and food sources. It is not His Will that a woman bully her child or a teenager torment a fellow student. Yes, these things happen. But God isn't waving His magic God wand, creating terrors with the intent of tormenting us.

This, then, is what I've come to believe regarding our Creator and suffering. God has given us everything we need to make things better for each other here on this planet. We possess countless talents, perspectives, intelligences, curiosities, and passions. We have wonderful people working to find ways to predict and protect us from the dangers of natural disasters. There are wonderful people who are working to make our world safer when it comes to cars, planes, our places of business, and our homes. There are wonderful people working to cure myriad diseases. And each of us must face up to the hurtful things we do intentionally or carelessly to one another and ourselves. We must acknowledge and claim them. Then, we must act to change them. God has put a huge responsibility in our hands. He has given us the opportunity to do all we can, of our own accord, to make things better, to be unwavering and compassionate in our actions. We are to get to know one another – the loving and the hate-filled, the friendly and the distant, the mentally competent and the mentally challenged, the generous and the selfish, the brave and the terrified. We must embrace our incredible God-given connection with one another. Then we must put what we've learned to work toward a peaceful, more aware, more courageously loving world. We are all members of God's family. When we realize this, our perceptions change profoundly.

We may never eradicate everything that is hateful and selfish. We have an enormous mountain to climb. The terrain is brutally steep and very rocky. But we can't just hope things will improve. We can't just image it. We must put into action that which we imagine. We will stumble. We will be wounded. Some of our steps will be very small. Some will be larger. At times we'll be standing still. But as long as we don't run fearfully back down that mountain, we'll learn. We'll grow. We'll become more of what we were put here to become as the bright, beautiful Summit of God beckons us upward. Individually. Collectively. Onward.

And what a beautiful, purposeful calling that is.

Deciphering and Following God's Will

I remember sitting in pews in the United Methodist church of my childhood and youth and then the Presbyterian church during part of my young adulthood, listening to the songs, readings, and sermons. I have warm memories of favorite soul-stirring hymns such as "Be Still My Soul," "Abide With Me," and "Let Us Break Bread Together." I recall some powerful and comforting passages from the Bible. They spoke of love, mercy, and forgiveness:

"The Lord is good to all; he has compassion on all he has made." Psalm 145:9

"And when you stand praying, if you hold anything against anyone, forgive him, so that your Father in heaven may forgive you your sins. " Mark 11:25

"Love your enemies, do good to them, and lend to them without expecting to get anything back." Luke 6:35

"Blessed are the merciful, for they shall obtain mercy." Matthew 5:7

I remember passionate sermons on the commandment to love and care for one another, to love one another as we love ourselves. I remember sermons about the life of Jesus and the Biblical prophets.

And then there were the sermons about following God's Will for our lives. Just what was God's Will, we seated in the pews were asked? Well, it was up to us to be still and quiet. It was up to us to pay attention and it would be revealed. We were assured that everyone had a purpose in life, no matter how short or long that life might be. And once we knew what it was, we were to submit to it. We were to let God's Will for us guide and direct us. I believed that then and I believe that now.

But that early into my spiritual journey, the idea of God being in charge of me was scary. I mean, really. Look at what has happened to some people who have followed God unflinchingly, striving to serve Him with their minds, souls, and bodies. We've heard about martyrs and their agonizing tortures and executions. We know about those who have gone to wild and dangerous places to serve the Creator and have contracted terrible diseases. We've read about those who have suffered extreme poverty, loss, hardship, and alienation from family and community as they did their best to follow God's Will in their lives.

So, nope.

No, thank you.

Seeking and following God's Will in my life sounded less than appetizing.

It took me years to reconsider what it might mean to seek and follow God's Will and I'm still learning. The most important thing I've realized is that His Will is rooted in His Basic, Most Wonderful, Most Important Truth – He is the Creator of all that ever was, is and ever will be, and He loves His creation with a profound, unconditional Love and it is His Will that we love and care for each other. And there it is. No matter who we are, this is His Will for us. No matter where we are, this is His Will for us. It's that simple. It is that deep. His Will may take us different places. We will encounter different people and situations. We will face our own troubles and fears and reap our own joys. But the Basic Will is the same for all.

It's not easy to put into practice. I know He wants me to be patient and understanding, but damn, Sam, at times there are people who get under my skin and set my teeth on edge. I know He wants me to be generous and unselfish, but it's so easy, so comfortable think more of my wants than the needs of others.

Yes, His Basic Will is simple and deep. Simple, deep, and the most beautiful calling anyone can embrace.

Back to those who have been ridiculed, tortured, or killed for sharing their beliefs in God. Was it, or is it, God's Will that they be abused or killed in His Name? Does He demand that kind of ultimate sacrifice from some of us to prove our faithfulness to Him or to inspire others to conversion or reaffirmation? I don't believe so. It could never be His Will that any of His children damage or destroy another of His children. Yet many martyrs have been willing to endure suffering because they believed it was a way to advance the cause of love and compassion (and no, I'm not speaking of those who were killed in response to their own brutal methods to steal land or force others to convert.) I've no doubt that selfless, loving sacrifices are held in a most tender regard by our Creator. He knows the trust these people have put in Him and their willingness to risk everything. I am sure that at their deaths they were caught up in the Eternal Ecstasy of His Love. But the violence directed toward someone who may then be labeled "martyr" is never part of God's Will. To die violently at the hands of another human being is counter to Love. That which is counter to Love is not the Will of God.

To take it a bit farther – does that mean those who love God should never risk their safety in order to tell others about their love of God? No. There have been people throughout history who have bravely shared the gentleness of God's Love with those who they knew would bring down the axe or the whip. People will share their love of God based on how they feel guided – through spoken word, through written word, and through actions. It is up to them. It couldn't be more personal. I am in awe of those who will do so in spite of mortal danger.

When God's Will Always Prevails in Our Lives

Many times our wills prevail. Sometimes our wills are God's Will. Other times they aren't. We can identify actions and situations that are not God's Will. These actions and situations are everywhere. We encounter them daily. They seem so prevalent that if they are the only things we tune in to we become depressed, overwhelmed, apathetic. Maybe even suicidal.

Yet there are pure examples of God's Will in our lives here, in this day and age. Things that, no matter what we want or do not want, no matter what we do or do not do, simply *are*, and they are beyond measure. Examples of God's Will outweigh the other more than we could imagine.

The existence of the Universe/Multiverse is an awesome example of God's Will. The facts of light, of space, of matter and anti-matter; the galaxies, stars, moons, planets, black holes, pulsars, quasars, asteroids, comets. The realities of physical life and its countless, incredible varieties. Our Earth and every other planetary body that is able to sustain life. The physical laws that govern nature. All of these are astonishing. Some would say miraculous. God willed these to be, and they exist because of His Will. These were all conceived in the Divine Mind. These were created by God and God alone.

But in looking at our individual lives, where does God's Will totally and utterly trump ours every time?

1. Birth. If God didn't want us to live, we would not have been born. If it wasn't His Will that we exist, we would not be here. There are some people who wish they had never been born. But here they are. Here I am. Every single human from the dawn of time – including earliest hominids – was born through God's Will. And that goes for every living thing that ever was, is, or will be. If He did not want me to be, I wouldn't be. If He didn't want you to be, you wouldn't be. Thinking about that is really quite awesome. We exist because God wanted us to. And each of us has a reason to be here, a reason in addition to the fact that God loved the idea of us. Our purpose may be to solve a problem, create music, teach, preach, share, listen, grow crops, tend animals, nurse the sick, love the elderly, build a bridge, care for children, stand up against

injustice, create art, write a story, clean something that needs cleaning, sell home improvement goods, construct a house, inspect a bridge, deliver mail, manage a warehouse, fix something that is broken, organize items, share laughter, feed a family, bandage a wound, comfort the grieving, give a hug, offer a listening ear, or give a helping hand – or any combination of those. Your purpose for existence may well be one beyond those few I listed, a purpose that will draw on the unique individual that you are.

And then there are some of us who were born to be cared for, whose mental, physical, or emotional disabilities are such that they are here to be loved, sheltered, and healed through the efforts of those of us with the abilities and willingness to help. There are huge lessons to be had through this kind of caring outreach.

2. Personal, uniquely individual experiences. I have no doubt that every person who has ever existed has had or will have God's Hand move in their lives at some point in time. He doesn't create us and turn His back on us. He is conscious of each of us. His Love for each of us is more complete than we can ever imagine. It is His Will to relate to us all, whether it be through the human compassion He's given us that compels us to help someone who is suffering, through an apparent miracle when an illness for which no hope is given is healed, through a startling revelation through a particularly moving dream or vision, through a moment of awe when looking at nature, or through a Whisper in our ear or Hand upon our hearts when we feel especially vulnerable or hopeless. The experience may be a moment or there may be many moments. It may occur in our youth, adulthood, or even on our deathbeds. We may not realize it is God, yet we may. God will never forget His own, and we are all His own. Atheist, agnostic, "none," churched believer, un-churched believer, it doesn't matter to God. It is His Will that He connect with each of us in a specific way during our lifetime. And that connection will be sacred.

3. Death. If God wanted us to live forever, He could fashion it so we did. But it isn't His Will that physical life continue forever. Many Christian denominations teach that, "The wages of sin is death." That line is in the Bible, Romans 6:23, specifically. I interpret the passage to mean that being cruel, selfish, and destructive results in a dying of the spirit, the hardening of the

heart. Others the passage as meaning a literal, physical death, based on the story of Adam and Eve in the Bible and their original sin.

Yet little children die. Kitties and mice die. Ants and crickets and mudskippers and gorillas and mosquitoes die. Cacti and ferns and volvox colonies (remember those weird little round communal life forms from science class?) die. They didn't sin. We live in a world that works based on God's natural law. Because of this we will all die. We cannot not die. No matter how much we will ourselves to stay alive, ain't gonna happen. We will die because God wants us to die. Technologies and medical innovations may extend our lives greatly, but we'll still die. I like the way Prince summed it up in "1999": "Life is just a party, and party's weren't meant to last."

Regardless of how old we are when we die, whether we've lived a single moment or 100 years, we're equally precious to the Creator. We are each as precious as if we were the only soul to have ever existed. God knows us and cares for us. Which leads to the fourth instance of God's Will prevailing in our lives.

4. Eternal life beyond the physical. I believe with total confidence that our souls, which were created along with our physical selves, will continue on after death into eternity. Our awareness and consciousness isn't temporary. They are created of spirit by God, whose Will it is that we do not become nothing. How amazing and glorious is that?

An Aside: What About Death through Miscarriage or Abortion?

I can imagine some mutterings regarding the mention of death as God's Will, with the word "miscarriage" or "abortion" somewhere in those mutterings. As most people know, miscarriage is nature's way of ending a pregnancy that wasn't going well. A fetus that cannot survive in the womb can't survive beyond the womb. It is nature's way of taking care of it. It's very sad for those who experience it. God knows it is sad, but it's in His Hands.

Abortion, however, is another matter, highly charged, highly emotional, highly politicized, highly spiritual or religious. There are solid arguments for and against. Personally, I do not like abortion. I think it's a very sad thing. I know of some young women who have used the procedure in place of responsible conception prevention. On the other hand, I believe safe abortion must absolutely be legal. There are instances in which, when seriously and carefully considered by a woman and her doctor, it becomes the only true option. As to God in these matters, He knows and He understands all that is involved. And He loves.

God's Will and Happiness

There was a time in my life when I believed it wasn't God's Will for me to have any true happiness. That it wasn't His Will that I take time off to chill out, to be still, and find the beauty in the mountains or the beach, to savor a good meal, to enjoy a movie or just kick back and read a novel. Not that He condemned those things exactly, but that since there is so much suffering in the world why should *I* be happy? Why should *I* take pleasure in something when I knew, at that very moment in time, someone somewhere was being abused? Was starving? Was lonely? Was gravely ill? There are others who embrace that same belief – that God doesn't want us to be happy because it's not fair to those who aren't happy.

My mother was fifty-seven when my precious dad, whom we called MeDot, died during open-heart surgery. Mom married again when she was fifty-eight. She had never lived alone until MeDot passed away and the prospect of living by herself was scary. Within the first month following my dad's death, Mom was romanced off her feet by a man (who will remain nameless) twelve years her senior. He was quite charming during their nine-month engagement period. But the charm was a thin veneer. Even before the honeymoon was over he was emotionally and verbally abusing Mom. Her new husband was a miserable soul in need of emotional help (bless his heart, as we say here in Virginia), prone to sit in the family room and criticize most things and most people. He was especially angry at Thanksgiving and Christmas, blaming his mood on the fact that poor people couldn't enjoy the holiday and so he couldn't, either. And so he treated my dear mother like either an enemy or a servant, holed up in "his chair," expecting the rest of the family to come find him in an attempt to cheer him up, which was impossible to do. After a while we stopped trying. While I understood the sentiment regarding poor people during Christmas, it became very apparent how his misery affected those around him, especially Mom. His unhappiness a brought a heavy pall over family gatherings, gatherings that had once been relaxed and cheerful. My mother's sweet disposition was squashed and it wasn't until eleven years later, when she filed for divorce, that she was able to start shaking off the heavy coat of gloom and pain he'd brought to the marriage. (Note: My mother stayed with him as long as she did because she said she'd made a promise to God to love the man and to honor him "for better or worse." It wasn't until a wise minister told her that her husband had already broken the vows by his abuse that Mom realized she could move on to save herself. And later, after Mom died, we found her marriage license on which she had written in big red letters, "Worst mistake I ever made.")

I didn't want to emulate the man's negativity and his inability to find happiness. So I tried to keep my sadness to myself and put on a good face. While I still doubted I deserved happiness while others suffered, I began to realize there was something screwy with that belief. I could see how one person's misery can, in turn, cause other people's misery. One person's self-embraced suffering can make others suffer. And as sad as I might feel at times, God not wanting us to ever be happy didn't fit into what had become my deepest belief about the Basic, Most Wonderful, Most Important Truth of God – that He loves His creation with a Profound, Unconditional Love and it is His Will that we love and care for each other. If love can't include joy, that's a pretty crappy love. The whole thing seemed completely out of whack.

But on the other side of the coin, I knew there were those who embrace the idea that the purpose of life is to be happy. That happiness is God's (or the Source's or the Universe's) primary Will for us. And that if we aren't joyous or ebullient then we're doing something wrong – we are thinking or behaving incorrectly. We're not vibrating at a high enough level or we're attracting the wrong energies. As a believer in God the Creator, could I embrace the idea that we were made for the sole purpose of being happy? That point of view also seemed a bit screwy to me. A 2012 article in *Psychology*

Today by Nancy Colier, a psychotherapist and interfaith minister, discussed how we become unhappy in our constant search for happiness. We get into a mindset that there is always something better to be had or found, and so we can't be satisfied with the here and now. Show me someone who claims he is perfectly happy all the time and I'll show you someone who is either a most rare and amazing spiritual being or someone who can't admit the truth. If it is God's Will that we should always be happy then the goal of being perpetually happy would be attainable for each and every one of us.

So, I thought, perhaps the truth falls somewhere in the middle. Or perhaps I was overthinking it. Yes, of course, happiness is important! We need happiness. I love to be happy. I love to be joyful. Most of us do. Yet what was...what *is*...God's Will regarding our happiness? What defines happiness, anyway? And maybe happiness isn't the right word. Maybe "sense of well-being" or "a sense of positive purpose" is better. That's different from ebullience or joyfulness, which is a glorious, necessary part of life but isn't sustainable or even intended to be sustainable.

In the Bible, Psalm 37:5 says, "Trust in the Lord and do good; dwell in the land and enjoy safe pasture. Delight yourself in the Lord and He will give you the desires of your heart. Commit your way to the Lord; trust in Him and He will do this." Is this passage saying that it is God's Will that we have everything we desire? That if we do good and trust Him, we will receive all we want, which should, of course, make us overjoyed? It can be read to mean that.

But let's admit it; some of the desires of our heart aren't all that great. It may be that we truly, earnestly desire the next-door neighbor's dog to run away because it barks all night long. We may truly, earnestly desire to bomb another nation "back to the Dark Ages" because they have hurt people or threatened us. It may our earnest desire that one child get a solid thrashing because he has bullied our own child.

Other desires may not be harmful but are still quite self-centered. We may truly, earnestly desire the job that makes us millions of dollars. We may truly, earnestly long for a trip around the world. It may be our earnest desire to own all the newest electronic gadgets on the market.

And then some desires are more others-centered. We may truly, earnestly desire our drug-addicted friend to accept treatment. We may truly, earnestly desire the money to send our children or grandchildren to college. We may truly, earnestly desire peace of mind so we can function better with our families, our friends, our community, ourselves. In many cases we know deep down what would be best but in other cases we really don't.

So here's my heretical suggestion. I would alter the passage of the Psalm slightly to read: "Trust in the Lord and do good; dwell in the land and enjoy safe pasture. Delight yourself in the Lord and He will give you the desires of His Heart. Commit your way to the Lord; trust in Him and He will do this." (And perhaps that's what the author of the Psalm meant?) Because what could be better than God's Perfect, Love-based Will replacing the desires we have that are sometimes selfish, foggy, or even destructive? What could be more peaceful and powerful than the desire of God's own Heart awakening in us and guiding us? In fact, I believe that in the deepest part of our souls, in the "souls of our souls," what we want really *is* the same as what God wants. We were created with souls that breathe in harmony with God's Will of Love. Even if we don't know it now, even if we are so anxious, angry, or sad that we don't sense it, it is there. Beneath the desire for that bigger house, that beach vacation, all those electronics, that fame or fortune, lies the desire to love and be loved, to accept and be accepted, to find purpose and have purpose. And when we are able to be still, to become humble before our Creator, to let go – through prayer, meditation, contemplation – of whatever has us tangled and confused, we will begin to know the truest happiness.

Prayer, God's Will, and Miracles

Earlier I mentioned the Gloria Copeland booklet; she and others hold to the belief – based in passages of the Bible – that it is God's Will to always reward faithful Christians' trust, faith, and worship by giving them whatever they ask for. Others believe that

God's Will changes based on the strength of the faith of the one who prays.

I would think that any Christian believer, if he or she is going to be completely real about the matter, must realize that, yes, there are those who have prayed earnestly and with perfect faith yet still didn't receive what they asked for. Case in point – me.

My sister Barb and I shared a room when we were growing up. She is two years younger than me. We were and remain best friends. When I was ten and she was eight, we liked to dress like twins. We would wear matching shirts, shorts, and bright red bandanas over our hair. Though we didn't look alike, we wanted people to think we were twins. Once, when hiking in the mountains with our family, a woman passed us and asked, "Are you two twins?" We were thrilled! And so, that night, in total earnestness and absolute, trusting faith, we prayed to Jesus (whom we believed was also God) to make us twins. That we would wake up in the morning and voila! We would look in the mirror and not only would we look the same but we would be the same age (we'd decided we should both be ten, not eight, because I didn't want to go through second and third grades all over again.) We prayed and *knew* it would happen. We trusted with utter faith that Jesus would do this for us. And when we woke up...well you know how that story ends. Our faith didn't get us what we wanted, in spite of the promise in the Bible that says if anything is asked with perfect faith in Jesus' name and power, we'd receive it. That we could even tell mountains to move and they would pull themselves up and hike wherever we told them to go. I'm sure there are Christian apologists who could offer excuses as to why our prayers didn't work, but bottom line is this. It wasn't God's will that my sister and I be twins. He wasn't going to defy His laws of nature for us. And, thank God, He didn't. (Though it would have been fun for a while.)

Many of us have found ourselves, in times of dire necessity, grave fear, or intense longing, praying to God, pleading with Him to help us by granting us a miracle. Prayer is precious communion between our Creator and ourselves. And so when we are crushed down, hopeless or terrified, we fall to our knees figuratively or literally in surrender and supplication, begging Him to intervene and make things better. Our prayers are earnest and uttered with great faith. We ask God to help us. We tell Him what we need.

Then it is up to us to trust the Creator to do what He will do.

Sometimes nothing seems to change whatsoever. Sometimes there are shifts in perception and circumstance. And other times, God intervenes with recognizable miracles. Illnesses are cured. Hearts are softened. Minds are changed. Money is raised. Tragedies are averted. Sometimes other people will see and acknowledge our miracles while other times only we know for certain that our prayers were answered. But no one else needs to tell us whether there was a miracle or not. We know. It's that personal. It's that breathtakingly awesome.

So does our faithful prayer cause God to change His Mind – His Will – about something? I don't believe so. God's Will won't be changed by human petition because His Will is already perfect and ready. We can't lure Him with breadcrumb trails of promises into doing what He would not otherwise do. We aren't His puppets, and He certainly isn't ours. However (and this is a very *big* however) when we are moved to pray, when we are beaten down, hopeless or terrified, and when we fall to our knees or bow our heads in surrender and supplication, God has already opened our hearts to Himself and His Power. He reached out first. He already knows what scares us, what saddens us, what depresses us. Even when we feel utterly alone, ripped apart, distraught, God is there. His Arms are around us. We are never on our own. And in this, because of His Loving Will, God may help us change our attitudes or perceptions. Because we have opened to Him, the beautiful Divine communion is complete. He may show us new opportunities that we will take advantage of or ignore. He may offer a breath-taking miracle that lifts us from anguish into pure, unadulterated joy. And for a reason known only to God, He may let us be as we are in that moment. Yet even when He leaves us on the floor or crying into our pillows, He is still there. Still hearing us. Still loving us, surrounding us, kneeling with us, breathing into us. For no matter what we suffer, no matter how we struggle or weep in the now, there will be Light. There will be True Peace. Maybe not in this second or minute. Maybe not tomorrow or next week or next month. But in God's perfect timing there will be Light and there will be Peace for each and every one of His children. Regardless of the darkness that might fall due to natural circumstances or the heartless actions of others. The Great Light, the True Peace will come. This is the Miracle of God that will dry every tear, comfort every sorrow.

Because of this, no one should ever be criticized or dismissed for not having enough faith or not praying hard enough if a bad circumstance remains so. God doesn't bless us with a miracle or withhold a blessing based on the perfection or lack of perfection of our faith or our human insecurities. The miracles He gives us are done so because He loves us and it is His Will.

An Aside: What of Miracles and Those Who Don't Believe?

Atheists don't pray. Most agnostics probably don't (though Roger Zelazny, in his *Creatures of Light and Darkness,* crafted a lovely agnostic's prayer in 1969). With a lack of two-way communion between non-believer and God, does this mean God does not offer the non-believer miracles? Does He withhold miracles from those who do not pray?

No, of course not. We're all His children. He loves us equally. The non-believer may well experience miracles, both large and small. He or she won't interpret it as a reaching out of the Creator, but the gift is still there.

Should God gifting the non-believer lessen our desire to pray or diminish our relationship with our Creator? Aren't those of us who believe "special" in God's eyes?

No, of course not. That God cares for us all equally should be celebrated. These are our brothers and sisters. Let us be thankful for Divine, Unconditional Love.

A Final Thought on God's Will

There are circumstances during our lives when God's Will prevails. There are plenty of times when our free will prevails. Too often this makes our world seem like a heartless planet and humanity seem like a hardened, hopeless species. The wills of fearful, power-crazed people seem to crush the wills of good-hearted, loving people. But we must learn from this; we must grow in courage and understanding. We must discover in ourselves the strengths to stand up against terrible behaviors, to circumvent terrible events. Yes, it's a life-long chore. Not only life-long for one but for all humankind.

Yet even as we struggle, there is the Biggest Picture above it all, the Picture of God's Ultimate Will. Though our wills often reign on Earth, everything, absolutely everything, will return to God's Will in the End. He will always have the final say...not some imagined devil, not hatred, not cruelty, not despair or greed. People may fear that God's Will for them is harsh and cold, that it will be little more than suffering and oppression. I'm here to assure you that is not God's Will. We are here because He willed us to be here. He wants us to live, love, struggle, and grow as humans. Sometimes we will be profoundly happy. Sometimes we will be miserable. Sometimes we will be successful and sometimes we will fail. It's all part of life on God's good planet, a partnership between humanity and the Creator. And in His Time we will all – *all* – be brought around, bought back, to His Love, Forgiveness, and Absolute and Eternal Peace and Joy.

A Quote

"Seek God's Will in all you do, and He will show you the path to take." Proverbs 3:6

7

Evolution, Human Sexuality, and other Sciencey Stuff

This is my Father's world, and to my listening ears
All nature sings, and round me rings the music of the
    spheres.
This is my Father's world: I rest me in the thought
Of rocks and trees, of skies and seas;
His hand the wonders wrought. – Maltbie Babcock, 1901

    In 2007 in Petersburg, Kentucky, a tourist attraction called the Creation Museum was opened for business. I've never been there. First of all, it's 461 miles from my home according to Google Maps. Secondly, I don't think there is anything at the museum that would appeal to me except perhaps for what looks to be a pretty cool bug collection and the fact that I have "ride a zip line" (make that a "ride a not very high zip line") on my bucket list. For those who haven't heard of this museum, this is it in a nutshell:
    The museum was conceived, funded, and is maintained by a group called "Answers in Genesis," whose president Ken Ham was a major force in the creation of the Creation Museum. It seems to be fairly popular, too, with what they estimate to be close to two million visitors a year. From viewing the museum's website I can

see that it is quite expansive and well maintained. The employees and visitors, based on viewing the photos, look happy and engaged. I have no doubt they are. I say most sincerely, "God bless them."

Everything about the museum is grounded in the Biblical account of Creation. This includes the belief that God fashioned the world and everything in it during a period of six days, and that it was all done in the relatively recent past (6,000 – 10,000 years ago). Adam and Eve are taught as the first two humans on the planet. The museum even has its own Allosaurus fossil, a fossil that, claims Mr. Ham, offers proof that humans and dinosaurs lived side by side a few thousands years ago. The fossil is also pointed to as proof of a worldwide flood since the bones were found in northwest Colorado. The conclusion is that about 4,300 years ago, this dinosaur ran off in an attempt to escape the global floodwaters but drowned, was washed away, and was covered by debris and sediment, and then unearthed in the early 21st century.

In February 2014, Bill Nye, the bow-tied "Science Guy," agreed to debate Ken Ham at the Creation Museum. Talk about Nye stepping into the other camp – these two men are as different in their beliefs on the existence of the Universe as night from day. The debate went for close to three hours, with Ham giving passages of the Bible as the source of his understanding of how things were created and Nye giving scientific discoveries as the source of his understanding of how things were created. I watched a good chunk of the debate online (watching three hours of anything on the computer is beyond my level of physical or mental tolerance) and found it to be on a fairly even emotional keel. Each man was fervent yet steady in his delivery. It seemed that each had ample opportunity to say what he felt he needed to say. I heard no name-calling, mudslinging, or heckling from the audience.

That's rarely the case, though.

There is a lot of white-hot emotion when it comes to the topic of Evolution vs. Creationism. I've seen blogs online (I'm sure many of you have, too) in which those who believe in evolution are called "Satan worshippers," "deluded," "doomed," and "Hell-bent." And there are blogs in which those who are Creationists are called "ignorant," "sheeple," and "clueless."

Bible Stories About the Beginning

"And God said, 'Let there be light,' and there was light." – Genesis 1.3.

A very simple yet powerful verse. Though the authors of the Bible would have had no clue about current scientific concepts of the beginnings of all there is, they knew that the force at the dawn of creation must have been stunning, indeed. Nothing could be more dazzling than Light proceeding from the mouth of God!

I am a creationist, a label some liberal believers will run from like a Biblical plague. I'm not a creationist in the way many fundamentalist or traditional monotheists are creationists. To be more specific I should say I'm a creationist-evolutionist. I believe God created everything that ever was, is, or ever will be. I love to imagine the Light, the Power, and the Wisdom of God willing what would be into being 14 billion years ago.

There are stories in the Bible about the beginning that resonate sweetly. And then there are others.

Attending Sunday school as a little girl, I was taught about the seven days of Creation, Adam and Eve, mean old Satan and the forbidden apple, Noah and the Great Flood, the Tower of Babel, and so on. And like most kids I knew at the time, I didn't think much about them or evaluate them. Still, there was fun to be had with these tales. We got to color pictures of Bible heroes and adventures, make dioramas, and create costumes then act out the stories as skits. Beyond Sunday school there was Vacation Bible School (a week long summer day camp) where we made puppets of the featured Bible players – Adam, Eve, Noah, Moses – using paper, markers, glue, and popsicle sticks. In Brownie Girl Scouts (we called ourselves Girl Snorts) we sang lively Bible-inspired songs like "Dem Bones Gonna Rise Again" ("I know it know it, indeed I know it, brother, I know it, whee! Dem bones gonna rise again!") Mainly, though, since those Bible stories happened so long ago, they didn't concern me. I had more important things to think about, like earning new Brownie patches and pins, playing Civil War with the neighbor kids, and pretending to be a horse.

Then our mother gave my sisters, my younger brother, and me a children's record album that told the story of Noah's Ark. We gathered around the record player on the floor (me with my blue stuffed dog, Barb with her purple stuffed hippo) to listen. The narrator had a charming voice and the animal sound effects were adorable. And at the end, when God revealed the rainbow and promised not to flood the world again, the accompanying music carried the story to a powerful conclusion. But, since this was the first time I'd paid close attention to the story, something stuck in my craw. As cute as the animals were as they squawked and bellowed and squealed as they clambered onto the ark, and as pious and loving as Noah sounded when talking to the Lord, there was God Himself – drowning everybody and everything else. It was so mean. Hadn't I been taught that God was loving? Surely not everyone and everything that was drowned were so bad they deserved to die. The image of kids and moms and dads and ponies and dogs and hippos swimming for their lives but getting pulled under, swirling around, inhaling filthy water, and then dying gave me nightmares. God couldn't be that hateful, could He, to kill almost everything He made? Or maybe He just didn't love any of them from the beginning. I didn't like the story of Noah.

That made me think about other Biblical creation stories. Adam and Eve, for example. If God really didn't want them to eat fruit from the Tree of Knowledge, why did He plant that stupid tree in the place? As God He surely would have known that Adam and Eve would give in to temptation (He knows everything, right?) and that He would then boot them out of the Garden of Eden. He knew with certainty that the first couple would screw up that test and yet He purposefully set them up to fail. I didn't like the story of Adam and Eve.

Then there was the story of the Tower of Babel. God was angry that people, who all shared a common language, were working together to build a tower to Heaven. He didn't like that their focus was on the tower and not Him. He was also concerned that the people would learn things they shouldn't know. And so in the blink of an eye he made them speak different languages. No longer could they understand each other. Even as a child, I knew that things would only be worse for people if they couldn't understand each other. I didn't like the story of the Tower of Babel.

As an adult, I've come to know that Bible creation stories have more to them than I thought as a child. The authors of the Bible sought to honor God and His Handiwork. Those who wrote Noah's story tried, in a very visual, visceral way, to explain how much God loves goodness and does not love evil. How bad behavior can lead to calamity. It also adds that sweet bit at the end about this being the first rainbow ever seen. I don't believe the literal, whole-Earth Noah flood (though studies suggest there was a large, catastrophic flooding of the Black Sea about 12,000 years ago), but I don't begrudge the storytellers their imaginations. The tale of Adam and Eve attempts to explain how people came to be and why (by disobeying God through the "Fall") they suffer and struggle to this day. It has similarities to the Greek tale of Pandora, the first human woman created by the gods, who opened the forbidden jar or box and let all the terrible things out into the world. The tale of the Tower of Babel tried to explain why there are so many various languages across the world (a world that, in the minds of those who created the story, only included the portion of the world with which they were familiar. To them there was no North America, South America, Australia, or Antarctica.) The Tower of Babel story also makes a point that if a people have a collective yet delusional goal, not only are they wasting their time, but they also may cause harm to each other.

Biblical scholars have analyzed and will continue to analyze these and other Bible stories to find relevance in today's world. I'm no scholar. I believe these stories to be creation and early-life allegories that don't need to be taken literally. But they might offer some things to ponder and, yes, to appreciate.

Evolution and We, the People

I've believed in evolution for as long as I've known what it is, which was at some point in my later childhood. It is frustrating and unfair how evolution has become a hot topic for politicians running for office ("Do *you* believe in evolution, Senator-who-wants-to-be-president?"). And then there is the issue regarding the teaching of evolution in school systems ("Let's not include evolution in our science curriculum or let's at least require science teachers to include creationism along side evolution because some parents will protest otherwise.") No political official or school system seems to debate gravity or the fact that the Earth revolves around the sun, possibly because those doesn't include the "where we came from" issue. I don't consider evolution a theory. Most scientists don't, either. National Academies of Science states: "In science, a 'fact' typically refers to an observation, measurement, or other form of evidence that can be expected to occur the same way under similar circumstances. However, scientists also use the term 'fact' to refer to a scientific explanation that has been tested and confirmed so many times that there is no longer a compelling reason to keep testing it or looking for additional examples. In that respect, the past and continuing occurrence of evolution is a scientific fact. Because the evidence supporting it is so strong, scientists no longer question whether biological evolution has occurred and is continuing to occur. Instead, they investigate the mechanisms of evolution, how rapidly evolution can take place, and related questions."

So what is evolution? I'm sure most of you reading this already know, but for those who don't, here it is in a nutshell. According to Dictionary.com, it is "the change in the gene pool of a population from generation to generation by such processes as mutation, natural selection, and genetic drift." Basically, organisms with certain beneficial traits will be the ones to survive and pass their genetic material on to the next generation. Those with traits that aren't beneficial to survival will die off or be killed and therefore not pass their genetic material along. This is how species change over long periods of time – they adapt to better survive due to the traits their ancestors passed along to them.

Over the years I've encountered religion-based arguments against evolution. The larger two umbrella arguments are these:

1. The Bible gives the story of Adam and Eve, who are the first people, and they were people from the outset, not a "lower animal." God created them, whole and complete, and placed them in the Garden of Eden.

2. God created people in His image. Only people are created in His image, and therefore we had to have been placed on this

earth as humans from the beginning. One-celled organisms in the sea or soil could not be considered in "God's image."

The various sub-sets of arguments against evolution can be very pointed. Examples of wingless birds or the symbiotic relationship between termites and microbes are given as proof that evolution is nonsense. The Evidence for Creation website has even suggested that "...Satan inspired Darwin with evolution."

I don't agree but I won't debate it. I won't debate evolution. I don't debate well, and I find debates more often than not just lock people down in their own views. However, I will discuss it.

If God is as infinitely intelligent and powerful as I believe He is, He certainly could have created what we see, in all its vast variations, through a process that has taken more than 13 billion years. His Spirit is certainly creative and powerful enough to have spoken or imagined into existence the first spark of life then guided life as it expanded outward and evolved into the 8.7 millions species of living things that now occupy Earth, not to mention any other forms of life that likely exist elsewhere. It is mind-boggling, to put it mildly. It is absolutely awesome and glorious. He loves His Creation with a Perfect Love, every single-celled organism, every fern, every gnat, lizard, dog, and human.

Evolution will continue as our Universe – this portion of God's Kingdom – continues to exist. Humans are no longer bushy cave-folks. We evolved from extensive hairiness to the relatively hairless forms we are now. If humans continue another million or so years, what might we have evolved to by then? Totally hairless? What might our skulls look like? Larger? Smaller? Will we still have appendixes or earlobes? Will we have lost our little toes? Will our skin tones change to adapt to the Earth's climate? Will we all have the same color hair and eyes? Will we have developed better or worse hearing or eyesight, based on our dependence on technologies? Or will we have become extinct, with other animals and plants taking over the planet? I have no clue. Science fiction authors speculate. Scientists hypothesize. What I can know with certainty is that however God directs life throughout the eons, He is the Creator, He knows how this is going, and He loves us. He loved us as bushy-cave folks, He'll love us as hairless, earlobe-less, four-toed people, if that's what we become in our adaptations.

Even if we cease to exist as a species, God will have loved us during our time on Earth and will continue to love us utterly and perfectly in the glorious realm of Spirit and Eternity.

An Aside: Teaching Biblical Creation in Public Schools

As much as I respect people's various religious views on Creation, we must make sure that those views are not taught in public schools as scientific fact. Teaching classes on comparative religion is one thing; teaching religious beliefs as challenges to science is another altogether. If those who demand their religion's views be taught in public schools were truly aware of all the implications that come when that door is opened wide, they'd want to slam it back and prop it shut with a big, big stick.

The Big Bang or the Bang-less Biggie

For those who missed science class that day or who never heard of Sheldon Cooper (!), the Big Bang is a theory regarding the creation or beginning of our Universe. According to a National Geographic webpage: "Big Bang proponents suggest that some 10 billion to 20 billion years ago, a massive blast allowed all the universe's known matter and energy – even space and time themselves – to spring from some ancient and unknown type of energy. The theory maintains that, in the instant – a trillion-trillionth of a second – after the Big Bang, the universe expanded with incomprehensible speed from its pebble-size origin to astronomical scope. Expansion has apparently continued, but much more slowly, over the ensuing billions of years."

This makes perfect sense to me. I can imagine God, preparing to set Creation into motion, speaking with a voice so Powerful and Almighty that it, itself, was the Big Bang from which all matter and energy and space exploded and expanded. What Authority. What Vision and Purpose!

Another scientific theory suggests that the Universe might not have begun with the Big Bang, after all. According to a recent article on Phys.org, "The universe may have existed forever, according to a new model that applies quantum correction terms to complement Einstein's theory of general relativity. The model may also account for dark matter and dark energy, resolving multiple problems at once." Basically, this theory says the Universe has always been and had no beginning. I wouldn't ever suggest that I understand even a fraction of what went into coming up with this new theory, or that I understand much about quantum mechanics or general relativity. But if it's true, it is true. Just like the Big Bang; if it's true, it is true. No amount of wanting it to be true and no amount of wanting it to not be true will make any difference. Truth is Truth.

I'm intrigued with each new discovery and theory posed by scientists and others who investigate, study, and speculate. And nothing ever discovered will threaten God. How could it? He is the Author of all there is. Talk about a Master Mind. Nothing science has discovered or will ever discover will cause me to question the existence of God. In fact, every new discovery is only additional proof to me of the Greatness and Creative Genius of the Divine.

Human Sexuality and the God Who Created It

Sexuality. Where would we…or most other living things…be without it? Nowhere in the physical realm, that's for sure. Sexuality is everywhere, from humans to squirrels to hummingbirds to bumble bees to catfish to dandelions that bloom in the yard. A wonderful aspect of life and the continuation of life imagined and devised by the Creator.

Some early cultures openly embraced or celebrated human sexuality. In Mesopotamia, voluptuous Ishtar was worshipped as the goddess of sexuality, fertility, love, and war. Ancient Roman religion encouraged sexual behaviors as beneficial for the state, and paintings or mosaics that people today might consider pornographic could be found in plain view in respectable Roman homes as well as other public venues. According to the article "Drinking From the Jade Fountain" by John Amaro, in ancient China "…the sex act was considered preventative and energetic medicine assisting with longevity, stamina, immune enhancement as well as a positive influence to a host of physical, emotional and spiritual factors." Six thousand years ago in India, the concept and practice of tantric sex emerged. It purported that sexuality, along with other earthly pleasures, was a doorway to the divine. Graphic paintings and sculptures from the period depict peaceful, smiling men with large, erect penises penetrating the large vaginas of equally peaceful, smiling women. Take the penises and vaginas out of the equation, and the expressions of happiness could as easily come from enjoying a wonderful meal, witnessing a colorful sunset, listening to beautiful music, or talking about how proud they are of their kids.

Few cultures or religions openly celebrate sexuality these days. Some Western religious traditions teach that sex, while necessary, is also a dangerous desire that can lead us down the path of destruction. Some teach that sex is a base, even dirty passion with the power to throw immortal souls into Hell if indulged in incorrectly. Unless, of course, the act is performed within the bonds of holy matrimony, the one man, one woman variety of matrimony, that is. And even then, some that teach that certain sex acts that are immoral or harmful or even that sex should only be done if the possibility of procreation remains open.

First, to those who say, "Well, yeah, sex *can* be dangerous." That's true. Sex can be used to subjugate or abuse others. For eons, rape has been a tool of war against women. When sex becomes an addiction, the addict has a difficult time functioning in other areas such as work or family life. Pedophiles use sex as an abhorrent, destructive act that crushes the spirits and damages those who are its victims. There is no question that sex, used in those ways, it is destructive. Sex can also be the venue for diseases and infections – HIV and AIDS, syphilis, human papillomavirus, gonorrhea, herpes, and more. Any time sex is dangerous, serious help always is needed.

Now back to non-dangerous sex.

Coupling is a powerful force, a driving force, and intentionally so. Why did the Creator make sexual foreplay and intercourse such pleasant experiences? Why is the sensation of skin-to-skin contact, penetration, and orgasm, for both men and women, so rewarding? For several reasons – so we would come together to procreate, of course. Life yearns for life. But it's not only about making babies. Having sex allows us to form the most intimate bonds with another loving person. Having sex releases and relieves stress. It boosts immunity, improves heart health, and lowers blood pressure.

So it's okay to have sex for reasons other than producing another little me or another little you. With someone we love, sex is an act of healing and communion. It offers a fun and very pleasant cardiac workout. And that's all part of God's Plan.

Must sex be within the confines of marriage? That's up to each individual based on what he or she feels is right. My views? Let me just put it this way. I lived with Cortney for thirteen years before we got married.

An Aside: Sexuality and "Purity"

A "purity ball" is a formal dance attended by fathers and their teenage or pre-teen daughters during which the girls make a "purity pledge" – a promise to remain a virgin until they are married. These promises are made both to God and to the fathers. In some cases, the fathers (the "High Priest" of the home and family) pledge to cover the daughter as her authority with the goal of protecting her purity. The fathers then give the daughters a "purity ring," a simple gold band that resembles a wedding ring and is placed on the ring finger of the left hand. The girls are to wear the ring as a promise to God and their fathers that they will abstain from any sexual activity until they have a husband.

I have my own personal reactions to the idea of a "purity ball" and a "purity ring," which I won't discuss here. But what I will say is this: I find the belief that sex before marriage makes a girl "impure" to be cold and unfair. It attempts to turn the sex act into something inherently foul that can only be un-foul following the "I do's." Yet sex is not an impure act. It is a normal and beautiful aspect of our humanness.

Now of course, absolutely, girls *and* boys should be taught about sex, about the emotional, mental, and physical aspects of sex, about the wonder and power of sex, about the serious responsibilities that come with physical intimacy and about the maturity one should have before taking part. And yes, two loving, consenting, of-age people waiting until marriage to have sex is good and right. But two loving, consenting, of-age people enjoying sex prior to marriage is also good and right. "Purity" or a "loss of purity" is not even part of the equation.

Homosexuality, Same Sex Marriage, and the God Who is Ready for Us to Get Over Ourselves

With the exception of organisms that reproduce by an exclusively asexual manner (such as the tiny bdelloid rotifers, freshwater animals that have existed for nearly 80 million years), species have males and females. If not individual male and female organisms then at least specific organs that produce male or female sex cells, as is found in most flowering plants (you might remember middle school life science class and that cut-away diagram of a bright yellow daffodil with its labeled stamen and pistil.)

Humans are members of the Animalia kingdom. Break it on down and we find we are also members of the mammalia class. Mammals are warm-blooded creatures that have hair; the females produce milk to feed their young. Other members of our class include fruit bats (could fruit bats be any cuter? HONEYS!), whales, zebras, cattle, cats, foxes, moles and voles, and duckbilled platypuses. The highest percent of mammals are heterosexual. Yet in some mammal (and some bird and even some insect) species, there is a percent that apparently prefers to couple with those of the same sex. Domestic sheep are one example. According to 1994 studies (reported by BBC), neuroscientists found that in "flocks of sheep, up to 8% of the males prefer other males even when fertile females are around." A 2006 study by Paul Vasey (University of Lethbridge in Alberta, Canada) and his team suggests that female macaques frequently seek sexual pleasure with other females.

There are disagreements on what percent of humans prefer to bond physically and emotionally with someone of the same sex. An older estimate put it at 10% of the population. A 2013 survey released by the CDC (Centers for Disease Control and Prevention) reports that about 1.8% of men identify as gay and 1.5% of women identify as lesbian. 0.4% of men and 0.9% of women identify as bisexual. This survey was conducted with specific questions regarding one's sexual attractions. However, another 2013 survey by the National Bureau of Economic Research (and also reported by Smithsonian.com) got different results. On their website they note that, "Measuring sexual orientation, behavior, and related opinions is difficult because responses are biased towards socially acceptable answers." Using new survey techniques that allows for participants to be more safely honest, the results indicate that about 20% of humans are attracted to their own gender.

But here's the bottom line. What difference should it make? It should make none. Whether it's .01% or 20% or 50%, some people are gay. It's not a "lifestyle." It's not a choice, though if it was a choice that should not matter, either. Being gay is not a way of being that someone was coerced into or corrupted into adopting. It is not unnatural. Anything that exists in nature is natural. Being gay is as normal as being straight; it is as God-crafted as heterosexuality. Why did God create some of us gay, some straight, and some bisexual? I don't know. But it doesn't matter. How sad, shortsighted, and destructive that some of us, due to religion, culture, or society discriminate against, abuse, or even execute those who find their emotional and physical needs met in the arms of someone of the same sex. It just shows how far we still have to go in order to grow up as God's children.

Marriage customs evolve over time as social structures bend or mesh with others' marriage customs. We are a blended world, as much as it often seems we are far apart from one another. But with communication and transportation so readily available, it would be strange indeed if there wasn't a great deal of blending. People marry across racial lines, religious lines, economic lines, and social or cultural lines. Sometimes these marriages work, sometimes not. I wonder what marriage might be like 100 years from now? I can only speculate, and all sorts of things yet to happen could easily throw the trajectory of my speculations way, way off.

As I write this today, same sex marriage remains a hot topic for some people and politicians in the United States. In June 2015, the Supreme Court confirmed same sex marriage as a right in all fifty states, Washington DC, and four of five US territories. Thank God. How wrong for a government to disallow loving, of-age, same sex partners to marry.

But just because the Supreme Court made the ruling, that doesn't mean that we will all peaceably agree on the matter. Some are still fighting to make same sex marriage illegal in their particular state. There were prayer vigils and protesters – some peaceful, others enraged – outside the Supreme Court in May 2015 as the Justices inside discussed and debated the matter. Remember Kim Davis? She had a few months of fame as the county clerk who refused to issue marriage licenses to gay couples (and also to straight couples, in a strange attempt to prove she was not discriminating) in Kentucky because of her strictly held fundamentalist Christian beliefs against homosexuality. Others felt and still feel as she does, though happily as of 2016, 61% of Americans support same sex marriage (Gallup Poll).

The Family Research Council, which is adamantly anti-same sex marriage, gives a variety of reasons why it is wrong. Yet they boil it down to one main point: gays as a couple cannot produce children without help from someone else. When challenged regarding opposite sex couples who don't want or can't have children, the council responded on their website in 2015:

"A couple that doesn't want children when they marry *might* change their minds. Birth control might fail for a couple that uses it. A couple that appears to be infertile may get a surprise and conceive a child. The marital commitment may deter an older man from conceiving children with a younger woman outside of marriage. Even a very elderly couple is of the structural type (i.e., a man and a woman) that could theoretically produce children (or could have in the past)." I do have to chuckle at the last sentence. They had to squeeze in that elderly couple because they have the right physical structures to have produced a child if they were younger, and so that answers that. Right? Talk about a force fit (in more ways than one!)

God doesn't expect every married couple to produce or be able to produce children. For certain not everyone is meant to be a parent. Unlike other animal species, humans have the ability to think and decide whether or not they have what it takes to be a parent, or if they have the desire to be a parent. I have friends – couples as well as individuals – who are childless by choice. It is the right decision for them.

And, of course, there are same sex couples who want children and can make it happen. Just as mothers and fathers can be wonderful parents who raise healthy, stable, compassionate, and productive children, so can mothers and mothers and fathers and fathers. My cousin, John, and his husband Joseph, together seventeen years, have adopted two beautiful children and are doing an incredible job as parents. Likewise, single moms and single dads can be wonderful parents who raise healthy, stable, compassionate, and productive children. I do believe that all children need strong, positive adult male and female role models. Yet these role models do not necessarily have to be the child's custodial or biological parent. They might be a grandparent, aunt or uncle, family friend, or teacher. Bottom line? Parents are those who lovingly raise children. Who loves is not the issue but rather the fact that there is love.

I respect the right of those who believe any sexual orientation other than heterosexuality is wrong due to their religious teachings. But the right to believe that way should never extend into the public realm where they bully and deny the rights of others. I pray that one day sexual orientation will no longer be an issue, and we can turn energies toward things that truly need addressing such as poverty, violence, inequality, education, the environment, and health care.

"...male and female He created them..." – Genesis 1:27

God created males and females. He also created some of us inter-sexed. According to the Intersex Society of North America, intersex is "a general term used for a variety of conditions in which a person is born with a reproductive or sexual anatomy that doesn't seem to fit the typical definitions of female or male. For example, a person might be born appearing to be female on the outside, but having mostly male-typical anatomy on the inside. Or a person may be born with genitals that seem to be in-between the usual male and female types – for example, a girl may be born with a noticeably large clitoris, or lacking a vaginal opening, or a boy may be born with a notably small penis, or with a scrotum that is divided so that it has formed more like labia. Or a person may be born with mosaic genetics, so that some of her cells have XX chromosomes and some of them have XY."

God has also created some of us transgendered or non-binary. Transgendered persons may have typical male or female anatomies but feel very strongly that they are in the wrong bodies. A boy or man may be certain he is actually female. A girl or woman may be certain she is actually male. Non-binary individuals may have physical characteristics of either male or female but don't identify with either gender. How freeing to be able to then embrace the gender we know we are, or to be free of gender labels, without criticism, restriction, or ridicule from anyone else.

Beyond physical sexual features, there are hormonal, emotional, psychologically-based differences, as well. Some of us are asexual, with no sexual attraction to people of either sex. Others are pansexual, with potential attraction to a wider spectrum, including those of both sexes and those who identify as intersex or transsexual.

We are quite the variety, we children of God. There is no one rigid standard or blueprint when it comes to our physical bodies or our sexual orientations. We should not frighten each other because of who we are. We are all God's children. We cling to old misconceptions. We make too big a deal as to the physical mechanics and not enough of the emotional wellbeing that loving intimacy brings.

God made us and loves each of us completely.

Tenderly.

Compassionately.

Let us do our best to live up to His Will that we love completely, tenderly, and compassionately, too.

An Aside: Religious Schools and Religious Rules

I may be in the minority here, but when I come across an article about a student who has been kicked out of a religious school or asked not to enroll because the student is openly gay (or the school staff discovered later that he or she was gay) or the parents are openly gay (or the school staff discovered later that the parents were gay), and the angry parents want to take the school to court, sue the school, or otherwise have the school's name dragged through the mud, I sigh and shake my head. Yes, I wish all schools....all people...could accept the fact that homosexuality is a normal orientation for a certain percent of humanity. But a religious school is going to be true to its doctrines. If the personnel believes being gay is against God's Word and they discover a gay student or gay parents in their midst they will either:

1. have a difficult time treating the student or parents fairly
2. try to change the student's or parents' orientation, or
3. expel the student or deny him/her admittance.

None of these reactions are good, but none should be a surprise. Private religious schools have a right to decide who attends based on their particular standards. Parents of gay kids: don't send them to religious schools that have issues with homosexuality. Gay parents: don't send your children to religious schools that have issues with homosexuality. Unless, of course, you think that particular battle is worth your time and energy. You're certainly free to choose as you will.

Science and the Sacred

Science, which is the study of the physical, offers more than enough to investigate, explore, and analyze. And regardless of how thoroughly we investigate, explore, and analyze, the sacred aspect of creation is never lost or diminished. The sacred is the spiritual essence of that which is physical. The sacred – God's Imprint, His Touch – is what tunes us into the beauty that is there, what generates the rush of awe for the endless wonders that exist. The sacred is what silences us and makes us melt in love with creation. Billowing clouds in a blue sky. Leaves shuddering in the wind. Butterflies on dandelions. Sunlight on ocean waves and moonlight on a pasture. The down of a baby's cheek. The scent of pine needles. A beloved's smile. The splash of stars and planets in a velvet-black sky. I could list countless things that cause me to pause in silent appreciation or laugh out loud in amazement. Science delves into that which is sacred. That which is sacred can be explored through science. Nothing is threatened. Nothing is diminished.

A Prayer

Dearest Creator,

How Profound is Your Wisdom! All of Creation is the Artwork of Your Hand! May we, Your children, open our hearts, minds, and spirits to the wonders that surround us. All that was, is, and shall be comes from Your Hand. Help us to see that the world and one another through Your Eyes. And then we shall be able to focus more clearly on your Most Basic, Wonderful Truth. We will know love. We will love.

Amen

8

Mortal Bodies, Mortal Fears

The Dizzying Tightrope of Life

When I began this particular chapter I was in the grips of a painful bout of pink eye. It felt like someone was rubbing the right eyeball with a wad of sandpaper and I couldn't make it stop. My vision was quite blurry in that eye, which added frustration to the pain. My tolerance was pretty slim, with little patience for anything. I didn't want to talk to anyone. I wished I could pop the eye out with a spoon, soak it overnight, and return it to its regular place once it was all cleared up. I had no insurance to get a prescription from a doctor (I've since been able to get some insurance, thank God), but had a bottle of over-the-counter drops. They didn't work very well.

I don't mean to sound like a whiner. Pink eye is certainly no big deal in the grander scheme of things.

But *ugh!* Pink eye sucks!

So I started thinking about pain. Isn't it curious how one small portion of the body, when hurting, affects not only our body but our emotions as well? How we can be mightily distracted or even stopped in our tracks by something that seems, from a vantage beyond ourselves, to be a relatively small matter? Pink eye. A broken toe. A splinter under a fingernail. A toothache.

Most of us understand that pain is a good thing. Without a sense of pain, we might step on a shard of glass, driving it into our foot, and never know. That could lead to infection and possible death. Without pain, we might develop a deadly disease but would not detect it until it was too late. Pain is a warning system, and a very effective one. I can't remember the last time I put my hand on a red-hot stove and left it there because I was thinking about something else.

Still, as valuable as pain is, we don't like it. It's not meant to be likeable. We fear the pain our bodies might put us through. It's as though our bodies are turning on us, as if they have minds of their own.

Of course, our bodies can turn on us in ways that might not include physical pain. I watched as my grandmother and mother struggled with dementia and then pass away several years after the onset. This was one of Mom's greatest fears…to end up confused, forgetful, and put into a nursing home where those trained in such things could watch over her as our family came to terms with her condition. It was more terrifying to her than cancer.

Sometimes carelessness or intentional abuse by others can wound us, causing fear. When I was a young girl, I was sexually abused by my maternal grandfather. So were my sisters. I believe Mom was, too, though she was of the "if you can't say anything nice, don't say anything at all" school and so we never knew for certain. Every once in a blue moon she would mention how she didn't like her father when he was drinking. But that was it. As a child and teen, I never saw him falling down drunk, but knew he over-indulged. I could smell it. I could sense it. Things he said went from mundane to dark, suggestive, and troubling. My grandmother was a wonderful woman but I think she didn't have a clue. To this day I don't believe she knew that when she went visiting her friends or went to her garden club meetings and left us alone with him he would remove all his clothes but his boxer shorts, climb onto his bed, lie down, and then, one at a time, make us strip to our underpants and climb on top of him to "wrestle." I don't think she knew he would at times sit beside us on the sofa and poke his finger between our legs, or rub us there, and force us to tell him it "felt good." He never actually raped us as in penetrating us (I don't think he did…maybe I can't remember) but I recall clearly those disturbing, disgusting times. I will never forget, though I have gotten past the fear.

There are frightening circumstances that don't directly or immediately affect our safety, but rather threaten the conditions of our lives. Many of us know what it's like to lie awake in the silent hours of night, afraid of losing our homes, our jobs. Little or no money in the bank, asking for extensions on payments and hoping the companies will understand. Aware that bills, like waves on a beach, will continue to crash into us over and over. I've been there and may be there again. I know the worry, the dread, and it can be overwhelming.

The natural world at large can also be terrifying. Natural disasters occur regularly. Diseases are rampant, sometimes creating epidemics or pandemics. People in power take advantage of others. Industries and individuals pollute the environment and take more than they would ever need just because they can. Leaders wage wars. None of us is immune to fear. We all, at times, feel utterly vulnerable and weak. It's enough to want to hide in a hole somewhere.

Why Suffer?

"Although the world is full of suffering, it is also full of the overcoming of it." - Helen Keller

We all suffer. Some more than others, but we all do. Any human being who has ever lived on Earth has experienced suffering. Religions acknowledge suffering. Buddhism's primary focus is that of suffering – its causes and how it might be reduced or eliminated. Some religions teach that suffering can be a punishment as the result of sin and that it can also be a test of faith. Some religions believe a devil or evil spirit torments us with suffering for his pleasure. *A Course in Miracles* says that suffering is an illusion, a projection of ego. The fact of suffering has long been explored, debated, defined, and explored again. As of yet there is no consensus between religions as to its meaning (if any), its purpose (if any) or means of elimination, and I would guess as long as there are so many understandings of God and life, there never will be a complete agreement.

Like most everyone else who believes in the Creator, I've struggled with the issue of suffering. And here is what I've come to believe – God created our natural Universe with its natural laws. He loves His creation. We are not meant to live forever (thus disease, accidents, natural disasters, and the infirmity that comes with aging.) More often than not we experience pain with disease, accidents, natural disasters, and infirmity. And pain hurts. That's the physical suffering.

As to the emotional and mental suffering we experience, that is very personal. About four weeks ago I was overcome with depression. I've been depressed before, sometimes for a day, sometimes for weeks or even months. During this recent bout, as depression dictates, I felt worthless. I felt that nothing I have done or will do will ever have any value. In a store, which was very crowded, I didn't feel compassion for the people who shared that space with me but rather anger and irritation. Lazy people! Thoughtless, selfish people! Pushing, arguing, looking for something to complain about rather than seeking something that is good and right. Then I thought about a friend of mine who is handling her family issues in ways that are more destructive than productive. I wanted to call her, yell at her, and tell them to stop being so stupid and self-centered! As I drove around town, running errands, I felt beat up and beat down by all the terrible things are going on in the world right now, by my inability to fix anything, by the fact that I'm aging and I don't know how that is going to play out in my life, feeling like a slug and a slob and a bum, and wrapped in that nameless, vague sadness that sometimes settles on us like a damp and heavy fog.

(Tell us how you really felt, Beth.)

Now, when I'm able to step aside and look at myself as I go through those awful feelings, I can see that I'm not as much of a bum as I might think. I have done a few things that had some benefit. The world is a mess but yes, as Helen said, there is a lot of good out there, too. But wow. When depression hits, I might know these things intellectually but I sure don't feel them. The feelings seem stronger than the knowings.

Within the last several years, two of my friends have had sons, both young adults in their twenties, die unexpectedly, one in a car accident and one from an undetected heart issue. While I've lost loved ones over the course of my life so far (my sister, my parents, good friends) I would imagine that losing a child is one of the most painful losses someone can experience. With such loss can come grave emotional and mental pain. It clings like a thorny coat that refuses to be shed. We seek ways to survive, to manage the suffering. Sometimes we are successful. Sometimes less so.

So yes, bottom line, we suffer. I can't think of a single religion or spiritual tradition that would deny or try to ignore our suffering. Back for a moment to Buddhism, which tackles emotional/mental suffering directly and clearly through their four Noble Truths:

1. We will all experience suffering
2. The cause of suffering is craving (we will constantly search outside ourselves for something to make us happy)
3. Through diligent practice, we can lessen or put an end to craving
4. The Enlightened Path will help humankind's suffering. This path includes Right Understanding, Right Thought, Right Speech, Right Action, Right Livelihood, Right Effort, Right Mindfulness and Right Concentration

As a monotheist, I have no trouble embracing the basics of these Noble Truths. They make a lot of sense. They go hand in hand with my understanding of the God of Love and the challenges and blessings He offers us all as we live our lives. I see the Basic, Most Wonderful Truth of God as the Enlightened Path.

But why, though? Why do we suffer? Why must we hurt? Why must we wander the wilderness? Why must we feel loneliness or endure sorrow or grief? Why can't we just be at peace and content all the time?

When I Googled "why we suffer," seven of the first eight websites to pop up were Christian websites. The other was Jewish. Many of these sites state that God allows us to suffer in order to make us stronger. That He allows us to suffer because suffering breaks down the barriers we set up between ourselves and others and so we might have compassion for those who also suffer. That He allows us to suffer because it humbles us to the reality of the physical life we are living and gives us a wider appreciation for all that life encompasses. That suffering creates ultimate surrender, and surrender can help us realize God. I have no doubt that some of our suffering serves those purposes. I know that some of my sufferings have made me stronger, more compassionate, more humble, and more aware of the fragility, impermanence, and beauty of life. Some of my suffering has also made me more aware of my need for God.

And then there is suffering that seems utterly and wholly without reason, pointless. As beings in mortal bodies, placed on this Earth, some of us are swept up in the worst of it. I don't know why God allows this, but He does. This kind of suffering should cause us to rise to the occasion and do all we can to alleviate it. Not to look away or ignore it, but to face the challenge as maturing, caring children of God. And "pointless" does not mean eternal. There is no suffering that is eternal. All suffering will cease, thank God.

Fear and Faith

Some years ago there was a television series – *The Tudors* – based on the life and times of King Henry VIII. There was a priest who was soon to be executed. He stood upon the platform, sweating profusely, his hands bound behind him. The headsman with the axe stood beside him. The priest said something like this to the crowd that had gathered, "My soul rejoices that I will soon see God, but my body is terrified. Pray for me!"

For those who believe in God, who trust God, it seems to be a paradox. God created us. He loves us. We trust Him. Yet our bodies seem to have minds of their own and greatly fear the things of the flesh.

Jesus said to his disciples "The spirit is willing but the flesh is weak." Even this Divinely insightful son of God realized that as much faith as we might have, we will still fall back into fear at times. Pain has its purpose, but pain is painful. Death has its purpose, but death is the loss of every physical thing we have come to know and love.

As I write this portion of the chapter, I'm also watching leaves fly past my window. It's mid-October and today is very windy. The leaves don't cling to the trees; when it's time to let go they do, and they let go and take their final journey. It's quite a wild sight out there – leaves of gold and amber, scarlet and umber, spinning, rising, and swirling as if in a dance with one another. Now of course, leaves don't have children or grandchildren, parents or spouses or friends to leave behind. They don't have regrets. They don't have business left undone. But they are part of God's natural world as we are and we can learn from the allegory they offer. Like us, their days are numbered. Every living thing will die. We don't know when our own October winds will blow and send us out from this world, flying home to the Realm of Pure Spirit with God. And so, to help us face and lose our fear of the inevitable, let's deal with our regrets in the moment. Let's not ignore our children or grandchildren or parents or spouses or friends. We could live for 1,000 years and still not accomplish everything we think we should. Knowing this, let's use the time we have wisely. Not anxiously or fretfully, but thoughtfully. Time is a gift. Let's share that gift with our friends and family. Let's also take time for ourselves.

There is a Buddhist saying (yes, I love a lot of Buddhist sayings!), "Make a friend of death." I don't find that morbid at all, but rather solid advice that offers a deep sigh of relief. Enjoy the leaves, the wind, the sun. During our lives lets do work that is of good and of benefit to others. Let's realize that we will not live forever so may we make our days count. Death will come, but we will be more able to accept that it will happen and less fearful of its inevitability. In fact we may look up to God as death approaches, smile, and, as the leaves do, let go our clinging and give our souls over to the Creator who loves us so.

In the previous chapter I talked about God's Will during times of suffering. Faith in God's Love and His Presence offers peace of heart, mind, and soul in the midst of pain or fear, struggles or loss. Trust reminds us that He knows each of us perfectly and completely, that He loves each of us with utter tenderness and compassion. Our faith, our trust may waver. Yet no matter what happens, I've come to believe that one of these will occur under God's Loving Care:

1. He will create a miracle and change the circumstances
2. He will create a miracle by changing our mindset or ability to handle the circumstances
3. He will comfort and guide us through the circumstance
4. He will let us stand on our own to endure the circumstances yet will never leave us.

Numbers 1-3 are the easiest to accept on faith. Number 4, though, that's much more difficult. Some might think that God remaining silent and offering nothing to guide or comfort us is proof He has turned His back. Imagine an abused woman, cowering in a corner as her husband prepares to beat her again. Imagine a man imprisoned for some social or political infraction in North Korea, having just been tortured and now alone in a filthy cell. The woman calls out to God to help her, to save her, yet the husband beats her and leaves her gravely wounded. The man in North Korea may cry out to God if he believes, or a spirit if he believes, or to whatever or whomever might hear him, yet he remains in agony. What of these precious children of God? The Creator is not punishing them; their fellow humans are. Why, then, is He silent? Does He no longer care for this person? Has He forgotten them? No. He never forgets His children, not a single one. The Bible says of sparrows, "...not one of them will fall to the ground outside your Father's care." If God is conscious of and is aware of every sparrow, every insect, every snake or turtle or fish or tree or flower or every single living thing He has willed into existence, then of course He is conscious of and is aware of us.

So again, why is He sometimes so agonizingly silent? Yes, He might offer an amazing miracle on behalf of the abused woman or the imprisoned man. But what if he doesn't? The Answer is an answer cloaked in Mystery. Yes, "mystery" is a heavy-laden buzzword. Skeptics claim it's a quick cover-all to justify faith in something we can't explain. I understand why they think that it is a cop out. I'm not offended by the legitimate challenge. Yet those who seek God realize that much does indeed remain a Mystery.

God's Knowing is not our knowing. His Understanding is not our understanding. His timing is not our timing. Believers will continue to wrangle with this question, and God's Answer is at once Universal for all and very personal for each of us. We will cry and beg and plead at times, only to feel He is not listening. But He is. Not only is He listening, He is by our shoulder. His Arms are around us. His Mercy and Love have never left us and never will leave us. So why the silence at times? Why do we sometimes feel abandoned? Can't there be some fragment of the Answer, the Mystery, that we can hold, that we can comprehend?

Here is a fragment of the Answer to the Mystery, a fragment that helps me release my anxiety and also challenges me on the most basic levels: God created time, the natural Universe, and the natural world. Over billions of years, Our Master Artist and Scientist brought into existence all the wonders that we know (and many we have yet to know). This includes our planet, Earth, which was perfect to sustain life. It is the home where we are born, live, and die. Not only has God created all this, He has given us everything we need to make life on this planet work. Everything we need to overcome challenges, to care for one another, and to take care of the Earth. We have creativity, intelligence, and determination. We have the capability to love and have compassion for one another. We have the abilities to work together as a positive, powerful collective force. And so when terrible things happen, we have the choice to act or not to act. This is a huge responsibility. We are not helpless infants who must have everything done for us, babies who cry and pout in the corner, waiting for the grownups to fix everything. We are to stand on our two feet, be bold, and take part in this challenging existence for the benefit of our brothers and sisters as well as ourselves. In spite of our fears, we are to rise to many occasions to overcome those fears and to help end the suffering of one another. The responsibility is enormous. It is a responsibility for us, collectively. It is a responsibility for us, individually. It connects us to God in a way unique to all others, and brings us around from feeling His Silence to knowing His Power, Presence, and Confidence in us once more. God loves with Perfect Love the woman whose husband is abusing her. God loves with Perfect Love the imprisoned man in North Korea. Now, what are we going to do about it?

Miracles in a Time of Reason

When we are mortally or otherwise afraid, we might pray for a miracle. "Dear God, please help me!"

But what is a miracle, really? The word gets bandied around a lot. "It's a miracle our team won!" "This anti-wrinkle cream is a miracle product!" "It was a miracle I passed this test!" Then there are miracles attributed to more solemn, serious events. "Our baby daughter is the miracle we've prayed for!" "It's a miracle I didn't die in that automobile accident!" "It's a miracle we raised the money for my husband's surgery!"

Of course, we can check out dictionary definitions. According to Merriam-Webster, a miracle is:
- an unusual or wonderful event that is believed to be caused by the power of God
- a very amazing or unusual event, thing, or achievement

As far as I know, most religious writings share stories of miracles, and those miracles are attributed to direct intervention by God.

In Exodus in the Hebrew Torah, Moses led the people of Israel out of Egypt. To help the Israelites escape across the Red Sea, God parted the waters, pushing them back to create "a wall of water on the right and on the left." This allowed the Israelites to escape safely to the other side. As the Egyptian army rushed down and across the dry seabed in pursuit, God returned the water of the sea to its rightful place, drowning them all.

In the New Testament of the Bible, Jesus blessed then transformed five loaves of bread and two fish into enough food to feed a multitude of people. When all were finished eating, Jesus' disciples collected the left overs, which filled twelve baskets.

In the Quran, Mohammed proved to some disbelievers that he was the prophet of Allah by splitting the moon in half by gesturing with his index finger.

In the opening passages of the Book of Mormon, Joseph Smith and witnesses tell how Smith, though a Divine gift of interpretation, was able to translate ancient, unfamiliar engravings on gold plates; the engravings were the text of the Book of Mormon.

(Interestingly, the Kitáb-i-Aqdas, the spiritual book of laws of the Baha'i faith, says there is no need for miracles to prove that Bahá'u'lláh was God's prophet. It reads, in part, "…first point of our investigation will be the education He bestowed upon mankind. If He has been an Educator, if He has really trained a nation or people, causing it to rise from the lowest depths of ignorance to the highest station of knowledge, then we are sure that He was a Prophet. This is a plain and clear method of procedure, proof that is irrefutable. We do not need to seek after other proofs. We do not need to mention miracles, saying that out of rock water gushed forth, for such miracles and statements may be denied and refused by those who hear them.")

These days, however, we don't hear about the moon splitting, a sea dividing, a small amount of food being transformed into a great amount of food, or someone with no understanding of an ancient language suddenly being able to accurately interpret volumes in that language. We don't see unedited GoPro recordings of water turning into wine, bushes on fire that don't burn, or donkeys talking. Does that mean God decided to cool it with the dramatics or to drop miracles all together?

Many of the miracles found in religious texts are beautiful and stunning. I remember as a child being fascinated with the idea of the Red Sea rising up and away, creating a path of dry land for the escaping children of Israel. Of course, it was impressed in my mind more by seeing the film *The Ten Commandments* than by reading about it. Then came the titular event on Mt. Sinai as God, with bellowing voice and fiery finger, wrote the commandments on stone to hand over to Moses. It was an awe-inspiring thing to hear and witness. It gave the young me a sense of the power of the Creator. And really, what kind of God would He be if He was unable to part a sea, make a donkey speak, or split the moon in half? As a believer, I want God to be able to do that. As a believer, I know God is able to do that. Without a doubt, I'm sure He could and He can. But I don't think He did and I don't think He will. I believe God tends to work within the laws of science that He Himself created.

The miracles in those ancient texts were, I believe, projections of what people believed God could do. These tribal humans wanted to record the absolute power and the supreme glory they believed...they *knew*...God possessed. They wrote from yearning spirits that longed for and reached for the Divine. Their beliefs in God were solidly based in their experiences and hopes. And what better way, in a time when mass communication was basically nil, to share those beliefs than to create amazing stories that would be well-remembered and well-shared?

So were there ever miracles...big or small? And if so, do miracles exist still?

We may not climb a mountain and find a burning bush, we may not witness a feeding of the multitude from a meal that initially could only feed a few, we may not watch a sea part or find ourselves suddenly able to comprehend a mysterious, unknown language. But if we pay attention, we might notice some of the miracles in our lives.

As a pair of self-employed people (writer and illustrator), Cortney and I have walked that swinging bridge called "freelance" for many years. We work six days a week, sometimes seven, to make our combined living, pouring our creative energies into the many projects we take on. We love our work and are thankful for it. We live fairly simply and don't spend frivolously. Still, there have been times we didn't have enough in the bank to cover the bills when they were due. In addition to our own financial obligations, my sister and I were, for a number of years, responsible for our mother, whose dementia had taken so much from her that we needed to place her in a memory care unit in a local nursing facility. That produced its own heartache and heartbreak. And so there have been times when I've felt hopeless and truly, deeply afraid. I'm not sharing this to gain sympathy. God knows millions...billions...of us struggle at some point in our lives.

But as I pray in my uncertainty or anxiety, I become still in God, remembering the beautiful saying, "Be still and know that I am God." Slowly, I let my trust in Him surround me. Sometimes the anxiety melts way. Sometimes the anxiety remains. Yet I know the anxiety isn't going to stop God from hearing me. No matter how clouded our minds are as we pray, God can see through those clouds. He is Strong. He loves me. I pray, "Dearest God, I know You are Lord of all. And I need help, though you already know that..." My prayers aren't coins I drop into a supernatural vending machine. I tell God what I fear, what I believe I need, and then ask for help in whatever form He will offer it. I pray that His Will be done because He knows better than me. I pray that He will give me new insights, new direction, will comfort me, stay with me, or bring forth a miracle.

And yes, sometimes God does bring forth miracles. There have been times when the miracle is a rush of joy or peace of mind that completely wipes out any fear and allows me the clarity of mind to figure out a new plan. Other times the miracle is more concrete. A few years ago, when funds were way low and our 10-year-old P.T. Cruiser started to smell like gasoline on the inside (very worrisome!), I took it to a new mechanic shop in town. I asked for an estimate and sat in the waiting room, praying that whatever it cost we might be able to pay in installments. The head mechanic came back a short while later, explained that it was a frayed wire (something to do with controlling fumes, something like that, I don't remember exactly) and that he'd replaced it. *Okay,* I thought. *Here we go. I wonder what this will cost me.* When I asked about the charge, he said, "Nothing." "Wait...what?" I asked, not sure I heard correctly. Smiling and nodding, he assured me there was no charge; he was just hoping to establish some goodwill with new customers and if I was happy, would I spread the word about their new shop? This was a miracle! I was stunned, thankful to the mechanic and thankful to God. And yes, the stinky-gas smell problem was fixed. A little while later, when we were told our little Cruiser had a cracked motor mount (oh, crap! but the mechanic showed Cortney, and it was, indeed, cracked), the mechanic quoted a price of half what others told us to expect. That was a miracle, too.

Then there was the miracle regarding our roof. Cortney and I live in a small house on land owned by my sister and brother-in-law. One morning about two years ago, we woke after a derecho (a powerful wind storm) passed through our region to find scads of roof shingles scattered around the back yard. Lots of shingles in the grass, caught up in the bushes, tangled in the fence. Oh, crap! Not good.

I called the insurance company and said we thought we needed to make a claim. I asked if we were covered for wind damage and she said, "Yes, with a $500 deductible." $500. Not something we had on hand. However, I figured we could sell some things on Ebay, Cort could offer some illustration work to new clients, and I could knit some more scarves and if all went well, we could raise the money for the deductible.

Next we looked for roofers. We found three, who came out to make the estimates. All of them climbed up, took a look around, then came down their respective ladders and said, "It's the worst roof we've ever seen." Oh, *crap!* Not good at all. Soon thereafter, the estimates came in the mail and by e-mail. $5,200. $4,750. $3,800. Okay, well, not to panic. The insurance will cover it. It's wind damage. And we'll raise the $500 deductible.

The insurance adjuster came two days later, crawled around on the roof, said very little, and then drove off with his clipboard and ladder. The following Tuesday, I got a call from the insurance company. "I'm sorry, but your roof is deteriorated. We don't pay for deterioration." Pause. I asked her to clarify. She continued, "It isn't wind damage. It's deterioration. The shingles came off because the roof is in such bad shape. We won't cover that." Pause. I held the phone and stared at Cort, who was standing by. There was a lot of dead air, and then I managed, "Okay. Good bye." I hung up.

Cort and I felt sick. There was no way on Earth we could Ebay, knit, or paint enough in a month (it was November; winter weather was on its way) to raise a spare $4,000. We went to a bank with our hats in our hands (okay, we weren't wearing hats but you get the picture) and they were very nice, and said we might be able to get a personal loan at a high interest rate. First, we'd need to give them our last two years of tax returns. And with our income as low as it was for those two years, we realized we wouldn't qualify.

Without a roof, our home was no good. Rain and snow would come through and destroy it. Without a home, we would have to seek other lodgings. But we couldn't afford to pay the rent on an apartment as well as monthly payments on worthless, roofless home.

We were scared, vulnerable.

Then one of our friends suggested we start an online fundraiser-thing. A "GoFundMe" campaign. I hesitated because the idea made me feel like a bum. Like we couldn't take care of our bills. Like we had a crappy little house I didn't want people (outside my good friends) to know about. Like we were begging. But we didn't know what else to do, so we set up a campaign, one to run several weeks. And I prayed, "Lord, it's in Your Hands. At this point there is nothing more we can do. Help us, God, if it is Your Will." Within minutes, literally *minutes*, the fund began to grow. After about 45 minutes I got a message from Michelle, a sweet young woman I'd met at a convention and who is a friend on Facebook. She had seen the campaign. She said she and one of her friends had decided to pray together steadily that we would have the funds we needed within four hours. I was humbled. What a sweet gesture, but what a big order! Four hours? Seriously? Little did I know that God would move in answer to those prayers, that it would be His Will to touch hearts on our behalf. And when three hours and forty minutes had passed, our GoFundMe account had a few dollars over $4,000. I broke down and cried, stunned by the love and compassion shown by so many, stunned by the Love and Compassion God had shown us. We would have a roof. We would not lose our home. A miracle. Absolutely. Thank you, Michelle and all who reached out. Thank you, God!

And then there was the miracle regarding Mom. Anyone who has dealt with someone suffering with dementia knows how the person so afflicted can be combative and angry, confused and resentful. Mom went through a long period of that, accusing me of stealing from her, accusing others of trying to take advantage of her or hurt her. None was true, but it was to Mom. It was such a sad, devastating time. Yet, during her final months here on this Earth, as her dementia increased, as more of her memory was lost to time, one thing returned to the surface and remained steadfast. Her love for us. When we visited her, as she lay on her bed or sat reclining in her wheeled chair, often with her eyes closed, the one thing she was able to whisper was, "I love you!" She was filled with pure, unconditional love, and we were the blessed recipients.

Yes. Miracles are there for the finding. They are in the healing of an illness, in the new job when it is most needed, in the loving compassion of friends who rally together to help, in the change of heart from anger to forgiveness and love. Some miracles are so profound they seem to push the boundaries of what could be. Many, though, are gentle surprises that, when we are aware of them, cause us to catch our breaths and release sigh of humble gratitude.

Something I experience as a miracle might not seem like a miracle to you. What you find miraculous may seem coincidental to someone else. It doesn't matter. I experience the prayer, the hope, and when it is God's Will, the miracle. Others will encounter their own miracles throughout their lives. Some they will recognize and others they will overlook. And, as I mentioned before, miracles aren't just for those who believe in God. God doesn't withhold miracles from some of us while rewarding others. God is God of us all. We all belong to His family. We are all benefactors of His Love.

Yet What of These?

What of infants who are sick or die? What of children who are murdered? What of teens and adults who are caught up in societies that abuse or kill them? Where are their miracles? Such questions can't be glossed over or ignored. God's Love and His Miracles must be true for all, because if they aren't, they are true for none. If they are not intended for every human, then they are nothing more than wishful thinking. So where, oh God, are their miracles?

And I've received a consistent answer, felt true and deep in my soul: "Be still and know that I am God." I can't read, think, or hear that answer, without experiencing a shuddering thrill of awe. It is at once perplexing, profound, and Divine.

The answer remains cloaked in the Mystery. But it is a reminder that everything is God's. If we can take part in the miracle of helping the infant or the child, the teen or the adult, we should never hesitate. That is what mature people do - whether we are believers or non-believers. We must stand strong and be courageous servants of one another. That is our sacred duty, our task given us by our Creator.

And yes, there are circumstances facing others that are completely beyond anything we might do. But those dear ones are never out of God's Hands, never outside His Love. They may experience miracles we will know nothing about. But what we can know for sure is that the Miracle that is the Divine will surround them throughout their lives and will carry them to His Heart when their time has come.

And there, as the Bible says, "He shall wipe away all tears from their eyes; and there shall be no more death, neither sorrow, nor crying, neither shall there be any more pain." There, in God's presence they will exist in glory, joy, and peace forever.

A Song – "Abide With Me" – by Henry Francis Lyte, 1793-1847

Abide with me; fast falls the eventide;
The darkness deepens; Lord, with me abide.
When other helpers fail and comforts flee,
Help of the helpless, O abide with me.

Swift to its close ebbs out life's little day;
Earth's joys grow dim; its glories pass away;
Change and decay in all around I see;
O thou who changest not, abide with me.

I fear no foe, with thee at hand to bless;
Ills have no weight, and tears not bitterness.
Where is death's sting? Where, grave, thy victory?
I triumph still, if thou abide with me.

Lift up Thy Hand before my closing eyes;
Shine through the gloom and point me to the skies.
Heaven's morning breaks, and earth's vain shadows flee;
In life, in death, Oh Lord, abide with me.

9

Death and Beyond

Death – The Great Fear, The Great Equalizer

In researching human beings' greatest fears, I found lists that put the top ones in various orders. These usually include rejection, public speaking, and flying. And, of course, death. Death is one of the greatest fears people face. One, because it is a major unknown. Another, because it may involve pain. Another, because it is permanent. Once gone we're not coming back and there is nothing we can do about it…we're along for the ride with no hands on the wheel or feet on the brakes. Another, because of the sense of loss we image it will bring, if not to ourselves then to those we leave behind.

Not a living soul can take a detour from the inevitable journey into death. No one can prevent it from happening sooner or later.

Death is defined medically as "the irreversible cessation of all vital functions especially as indicated by permanent stoppage of the heart, respiration, and brain activity; the end of life." There have been studies and different views on exactly when death occurs but it does occur. To everyone at some point in time.

Religions and philosophers have wrangled with the concept of death. Christianity says, "the wages of sin is death," which is based in the Genesis story of Adam and Eve. According to that story, temptation and disobedience condemned people, through God's Will, to sweat and suffer and struggle through life and ultimately to die. Yet as I suggested earlier, armadillos and dandelions have not sinned, yet they also die. Therefore dying is not a punishment from our Creator. It is merely a part of God's natural plan.

My question, then, isn't "why death?" but "why not death?" We are not meant to live forever in our physical bodies. Practically speaking, can you imagine how crowded our Earth would be is no one had ever died since the beginning of humankind? Or how so many could be fed? Wouldn't it suck to be starving or sick forever and never have permanent relief? Even if I could, I wouldn't want to live forever. Most of the time I love my life. I'm beyond grateful that God decided to create me. I've had experiences that have taught me a great deal and know still there is much, much more I should learn. I've had joys and suffering. I've loved and have been loved. But I can't fathom living forever. The idea is exhausting. God planned it that our physical lives be temporary and that our spiritual lives be eternal. That's beautiful and brilliant.

French Jesuit priest and philosopher Pierre Teilhard de Chardin once wrote, "We are not physical beings having a spiritual experience; we are spiritual beings having a physical experience." God not only created our bodies but He created our souls, breathing them into us with Divine Inspiration and Power. And when our bodies die, our souls will be released to God. How glorious!

God, being God, has a perfect understanding of life, death, time, and space. He would not see death as an ending because He sees both sides of the Great Door. He knows that while our bodies die, our spirits are whole and alive, and they move from the realm of the physical into the realm of the Spiritual with the ease of water flowing from a cup into a river, with the simplicity of taking a single step across a floor.

Yes, death is huge to the human mind. Some of us obsess over it. Some of us try to pretend it doesn't exist. We associate it with frailty, physical or mental decline, or violence because those are the causes of death. And death brings sadness for those left behind, even for those who are certain that God's Healing Arms await us when we pass on to the next life. But life is tough. Life is difficult. And life requires that we experience death at the end of what we know so that we might move on into the new and glorious knowledge of God, knowledge that was only partial during our time on Earth but that becomes whole when we move through the Door to Him.

Satan, Demons, and H-E-Double Hockey Sticks

We all cross over from physical life to life eternal. What will we encounter at that point? Some say we die, we die. End of story. Others say that the matter and/or energy that made us up is redistributed and used again in other forms, and so we will continue in a manner of speaking.

Yet many who believe in God find more to death than that. As for me, I believe we do continue, that our souls or spirits aren't limited by the physical world and therefore don't play by the same rules. I believe God didn't create us to dream and love and wonder and long and hope to have us then fizzle and evaporate into a final nothingness.

Believers have differing ideas on what happens to our souls once we die. Some say it depends on how we lived our lives. Ancient religions and spiritual traditions often held the idea that if you were good, you would find paradise or heaven. If you were bad, you would face punishment. Deities weighed humans' hearts to decide where their souls would spend eternity. Those who were evil were condemned to suffer in a dark, dreadful place (often thought of as "down"). Those who were good were taken to a beautiful place (almost always thought of as "up"), a heavenly realm where they would find peace, joy, and sometimes material rewards. Modern day monotheistic religions tend to agree to some point on this view of the afterlife.

We're human, so we often ascribe human attributes to the Divine. We may not do it intentionally, but coming from a human standpoint it's what we tend to do. When someone steals, kidnaps, tortures, murders, drives under the influence, burns down buildings, carjacks, or otherwise harms people or property, we naturally want justice. Justice in the human mind may involve shunning, restitution, prison time, or even torture or execution. And if those people were not punished during their lifetimes, then it's up to God to do the punishing, right? People want justice. They want fairness. The idea that God's Justice must be much like our own, only more powerful, gives a sense of satisfaction to many. "He'll get his in Hell!" "Just wait until she meets her Maker! She'll be more sorry than she ever was before!" God is seen as the One who will punish all who slipped by under the radar, those who got away with something during life, didn't embrace the right belief, or didn't ask forgiveness. God is also seen as the One who will add more punishment, for good measure, to someone who didn't suffer enough while alive.

According to some Christian denominations, one of the worst sins that can be committed and will certainly send a soul spiraling down that long dark tunnel to Hell is not accepting Jesus as one's personal Lord and Savior. Which leads us to…

The Devil. Satan. Old Scratch. Beelzebub. Lucifer. Prince of Darkness. The Beast. The Liar. All names for the very powerful, evil spiritual entity that is believed to be responsible for so much destruction and sin in the world, the entity that presides over Hell and torments unsaved, unrepentant souls for eternity. Satan is described as having once been a beautiful angel who challenged God and fell from grace. He is able to deceive people and entire nations into false beliefs and therefore trick them into a horrific, never-ending punishment. He tempts people into all forms of wrongdoings. Satan's power is described as vast and terrifying. According to a website called Jesus-Is-Savior.com, Satan "blinds unsaved people, i.e., those who believe not. This is accomplished through secular wisdom, false religion, evolution, and manmade traditions." The site also says that Satan removes God's word from people's hearts; that some people who follow Satan truly believe they are following God, and that most people will go to Hell.

Whoa. That's one powerful entity.

Many who believe in the Devil believe he is to blame for our selfish and destructive behaviors, or at least he found our weaknesses and lured us into acting selfishly and destructively.

After all, some believe that the serpent who tempted Eve in the Garden of Eden was Satan in reptile form. So had there not been that original temptation, that original sin, humans would have lived innocent lives as God intended.

There are those who claim to have actually encountered the Devil in the darkness or in the face of another human being. Satan has been described as either very handsome or quite hideous. I guess that's to either tempt or terrify someone into doing his bidding. And there are those who believe demons – Satan's minions – can wreak havoc on humans. Demons are written about in the Bible; they are said to be responsible for creating spiritual warfare, and they are said to possess people. And, yes, people of those times would also think that evil spirits were responsible for lots of bad things, including diseases and mental illness.

I was still a child when I came to the certain realization that there was no such thing as Satan. Or demons. Or Hell. They weren't things I struggled to deny, but rather concepts that faded into nothingness and drifted away as my understanding of God developed. In 1864, Charles Baudelaire wrote (in "The Generous Gambler"), "…the loveliest trick of the Devil is to persuade you that he does not exist." This saying has been repeated as a warning by those who believe it. Some have argued for the existence of Satan by saying, "You can't have God and not have His adversary. To believe in God you must also believe in His opposite." That's a fairly harsh demand that makes no sense to me. The opposite of God isn't Satan or a Devil. The opposite of God is no God. Just like the opposite of a tree is no tree.

God is Great, Beautiful, Perfect and Loving. His Compassion is so Profound and Sweet it encompasses everyone. He would never allow an evil being or beings to delude and destroy some of His children. I mean, think about it: our Loving God would let a hateful entity (whom He created) confuse His children, even those who truly want to do good, and therefore condemn them to eternal suffering? That's beyond mean spirited. That's cruel and cold. That's: "Ha, ha, ha, some of you people whom I created! Listen up! I will let a fallen angel have so much power that he can destroy you or twist your concept of Me to the point that you won't know what's right or wrong and then I will then punish you for eternity for being so weak. You're destined to be tortured forever because I set it all in motion to happen that way! Ha ha ha!" Good Lord, no. That is *not* God's Character. His Character is Love and Understanding. Love does *not* trick. It does *not* entrap. Love does not hate or destroy.

I've read the argument that claims God's Justice is equal to His Love and that His Love does not trump His need for "just punishment." According to a recent post on a Christian Apologetics website, "It would be an injustice to God's infinite righteousness and holiness to have the sinner's punishment be terminated." In other words, unsaved sinners must suffer eternal damnation because otherwise it negates our Creator's eternal "righteousness and holiness." Saved sinners, on the other hand, will be taken into Heaven and spend eternity there, surrounded by Joy and Love. I realize that these concepts come from particular interpretations of New Testament passages. I realize that there are those who embrace this with absolute faith. Their understandings of God and His Plan may well fill their hearts with certainty, direction, and hopefully, comfort.

But my understanding of God's Justice is quite different. My understanding is based in the Basic Truth of God: He is the Creator of everything that ever was, is, or shall be, and He Loves His Creation and it is His Will that we love each other and love Him. Simply stated or repeated: God Loves. That we know. God Understands. That we also know. Those two Divine Attributes are powerful enough and profound enough to completely negate the idea of Hell, a Devil, and his destructive, creepy little demon minions. There is *no power* greater than God's. He created no evil being with the ability to circumvent His Beautiful Will that all His children unite with him in the next life. Do not be afraid. He loves us wholly and compassionately!

But Why Not Hell? I Mean, Some People Are Really Bad, Right?

Hell is supposed to be for bad people, for so-called evil people. Those who commit terrible crimes. Those who commit terrible crimes and never ask for forgiveness either from those they wronged or from God. To many Christians, Hell is for those who never accepted Jesus as their Lord and Savior – "all have sinned and come short of the glory of God" – and so Jesus was punished in our place, paying the brutal, bloody price God demanded for our evilness. Our wickedness.

But what is "evil?" According to Merriam-Webster, evil means "morally reprehensible," though most of us don't need to look up evil to have a fair idea of what it means. There are people who do and have done morally reprehensible things. Pol Pot. Ted Bundy. Joseph Stalin. Timothy McVeigh. Josef Mengele. Kim Jong Il. Idi Amin. Jeffrey Dahmer. Hitler. Bernie Madoff. The members of Daesh and Boko Haram. Jesse Matthew. And on and on, today and back through history to the dawn of humankind. Some of these people seem to have no remorse or believe the inhumane things they have done are acceptable. We seek to capture, stop, and punish those who have done such dreadful things. And rightly so. We need to stand up for one another, to do what we can to protect each other and our world from the cruel actions of others.

Why do people do reprehensible things? We could sit down with psychologists and behavioral therapists, theologians, and sociologists and compare notes about chemistry, environment, character, conditioning, and trauma. The personal reasons anyone does terrible things are personal. What went wrong in Jeffrey Dahmer's brain that drove him to torture and murder? How did the members of Daesh become a brutally violent, single-minded force determined to control everyone they encounter (a very multi-faceted issue right there)? Why did Bernie Madoff willfully ignore the fact that he was financially destroying so many people?

There is greed and desperation. There is fear and selfishness. There is a sense of powerlessness. There is a feeling of disenfranchisement. There is loneliness. There is immaturity. There is anxiety and depression. There is rage. There are blendings of any or all of these. Some of these, over time, fester and grow into a mindset of hatred and superiority, so much so that one's own will and needs supersede those of anyone else. And, of course, there are mental and emotional illnesses that seem to have been there from infancy, illnesses that distort how one interprets or experiences the world.

We have some ideas as to why Ted Bundy murdered women. We have some ideas as to why members of Daesh proudly and loudly destroy artifacts, brutally butcher human beings and record them for the world to see, and demand perfect obedience from those they overtake. But only God knows with Absolute Certainty.

And so here's a question. People have done horrific things, but are the people themselves innately evil? Are there people who are born evil? I don't believe so. The only way for a person's soul to be evil is for God to have created them evil. And if God is truly Loving He would never have created anyone evil. Circumstances arise from the natural world that may converge into a situation in which someone does evil acts, thinks evil things. A man who is incredibly insecure may become a tyrant in order to prove he has power or value. An abused teen may grow up to become an abuser. An oppressed, disenfranchised young person may join a terrorist group to prove he has power. A bullied woman may withhold help from others in a sense of misdirected revenge. Someone who has been conditioned to believe she is more important or more intelligent than anyone else may emotionally or physically abuse others through a sense of entitlement and superiority. Someone who is mentally ill may harm others. None of these people are evil. They do dreadful things. And, of course, we must protect ourselves and others from their actions. But following the Basic, Most Wonderful Truth of God, we also need to love these people. We need to help and care for them as best we can without becoming harmed ourselves. How do we accomplish that? The answer is something we must continue to study, something about which we'll grow in understanding, something about which, with compassion and courage, we will act to remedy.

Some of us are here in this life to care. Others are here to be cared for.

God knows our mental and emotional makeups because He created us. He knows every single experience we have had. He knows the pain each has suffered. He knows the rejections, the rage, the insecurities, the selfishness, the anxieties, the hatred, the fears. He *knows*. He *understands*. How could He not? God is God. The Act of His Creation is an Act of Pure and Purposeful Love, it is

Art fashioned by the Almighty Hand. He Loves the grasses, the ants, the bacteria, the camels, the dogs, the people, the trees, the rivers, the moons and planets, the stars and black holes and quasars and the vast regions of nothingness in space. Everything He made is part of the Great Reality, a portion of the Divine Fabric He has woven. Therefore, there is not a single person He did not intend to exist. No one is a mistake; no one is an accident. As educator Zachary Clements once said, "God don't make no junk." Because of this, there is not one soul destined by God to be lost forever, to be damned without rescue, to be condemned to eternal suffering. For that *is not* Love. It isn't even love. Such a deity would be cruel and sadistic beyond words. The concept of God crucifying some of his children on an eternal cross of pain and anguish as a penalty for impermanent sins is a distortion, a human-conceived wish that flies in the face of Perfect Love. There are those who will argue for it, who have studied the theories of countless theological scholars. Yet no matter how complex some try to make it, I'll always return to the Basic, Most Wonderful, Most Important Truth of God.

So here's a biggie. Does this mean that in the long run it doesn't matter what we do?

Of course not.

I realize there will be some who read the above and poo-poo it with some variation of "So God just lets us do whatever we want and there are no consequences? Everybody gets to go to Heaven, so why bother being good? If that's God, He's a wimp! If Hitler's in Heaven, I don't want to be there." I just ask that readers consider what I'm saying without assuming I'm all sparkling unicorns and rainbows regarding harmful or hateful actions.

While there are always reasons for behaviors, not all reasons are excuses. There are some people who cannot make the right choice, the compassionate choice, the loving choice. Something has crushed them or distorted their thoughts to where they are unable to feel compassion or act lovingly. And then there are those of us who are able to make the better choice, the compassionate choice, the loving choice, and yet we don't. We are too enraged or self-centered or lazy or greedy and we let ourselves be swayed by opinions or by circumstances. Those are our reasons, not our excuses. So if there is no Hell to scare us into being good, does that mean God doesn't care one way or the other how we treat one another or our world? That He's a wimp?

No.

When we step over from this life into the next, when we move from the physical to the wholly spiritual, God is there. Of course, God is here, too, but in the realm of Spirit there is nothing to cloak Him from us. There is nothing to distract us from Him. Each of us will meet Him face to Face at our deaths. It will be the most personal, stunning, awesome moment we will ever experience. If we had breaths at that time, it would literally take our breaths away.

As to the harmful, hateful things we intentionally committed and for which we have not sought forgiveness, what then?

I had an online conversation a while back with a Christian (whom I'll call Rick) who had (maybe still has) a blog. In one of his entries, he discussed how sad it was that some people reject God and choose Hell over Heaven. His point was that there are certain people who actually prefer Hell over obedience to God. The two of us had a very civil, respectful discussion. I suggested that when we die, we become totally aware of God – of his Power, Glory, Understanding, and Unconditional Compassion. I said that no one, not a single soul, could face God at that moment and still reject Him. It would be impossible, for His Glory and Love is that profound, that great. This, I suggested, is the true Irresistible Grace. Rick disagreed; he said that human nature, human selfishness, human rebellion would still keep some people from acknowledging God even when face to Face with Him. That sin would have them so hardened they would never offer their hearts to God and they would choose Hell. I can't fathom that to be true. There are only two scenarios that would allow someone, when faced with God in the Whole of His Glory and Goodness, to still reject Him. 1. He created some of us so flawed that our souls don't have the ability to acknowledge His Power, Mercy, and Love even when up close and personal. Or 2. God is not as Powerful, Merciful, and Loving as we think He is, which allows some of us to blow Him off even when facing Him at our deaths. Neither of those can be true if the Creator is as we believe Him to be.

An Aside: I Love Jesus

Dear Christian friends, please don't think that because I'm writing about Jesus in an "aside" means I think Jesus is not important. On the contrary. Jesus' incredible life and teachings inspired one of the world's most beautiful religions. But I need to talk about Jesus here, especially when it comes to a discussion on death and the hereafter.

I often think about the beauty that is Jesus. He revolutionized the idea of God. His incredible relationship with our Creator lead him to proclaim the Loving Parenthood of God, and how we are to treat one another with love, and how the Kingdom of God is everywhere. We are to courageously return love for hatred. We are to offer forgiveness rather than revenge. We are to see in each person the precious soul, God created.

Those who didn't agree with Jesus' take on God or those who thought he was a threat decided he needed to be disposed of. And he was, in a most brutal way. Yet he didn't fight it. He was willing to suffer the agony of crucifixion rather than deny the powerful truths he shared about God. What an astounding, courageous act! I love that Jesus was so brave, so compassionate, so filled with the God's Love that he faced death with perfect courage, forgiveness, and certainty that death was not the end.

I may not believe Jesus was or is God but I believe he was a son of God. A child of God who had opened his heart so humbly, so trustingly, and so lovingly that God filled him to overflowing with His Holy Spirit.

I can't picture the Face of God. It is too Amazing. But for Christians, the face of Jesus is the Face of God. It gives believers a human countenance that is at once tender, recognizable, and powerful. What perfect, abiding peace there must be found seeing our Creator in a human face.

I've been greatly moved by stories of Jesus and the teachings ascribed to him. The thought of him dying in such a horrific way – because he taught of God's Love and wouldn't denounce his teachings – is both humbling and profound. Wanting to share something that might resonate with Trinitarian Christians, Unitarian Christians, and those with no religious belief yet who see in Jesus compassion and hope, I wrote a poem several years ago. I then gave the poem – "All the Babes on Christmas Born" – some minor edits and it was transformed into a lovely song by composer and singer Johnny Schaefer. We were honored when Johnny was asked to perform the song during Marianne Williamson's 2015 Christmas Eve service.

Here is the original poem:

All the Babes on Christmas Born

Through Bethlehem a harsh wind swirled
Past shed and stable, shop and inn
By window, doorway, dimly-lit,
And homes bent low 'neath sorrow's din.
It paused beside a humble place
Where in a manger lay a child.
His father stood in awe, and still;
His mother held her heart and smiled.

A heavenly light shown kindly down,
Piercing through the wind and dust,
God, the Creator, blessed His child
With Tender Mercies, Love, and Trust.
The babe was Jesus, who would teach
Of God's Compassion and His Care,
Who would live and who would die
For our Dear Master's Love to share.

And on that night, all 'round the world
Other newborns' cries were heard.
As hard winds wailed, the fathers knelt,
And mothers prayed with gentle word.
Warm or shivering, rich or poor,
Hopeful, lowly little ones;
All the babes on Christmas born,
God's own daughters, His own sons.

He placed His Hand upon each brow,
Each one to the Lord's Heart so dear;
Blessed, so on life's rugged road
His Voice, through hope and peace, they'd hear.
For every child since dawning time
Has been a flower of His Heart,
Here to live, to learn, to grow,
Side by side and not apart.

On through days of toil and joys,
Through trials of many thousand years,
Our God has kept us in His Sight,
Our Lord has washed away our fears.
And with the lessons Jesus shared,
Of Love, Forgiveness, Patience, Grace,
All God's children, everywhere,
Shall someday, surely, see His Face.

We'll live and love, we'll search, we'll find,
Rejoicing, praising, our Great King,
One in family, one in heart,
And then fly home, safe on His Wing.
Yes, up we'll rise within His Love,
Our voices joined, we all shall sing,
One in family, one in heart,
Flying home, safe on His Wing.

What, Then, of Death?

We will never know with absolute certainty what faces us at our deaths. We won't be sure until it is our turn. Yet there are powerful, beautiful insights that can lead us with serenity and confidence to that point in our lives. I feel that comfort deep in my soul. I don't fear what is to come. The fact that God is in control, that all is in His Hands, gives me the confidence that all will be well at my death. His Loving Will will prevail. How can it not? He is God.

Death is a natural part of the Universe as God created it. It is not a punishment for sin but part of the journey of life. It is one of life's most deeply profound experiences. It is natural, something we all share.

There are some beautiful spiritual concepts of death. Some look at death not as an enemy but as something to understand and welcome as inevitable and certainly not dreadful. St. Frances honored "sister death," praying in Canticle of Brother Sun, "We praise You, Lord, for Sister Death, from whom no-one living can escape." Kahlil Gibran wrote in "The Ascending" – "And I can hear naught but the music of Eternity, in exact harmony with the spirit's desires."

We experience time here in our bodies, here on our planet. We count minutes or hours or days or years. We see kids growing up, teens maturing, adults growing old. We mark birthdays and anniversaries. We celebrate holidays and talk about how things were different years ago. We imagine what things might be like in years, decades, or centuries to come. Time is a gift from God. But time is not the same to God. He is beyond time, outside of time, because He created time and He is Eternal. Time is without meaning within the context of eternity. God is, was, and always will be. He knows that at our deaths we will leave the physical world and the experience of time, and join Him where there is no time.

So what do I believe is certain of the experience of death?

Whatever we imagine is the sweetest, most peaceful, most glorious and love-filled is what surely will be, and more beyond that. First Corinthians 2:9 in the Bible says, "But as it is written, eye hath not seen, nor ear heard, neither have entered into the heart of man, the things which God hath prepared for them that love Him." And as every soul *will* love Him at her or his death. Each person, even those who never knew or acknowledged Him in their physical lifetimes, will experience the Perfect, Unconditional Love of God and will in turn love God. It's inevitable. It is the final act of His Will for us. It is beautiful.

Many of us have heard that our lives will "flash before our eyes" at our deaths, that we will have a life review and will see or even experience certain segments of our time on Earth. I believe this is true. And during this review, God will let us know how our intentional actions affected others. Every secret will be laid bare. Nothing will be hidden. We will understand the heartache and sadness we caused others. We will know the kindness and compassion we offered others. And there, in the Presence of God, stripped bare of any pretense or excuses, in perfect awareness of ourselves, of those we affected during our lives, we will judge ourselves honestly and purely. There will be a great flood of hope and sorrow and relief from our hearts and we will offer it all to God in repentance and awe. Then, filled with the utter ecstasy of God's Forgiveness and Love, we will soar into the Beauty and Light of His Eternity to be with Him forever. *No one* will burn forever. *No one* will be swallowed up in a lake of fire. *No one* will be sent to some distant, spiritual outer-region and shunned by the Creator. God's Justice is not our justice. God's Justice is rooted firmly and unshakably in His Perfect Knowledge of us and His Perfect Love for us.

Yes, God's Loving Will *will* prevail.

Love does not mete out eternal punishment for temporary wrongs.

Love does not hold everlasting grudges.

Love forgives.

Love is patient and kind.

Love hopes all things, believes all things.

When our lives are done, God is not done with us. He made us to Love us. It's no more complicated than that. At our deaths, God will lift us up and away from our physical bodies; He will draw us to Himself as one would lift a drowning man from the sea. And then, in His Presence, each and every soul – those who loved Him while living as well as those who did not love Him and those who did not know Him – will be, in that instant, awash with Divine Power and Glory, enfolded and blessed by the Perfect and Unconditional Love of the Creator.

As for Heaven, we don't need to die to taste of it. The Kingdom of God is everywhere. As with God, there is nowhere it is not. It is within us, around us, right this very moment in the physical realm as much as in the spiritual realm. To give generously of our time, our wealth, our wisdom, our compassion and sympathy, to feel unabashed love and caring toward those with whom we share this world, to act freely with mercy, forgiveness, and understanding – all these open our hearts and minds to the astounding joy that is Heaven on Earth.

A Song – Beyond the Sunset (Partial) by Virgil Brock, 1887-1978

Beyond the sunset, no clouds will gather,
No storms will threaten, no fears annoy;
O day of gladness, O day unending,
Beyond the sunset, Eternal Joy.

Beyond the sunset, a hand will guide me
To God, the Father whom I adore;
His glorious presence, His words of welcome,
Will be my portion on that fair shore.

10

Obeying, Worshipping, Praying, Meditating

Obeying

"Obey" is an emotionally charged word. When I hear or read the word, my initial gut reaction is to cringe. "Obey" brings to my mind a number of things. The secret alien signs that show up when Rowdy Roddy Piper puts on the special sunglasses in *They Live*. The command of Big Brother in George Orwell's *1984*. Abusive parents screaming at their children that they best do what they're told or face the consequences. Bright yet terrified women keeping their opinions to themselves because they have been told by their families, cultures, or religions that it's their duty to obey their husbands or other authority figures.

I grew up as part of the "question authority" generation and am glad for it. Questioning is a critical aspect of living a mindful, conscious life. Looking at the history of humanity, there are countless examples of authority gone bad, of power being used to oppress and abuse, and those in power are more often than not willing do anything to retain that power. A quote from *1984* reflects this: "We know that no one ever seizes power with the intention of relinquishing it. Power is not a means, it is an end." And so "obey" gets its negative reputation honestly.

Of course, there are the necessary "obeys." Obey traffic signs so you don't kill someone or get killed yourself. There are the more innocuous "obeys." Obey the rules of a game. There are the scientific "obeys." As far as we know, black holes obey the laws of physics.

And then there is the peaceful, wonder-filled "obey." This is the obey that refers to God and His Will for us as we live our lives.

My husband Cortney and I are geocachers. (For those who don't know, geocaching is a global scavenger hunt in which people seek cleverly hidden caches by using GPS signals....seriously great fun! Check it out.) Several years ago, we went geocaching with some family and friends. The adventure took us all over the area of Roanoke, Virginia, snooping around for hidden caches, doing our best to make sure no "muggles" (people who don't geocache and who might remove or destroy said cache if they saw it) noticed us. While following the coordinates to a cache on a rural road outside the city we passed a little white church. It had one of those big portable, wheeled signs in the parking lot out front. The sign read, "If you love God, obey Him." One member of our party said the sign was creepy. "They want to tell you what to do, what to think. They want control your life. All you have to do is obey." I didn't say anything. Maybe I should have. But the sign struck me in a different way. I didn't interpret it as the church being the authority, but God. What does God want us to do? To love others and love Him. To do so is to obey Him.

There are powerful, well-known stories of people's obedience to God's Will of Love. One such story is that of Maximilian Kolbe, a Catholic priest who died at age forty-seven in the Nazi concentration camp at Auschwitz. Kolbe lived and worked at a monastery in Poland. The monastery provided shelter to refugees, including several thousand Jews whom he helped hide from German persecution. In February 1941, the German authorities shut the monastery down, arrested Kolbe and four other priests, and they were imprisoned in the Pawiak prison. In May, the priests were sent to Auschwitz, one of the most notorious Nazi death camps, where Kolbe was abused and tortured with the rest of the prisoners. In July, a man from Kolbe's bunker attempted escape and was found dead in a camp latrine. To punish everyone for this man's "crime" of escape, ten of the men of the bunker were selected by the commandant to be locked in an underground starvation chamber and left without food or water until they died. One of the chosen, a Jewish prisoner Franciszek Gajowniczek, screamed in horror, "My poor wife! My poor children! What will they do?" At that moment, Kolbe quietly stepped forward and offered to take Gajowniczek's place. And so he went into the starvation chamber – a small, cold, bare room with only a tiny barred window near the ceiling – with the other nine men. As the days wore on, he prayed with and for the other men, comforting them, remaining calm and at peace, sharing his love of God and his love for them. Over several weeks the men died, and at last, frustrated that Kolbe was still alive, the guards came in with a syringe filled with carbolic acid. Kolbe held up his arm calmly and they injected him. He died. Gajowniczek survived Auschwitz and was freed after spending more than five years in the camp and he was reunited with his wife. Of Kolbe's sacrifice, he declared, "I want to express my thanks, for the gift of life."

The story of Maximilian Kolbe is one startling example of obeying God's Will that we love each other. It moves me deeply. But there are also countless, everyday examples of obedience to the Creator by acting with love. A teacher working patiently with students who are struggling. A young man sharing his food with a homeless man. A woman who is kind to the cashier who is having a bad day. The teen who offers a caring, listening ear to a distraught friend. A child who gives her toys to a child who has none. A police officer who helps a confused man find his way home.

And what of those who don't believe in God?

One Christian website states, "We cannot have God without love or love without God." Another claims, "We need to have a relationship with God before we can show love to one another for long periods of time." The authors of these sites reason that we cannot truly experience love if we don't know or acknowledge God, or that we can love but only for short times; that true, lasting love is not possible unless one is a believer. In other words, whatever love atheists claim they feel, well, it can't be real love, not *permanent* love.

Human beings were created by God with the capacity for love. Just because someone does not embrace the idea of God doesn't mean they lose their innate ability to love. Of course atheists are as likely and as able to act lovingly and compassionately as believers. For those who think otherwise, they don't know any atheists or if they do, they aren't paying attention or don't care to pay attention.

Back to obeying…I'm not talking about submitting to those who claim to speak for God. I'm not talking about obeying those who claim to be theological authorities but whose demands are questionable. I will question any authority. And I'll challenge any authoritative rule that crushes curiosity, tries to form us into mindless or frightened drones, and sates its need for power by imposing nonsensical or burdensome restrictions on us. I'm talking about the beauty, wonder, joy of serving and obeying God, for His Will is Love. I mean really, think about it. God's Will is *Love*. Obeying God means loving and caring for each other. Though rarely easy, that's what it means. What could be more beautifully challenging and spiritually fulfilling than such obedience?

Worshipping

"I cannot believe in a God who wants to be praised all the time," wrote Friedrich Nietzsche. I have read more recent comments by atheists and agnostics who echo the same sentiment: "What a weak deity God must be to insist people grovel and worship him all the time. Who could believe in something like that?'

Amen, Nietzsche. I agree with you, agnostics and atheists. I don't believe in such a deity, either. I don't believe God demands praise or worship. He doesn't need praise or worship. He isn't egotistical. Ego is not a Divine Quality. God is Who He Is, with nothing that can threaten, challenge, or diminish Him. He did not create us to gain accolades and puff Himself up. He did not create us in order to reveal His Glory, because His Glory Simply Is. Rather, He created us as part of His eternal plan; He created us to share Love. When we encounter God and have the astounding sense of Him, when we are touched by or confronted by God we instinctively rise into Him, and worship is a natural expression of the awe, love, hope, and even uncertainty that fills us when we become aware of the Creator. Worshipping is a transcendent experience that is at once profoundly personal and deeply, beautifully universal. It is expressed out of our humanness, out of our longing for beauty, for something greater than ourselves, something perfect and peaceful and astounding, something to which we are all destined and will all experience.

Drive by just about any church in the United States and they will have some variation of a sign reading, "Worship Service, Sunday 11 a.m." Or 10 a.m. Or Wednesday night at 7 p.m. The weekly gatherings of believers are often called worship services.

A United Methodist and Presbyterian worship service includes hymn singing, readings from the Bible, reciting creeds, prayers read collectively or by the minster, announcements, a sermon, and songs presented by the choir. I remember sitting in the Methodist Church of my youth during the announcements, the Bible readings, reciting of the creeds, the sermon and hymns. If the prayer was particularly moving or the choir offerings especially beautiful, I would find my soul lifting in a spontaneous state of worship, a rush of awe, surrender, and adoration that had no specific words. This was my soul's acknowledging God. This was worship. Those in the pew beside me, behind me, or in front of me may have been experiencing worship at a different moment and in a different way. A warm glow of candles, a stained glass image, a floral arrangement, a scriptural reading, a sermon – any of those may deeply touch the spirit of the person encountering it and lift their souls to indefinable and glorious worship. I love that churches offer opportunities for people to gather to experience a community of believers and uninterrupted moments of worship. Services may be filled with shouting and dancing. They might be quietly reverent. But they are times set aside to ponder God, seek God, and worship Him as we feel moved by His Presence.

Worship isn't limited to a community of believers. God is there, is here, whether we are alone or with millions, whether we belong to a particular religion or not. And worship is not merely words or emotions. It is also action. It is obeying the Will of God to love courageously and share active compassion. It is being bold enough to be gentle, to be patient, to be giving, to be forgiving, to step out of our comfort zones to help, to be empathetic and sympathetic to others to help reduce their suffering.

Just as love is both an emotion and an action, worship is both an offering to the Creator and an honoring of the Creator through what we say and what we do.

Praying

Prayer is communion and communication with God. It is an innate reaching out of the human spirit to the Divine Spirit. It's a conversation. It is a discussion. It is a relinquishing, a quiet reflection, a time of silence, an appeal, a giving of thanks, sometimes even an argument. Prayer can be spur-of-the-moment or intentional. It can be thankful, hopeful, or desperate. Prayer may be conscious, when we are aware of what we are thinking and saying. It may be subconscious, when our spirits call out to our Creator even as our minds are too tangled and confused to think clearly. That we can converse with God is an astounding thing. That He hears and knows our every word, thought, and need is awesome. And absolutely nothing we pray surprises Him.

It isn't hard to pray. There is no complex set of steps to follow or rules that must be obeyed. There is no required, prescribed formula. It is a simple reaching for God in thought, emotion, or speech. It's as natural as breathing. Prayer can be done alone. It can be done with another person or a group of people. It can be a spontaneous act or part of a beautiful, traditional ritual. We can pray in our rooms, in our cars, in our schools, in our places of business, in our stores, out in nature. For wherever we are, God is and so wherever we are, prayer is available to us.

Prayer is an opening to the Spirit and Presence of the Creator. As C. S. Lewis put so well, "He Himself is the fuel our spirits were designed to burn, or the food our spirits were designed to feed on." When we pray, we become humble before Him. Being humble before God doesn't mean we are, as one woman I know said, "nothing more than dirty rags covered in skin," though sometimes we might feel that way. Being humble before God means we know that we are His creations, His children. It means we are open to the Reality that is God, the Almighty Glory and Compassion that is greater than our greatest longings and needs. It means we are ready to be completely honest with Him and to be willing to receive whatever answer He might offer.

Prayer can bring indescribable peace. Talking with God and feeling His reply, in whatever way He chooses, is a most profound experience. We were meant for this connection.

Some religions have prayer rituals or traditions. As a member of the Methodist Church, I was taught to sit quietly and respectfully, shut my eyes, and bow my head. Other Christian denominations kneel to pray, honoring God by humbling themselves. Some religions teach members to stand and raise their hands to pray in open adoration. Muslims pray five times a day with faces to the ground, an act of supplication and remembrance of Allah. Some believers say grace before meals and offer nightly prayers before climbing into bed.

Believers pray to express our wonder and thanksgiving. Such gratitude draws us closer to God. Such awareness of God's Majesty is awesome, filling our souls with incredible joy. And no prayer is wasted except those that are blatantly selfish or mean-spirited. Prayers such as those are just noise on the air, blown away and forgotten.

We pray to ask forgiveness. Throughout our days we do things that are not loving and we withhold things that are loving. Asking forgiveness from God for our selfishness, or meanness, or laziness clears the air and helps us do better in the days to come. And in many cases, when we ask God for forgiveness, He in turn asks us to seek the forgiveness of those we have wronged. This is spiritual cleansing. This is renewal.

We pray to seek help for others in need. We have dear friends and family who suffer. There are precious people nations far away who are suffering. We pray for clarity in order to know what we can do to help them. We pray for courage to step out of our comfort zones if we can help them. And if there is nothing we can do ourselves, we pray God will inspire others to act to help them. And that He will enfold those who suffer His arms, to protect and comfort them. Yes, it is God's Will that we pray for others; it brings us into oneness, it allows us to be co-creators of healing and mercy. We may learn of a startling miracle following our prayer. Other times, we cannot know what God has done. Sometimes He will reach out in the physical realm, sometimes in the spiritual realm. Even if the ones we pray for lose their lives, God has not let go of them. He has drawn them to Himself where perfect peace and ecstasy will enfold them and hold them forever.

We pray for strength, help, and guidance for ourselves. We may be overwhelmed or depressed, frightened or ill. And we know God hears us and loves us. We know we can lean heavily on Him for His Strength is beyond comprehension. We may have lost our jobs and need direction in securing a new one. We may need to find a new place to live, new transportation, or the money to get through a scary financial drought.

The Bible says we should pray without ceasing. I like this, though it wouldn't work to stay on our knees every moment of the day. I believe it means that as much as we can, we should go about our daily lives in an attitude of prayer, an openness to the Spirit. We might lie in the grass in a state of transcendence, knowing He is aware of us, our minds silent but our hearts rejoicing. Or we might gaze out at the falling snow or rising moon and pray, simply, "You are my God." We might sit on the warm sand with our eyes closed, listening to the constant rush of the wave and feeling the pulse of it all as if it were the Heartbeat of the Creator. Or we might stand in a busy grocery store or on a crowded subway and think, "These are all Your children; every one of them, and they are all precious to You." Such a prayerful interface with creation not only brings us closer to our Creator but also lightens our emotional loads. It allows us to connect with the beauty of the world and the beauty of humanity.

I've heard non-believers say that prayer is a lazy person's non-solution; that instead of praying for things to get done, we should get busy *doing* those things. I understand that criticism. We *should* get busy doing those things. The saying, "God helps those who help themselves" isn't in any scripture I know of, but it has merit. When we can help ourselves, it is up to us to do so. God can provide us with direction, courage, insight, and more.

Answers to prayers aren't rewards but are gifts. Those whose faith is profound and those whose faith wavers, those who call on Him tentatively and those who aren't even certain He exists yet "put out an appeal just in case," are all heard by the Divine. So are the longings and hopes of those who would never consider praying. God sets up no competition to see who has the most faith. Answers to prayers both spoken and unspoken should not cause us to boast. They are benedictions from God, reminders that He is the All-Compassionate Beloved. This is our God we are talking to. His Full Glory and Power are profound. Our minds and hearts could never encompass it all. But His Love is also greater than our ability to understand. His Love is what opens the door between Himself and His children. And that the door never closes.

Sometimes when I pray about my own issues (family, financial fears, health), I feel a twinge of guilt. There is so much hatred, pain, and suffering in the world, and my problems thus far have been miniscule in comparison. And so I also pray for God to bless, comfort, and give strength to those who are in danger, abused, downtrodden, discounted or disenfranchised. Recently, when sitting in the car, waiting for Cortney who was in a store, I prayed, "How is it that with all the people in the world, with all the issues in the world, with all that is going on that needs your attention, You hear *me*? How is it that You can pay attention to *me*? I'm one of billions of people on Earth. And, if what I think it true and there are conscious, intelligent sentient beings in countless other places in the Universe/Multiverse, then I'm one of many gazillion-gazillions. How can You even be aware of me?" And then the most beautiful, simplest answer came to my mind. I heard – I *felt* – God's answer in my heart: "Piece of cake." It took my breath away. I knew what He said was true, and I know He offered it to me with a smile and perhaps even a chuckle. Of course knowing me and hearing me is a piece of cake. He's God, and there is nothing outside His Perfect Knowledge, His Understanding, His Awareness, His Power.

He is the Creator.

Piece of cake!

And so that twinge of guilt is only my doubt speaking. I should not pray for others out of a sense of guilt but out of a sense of love. I thank God for making this clear.

Once, in a profound moment of awe and adoration, I prayed, "I have nothing to give You but what You have given me, what You have made me."

And I sensed God answer, "Exactly."

Meditating – God-Given Tool or Satanic Seduction?

If you've read up to this point, I'm sure you know how I would answer the above question. But let me ramble a bit more.

When the word "meditation" is spoken in the West, what might first come to mind are the Eastern religions of Hinduism and Buddhism. Some envision skinny, aged men in loincloths sitting in lotus position on a craggy summit, intoning *"Om"* over and over. Others might imagine a bunch of elderly hippie ladies with flowing gowns and long, wild gray hair in a circle, same lotus position, also chanting *"Om."* Some might recall a statue of the Buddha in a meditation garden or on a shelf in a New Age shop with a price sticker on the bottom. Others may remember seeing art work featuring a black silhouetted human with those rainbow-color dots running up the center that represent seven primary chakras.

The word meditation is defined simply in various dictionaries as "continued or extended thought," "devout religious contemplation," and "reflection." In these earlier years of the 21st century, most people I know understand that there are various kinds of meditation and a wide variety of people who meditate or at least claim to meditate. Meditation can be religious or non-religious. It is used to relax, to become more mindful and in the moment, to deal with pain and insomnia, to gain better control over emotions, and to increase one's spiritual connections.

I've found no research at all to support accusations that practicing meditation is harmful. On the contrary. Science has solid evidence to support claims that meditation is beneficial. Yet to some more traditional or fundamentally religious folks there lingers the fear that meditation opens practitioners up to all kinds of bad stuff. There seems to be a misunderstanding of the practice and its functions.

When I was teaching in a local middle school, one of my fellow teachers mentioned using visualization in her classroom for the purposes of creative writing and peer relationships. Students were to sit quietly and use their imaginations to tap in to their creative abilities to deal with various issues and topics. I thought this was a great idea! But it was immediately criticized by another teacher who said – in not these exact words but very close – "That's meditation. If you open your mind like that, demons can enter!" Double-yikes. Likewise, some of the more fundamentalist parents of children at that school agreed. They saw visualization (which they equated with meditation) as a flirtation with the three Big Bad Ds – demons, danger, and destruction. The backlash from the one teacher and the parents was serious enough to require another approach. I suggested that my pro-visualization teacher friend continue visualization but to call it "daydreaming" instead. That seemed to calm the fears.

No, visualizing isn't the same as meditating. But the situation at the school reveals the misconceptions generated by the idea of quieting one's mind or letting it drift. I found a website that discussed meditation in a negative light: "No amount of chanting, breathing, visualizing...will melt away the sin that separates us from the Lord...however 'peaceful' these practices may feel." It goes on to say that the Apostle Paul warned that "Satan himself masquerades as an angel of light" and that pleasant, peaceful experiences may be portals to danger or hell. A post on another website claimed, "When you clear your mind you make way for demons to enter and control you." And another post stated, "...meditation can also be used as communication with the devil. If you're doing it to relieve stress please find another way to do so, having evil spirits in your home is never a fun thing. I really hope that you stop and I will pray for you."

I had never considered attempting meditation until Cort began extensive readings on Buddhism. What he shared with me piqued my interest. Meditation seemed to make a lot of sense regarding health and wellbeing. To claim meditation is anti-God is, sadly, to limit one of the greatest gifts we humans have been given – our brains.

Meditation isn't easy. It's damned hard to quiet our minds and not let random, stray, persistent thoughts take over, because they will. But the efforts are worth it. For those who have never tried any kind of meditation let me suggest finding a guided meditation video; it can offer help in learning to calm the mind and soul.

I'm learning to use religious meditation to reduce those unnamed worries that cling at the beginning of the day. Most mornings, before I get up, I lie in bed and meditate on God's Peace. I release the clamoring anxiety; I turn away from my insistent, persistent thoughts with the simple mantra, "Peace." I breathe slowly and with each exhalation I silently repeat, "Peace."

Peace.

Peace.

Peace.

Peace.

Sometimes it is easier than other times. Sometimes I even give up. But if I allow myself a good five or ten minutes, more often than not that it will be there. God's Peace. I am in it. God is holding me, loving me, thinking of me. I don't have to do anything but release myself into His Peace. His Peace has always been here, but I have much too often forgotten it or not trusted it.

Peace.

Peace.

Peace.

Peace.

Try it sometime.

Meditation isn't something I do instead of a morning prayer. But I find it to be a good way to start the day. It is a reminder God is God and I am in His Thoughts and in His Love. The indefinable anxieties and vague weariness fade away. I'm ready to get going with what I need to do. I won't be alone as I take on the tasks, both expected and unexpected, that come my way. I will stop and meditate and pray throughout the day and into the evening.

Prayer and meditation are two God-given tools that can put us in the moment, in awareness of Him, in His peace.

A Song, "Breathe on Me, Breathe of God" - Edwin Hatch, 1835-1889

> Breathe on me, Breath of God,
> Fill me with life anew,
> That I may love what thou dost love,
> And do what thou wouldst do.
>
> Breathe on me, breath of God,
> Blend all my soul with Thine,
> Until this earthly part of me
> Glows with Thy fire divine.
>
> Breathe on me, breath of God,
> So shall I never die,
> But live with Thee the perfect life
> Of Thine eternity.

A Prayer, attributed to St. Francis, 1182-1226

Lord, make me an instrument of thy peace.
Where there is hatred, let me sow love,
Where there is injury, pardon;
Where there is doubt, faith;
Where there is despair, hope;
Where there is darkness, light;
And where there is sadness, joy.
O Divine Master, grant that I may not so much seek
to be consoled as to console,
to be understood as to understand,
to be loved, as to love.
For it is in giving that we receive,
It is in pardoning that we are pardoned,
and it is in dying that we are born to eternal life.

11

Carry On – Life With God

God With Us, God For Us

    Close your eyes moment.
    Breathe in the Comfort that is God.
    Be silent in the Holy Presence, which has never left you.
    Feel the Divine Union that is your inheritance.
    Allow yourself this Blessing.

Throughout our lives, God is here. There is nowhere He is not, and we are never forgotten. There is never a day we are overlooked; not a single day we are out of His Thoughts and His Heart. There are times He will make His Presence known in ways that are beautifully familiar. There are times He will make His Presence known in wondrous ways that catch us by surprise. There are times when He will be silent. During those times we may feel abandoned or depressed. Yet there is a reason for His silence. He may be urging us to stand more courageously on our own two feet and face our fears. And there may be other reasons that are very personal and seemingly unknowable to the conscious mind. But be sure of this – God is always with us. He is always for us.

Those of us who are un-churched believers shouldn't feel we have to hide our connections to the Divine. Regardless of how we have come to understand God, we have as much right as anyone to share our beliefs. We should feel free to discuss Him whenever the spirit moves us. That doesn't mean preaching or proselytizing; we know that can drive others away and slam the door of communication. It means realizing that our spiritual pathways are no less than that of others, nor are they greater. God walks with us all. If we want to gather with others to praise and discuss God, wonderful! If we prefer to worship alone, wonderful! But more important than being free to talk about God is being confident and free enough to share His Love. May each of us wisely, thankfully use the life our Creator willed into being.

Day By Day

What can we do in our day-to-day lives that will help establish goodwill and reflect our relationship with the Divine?

Let's make the most of our time here. Love openly, generously, and joyfully. We hold a great power in our hands, and that power is love. Courageous, active love can heal misery, loneliness, and fear. Let's put love to work. Let's speak out for those who cannot speak. Reach out to those who stumble. Share with those who are in need.

When something flies in the face of compassion, mercy, equality, or fairness – whether it happens beside us, around the corner, in a neighboring city, or across the world – we shouldn't be silent and turn away. It doesn't matter if the hatefulness is condoned by a society. It doesn't matter if it is justified by a religion, a culture, a political party, or an individual. We must stand strong. Write letters. Rally. Protest. Create art that shouts or whispers messages of hope. Create petitions. Speak out. Act out. Let's do what we can when we can. Edmund Burke wrote, "All that is necessary for the triumph of evil is that good men do nothing." May our lives serve as a beacon of God's Light, which is Love.

Confined as we are to our own bodies, it's sometimes hard to remember that we aren't the center of our Universe. We aren't the brightest, most sensitive, most troubled, or misunderstood stars that shine. Our emotions can cloud actuality. We shouldn't think, *I feel this way and so should you. I want this and so should you. I understand it this way and so should you.* We must acknowledge the wide spectrum of personalities, created by God, and the equally wide spectrum of life experiences. Let's seek our commonalities so they can bring us together.

Let's be generous with forgiveness. There is no one on Earth who hasn't wronged someone else, intentionally or unintentionally. Resentment is a weight on top of the burden of the original wrong. Forgiveness is a blessing twice given. We release ourselves from the suffering of bitterness and release the offender from the suffering of guilt. Forgiving a wrong can be a big challenge. There are times we may feel it is unmerited. And in some circumstances, forgiveness does not replace justice. Yet forgiveness is always an option. It is one of the most powerful tasks we assume, and the spiritual, emotional, mental, and even physical outcome is one of the most wonderful.

We deserve the same kindness we would show others. Yes, you deserve it. I deserve it. We are all equal members of God's family, after all. Let's be good to ourselves. If you forget something or lose something, don't berate yourself. If you are late or careless, remember that we all are late or careless at times. We're human. It's okay. Let's let it go. Breathe it out. Let's be able to forgive ourselves as we forgive others. Let's try to see ourselves through God's eyes, and remember how much He loves us.

When we go into a grocery store, walk through a mall, stand on a beach, sit in a waiting room at the mechanic's shop or with our children at the pediatrician's office, linger on the sidewalk for a chance to cross the street, sit or stand in a classroom, or wherever else we find ourselves with other people, let's make a point of reminding ourselves, "Each of these people is beloved by our Creator." We should look at faces, see them, and acknowledge each of them in our hearts as precious fellow children of God. Regardless of age. Regardless of ethnicity. Regardless of clothing, of size or shape or tattoos or piercings or expressions of anger, arrogance, or detachment. Look. See them. Let's bless them in our hearts and ask God to bless them.

Let's slow down and tune in to the ordinary-extraordinary wonders around us. Notice the shifting shadows on the ground. Watch the branches of a tree bending in the wind, catching the motion, lifting, trembling, and arcing. Breathe in the fragrance of foods, the scents of skin, the perfumes of candles and pine needles and decaying of leaves. Trace an apple with your finger and feel the texture. Taste bread, don't just chew and swallow it down. Listen to the sound of footsteps, of rain, of deep breaths and human voices. How incredible is all this?

Let's allow ourselves time to be immersed in music that sings to the soul. Music is an incredibly powerful experience. It can lift the spirit and comfort the heart. It can soar us to incredible heights or open a floodgate of tears. I've been both held immobile and stirred to movement by Hezekiah Walker's "Every Praise," Libera's "You Were There" and "I Am the Day," Louis Armstrong's "What a Wonderful World," Alison Krauss' version of "Down to the River to Pray," and instrumentals by Helen Jane Long, Nicholas Gunn, and Bill Douglas. You have your own favorites. Dig out those vinyls or CDs. Turn up that station or turn on that player. Put on those headphones or plug in those ear buds if you must keep it quiet. Let the music flow in and work its magic.

In this, our God-given life, we should be free to laugh. To rejoice. To dress in our colors, our styles. To sing our songs! Dance our dance! Shed our inhibitions! Celebrate our existence! Embrace our creativity! Let's dare to experience and explore what intrigues and inspires us.

Let us do all we can, when we can, to help others. But let's also give ourselves time away from the suffering to rest in God's Gentle Hand. Spending too much time online, face to face with the terrors and agonies of the world, can leave us utterly overwhelmed or beat down with despair. This does no one any good. Let's permit ourselves to just *be* for a while and to let the goodness of the world and the kindness of our fellow humans flow through our veins. Though it may not seem like it at times, there is much more good in the world than bad.

Max Ehrmann wrote in his 1927 poem, "Desiderata" – "You are a child of the universe no less than the trees and the stars; you have a right to be here." We are as much a part of nature as mountains and rivers. As much a part as birds and bugs. As much a part as the wind, the moon, the fields, the thistles, the cliffs, the soft moss on a forest floor, and the determined dandelion growing up through a crack in the sideway. Knowing this, let's step out into nature as often as we can – into the forests or fields, up into the hills or the mountains, wade streams and walk along rivers, sit in a patch of cool grass in a park. We don't have to have a lot of money to do this; most of us can't afford a month-long mountaintop retreat or a sunny sanctuary in the tropics. Nature charges nothing and is here for us all. Let it speak to us and let's listen without interruptions. Nature has the power to help ease the soul, for it is our home.

Let's resist the urge to constantly consume material goods. Can we go a day without spending money? Do we really need more things or do we shop out of habit? Let's break the habit. Let's share what we have with those who need it, and bless it on its way. Letting go of things can make us feel lighter and less burdened.

And Now...

There will be times of doubt in our daily life with God. There will be times when we feel alone, angry, or overwhelmed. There will be times when our prayers seem to stay inside our minds or rise no higher than the ceiling. There will be times when we think, "I'm not so sure I believe anymore." There may be times when we scream at or even curse our Creator. Such feelings and thoughts are normal. God isn't holding a hammer over our heads, ready to whack us if we doubt or if we scream. Doubt gives us the opportunity to step back and see things from other perspectives. Knowing God can handle our anger is freeing. Both doubt and anger allow us to re-evaluate what we thought we believed and find out in new and perhaps more powerful ways that God is the Almighty Spirit, at once Unknowable and Knowable. That God is Compassion, Mercy, and our most Intimate Guide and Friend. That God is God.

Perhaps, someday, we will find churches that speak to us. If so, join! Perhaps we will turn away from the idea of God all together. Perhaps, if we are non-believers, we might find ourselves awakening to God and will seek Him. Yet however our thoughts may change, God never does. Do not fear. He Loves us and will never let us go.

At least once a day, no matter who you are – un-churched believer, Christian, Muslim, Jew, Hindu, Buddhist, Baha'i, Shinto, spiritual-but-not-religious, New Ager, questioner, agnostic, atheist, "none," anti-theist, or any other seeker – and no matter where you live – a big and bustling city, a small town, along a country road, in a suburb, or elsewhere – share a compassionate act with someone else. Offer a smile, a listening ear, or a hug. Open a door, help with a heavy load, pick up something someone dropped, clean up a mess. Let someone else go in front of you in line. Be patient with the fast food cashier who may be having a rough day. Forgive a debt. Find the good in a difficult person and focus on that. Don't be shy in sharing. We're all in need of each other.

And when we feel that pull to be kind, the impulse to do something to help, it is God tapping us on our shoulders. He is encouraging us to love. It's the reason we are here. It's the reason we are.

This is His Will. This is life with God.

Now may you be filled with the peace that passes understanding, the courage that overcomes fear, and Love of God that brings healing and joy.

A Prayer

Dearest and Most Loving Almighty Father,

My soul is at peace, for You are God. Struggles and troubles are certain, yet Your Compassion is more certain and more powerful than any trial. You lift me up in Mercy and save me in Love. My soul leaps for joy! Thank You!

Amen.

12

Prayers to God, From His Children

God hears every prayer – those we speak aloud and those we speak in our hearts. He hears prayers that are clear and well-thought out as well as our anxious, desperate "child's prayers." He knows us and it is His Will to commune with us. What follows is a sampling of the prayers I wrote for the group I hosted on Facebook, "Prayers to God, From His Children." May you find one or more that speaks to your heart, or may you find inspiration to lift your own prayers to The One Who is Divine.

Prayers of Wonder, Thanksgiving, and Adoration

When you are happy, pray to the Creator, who is with us always. Share your delight, for He rejoices with us. Praise Him for His Love, and do not hold back your delight. For in worship our souls recognize, honor, and adore the One who has made us with such Care and Divine Intent.

Dearest Merciful Father,

My heart rises up in wonder and awe. I worship You with my whole being. Your Majesty and Glory are far beyond words, yet You know me and care for me with a most amazing Love. I will do my best to love You with all I am, and to love and serve Your children as is Your Perfect, Most Compassionate Will. Praises to you, my Lord and my Hope, my God and my Creator!

Amen.

Dearest, Most Loving Lord,

You are our Strength, our Joy, and our Redeemer. We lift our hearts to You in thanksgiving and wonder, and we pray You will guard us and guide us each step of the way. Each day. Each night. We know there are many dangers in life. We realize sorrows will come. But we know that You are with us to comfort and lead us, to console us and hold us. Thank You for your Constant and Perfect Mercies. And may we never hesitate to share Your Tender Love with others, for that is Your Great Will for our lives.

Amen.

Dearest God,

My soul rejoices in You! My spirit dances with absolute joy, certain in the Love You share and the Merciful Attention You shower upon me. I marvel at the wonder and miracle of creation, blessed that You have made me a part of it all! Thank You!

Amen.

Dearest, Most Loving Creator,

Thank You for the gift of tears. Such perfect release can come through weeping, bringing us back to a simple state from which we can humbly see our way and our God. Let us not resist this gift when we need it. Let us trust and let go. Let us have faith and let You be in control.

Amen.

Dearest, Most Holy Lord,

    We thank You for the gift of work. Honest tasks we perform that allow us to earn our daily bread and give us a place to live are honorable in Your eyes. Whether we are sales clerks or physicians, custodians, teachers, plumbers, artists, construction workers, bakers, day laborers, babysitters, musicians, secretaries, farmers, seamstresses, lawyers, writers, receptionists, factory workers, mechanics, or truck drivers, we know that all are valuable in Your eyes when done with care, honesty, diligence, cheerfulness, and a sense of service. We all have something to offer Your world in what we do and how we do it.

    Amen

Dearest God,

    We worship You for the Tender yet Powerful Compassion that eases the fears and worries of our souls. You are God. You are Eternal, Almighty, All-Glorious. Help us share Your love freely and without judgment. Let us do so tenderly, boldly, and courageously. Thank You, Father. Thank you.

    Amen.

Dearest, Most Compassionate Creator,

    Thank You for the gift of sleep. Our bodies are mortal; our minds grow tired as the day grows long. You have willed it to be so with Perfect Intent. You mean for us to rest. If we did not, our conscious minds might well spin faster and faster, and we would plow ahead, never taking the time to let our bodies slow down, never knowing the sense of peace that such surrender brings. Yet You have blessed us with the imperative need to surrender to weariness. Sleep enables our bodies to rejuvenate and repair. How wise are You, Our Loving Father, to create us in this way! How Merciful, that You will be with us in our waking and our sleeping, ever near, hearing the prayers of our hearts as we go about the daily tasks of our lives, and hearing the praise of our souls even as we sleep.

    Amen.

Dearest Eternal Master,

I am filled with wonder today, blessed with certain knowledge that You are God, You are Eternal, and You love me with a Love that will never end. I trust my life to You now and to my life beyond this world.

Amen.

Dearest God,

Even when I lose sight and thought of You, You never lose sight and thought of me. When I turn back to You, You are always there, as close as my breath, loving me with a Love more Profound than words could ever express. I am awed. I am blessed. I am humbled and grateful. I love You, Glorious Lord! I praise You!

Amen.

Dearest, Merciful God,

We thank You for the gift of friendship. We are not on this Earth to be alone, but to share and care for each other. You, in Your Infinite Wisdom, have made us for the purpose of love and companionship. There is much to learn during our lives, much to experience. There is joy and heartache, sorrow and wonder, grief and glory.

Yet the greatest, most important lesson is that of love. True friends are a blessing in our lives. Together, we learn and grow. We comfort each other when we are sad, support each other when we feel weak, encourage each other when we are anxious, and rejoice with each other when we are happy.

Friends are an extension of and reflection of Your Perfect Love. Love is Your Glorious and Beautiful Will for us. Love shall surround us through life's journey, and when it is time to leave this world for Your Eternal Kingdom, Love will see us safely there.

Amen.

Dearest, Most Loving Creator,

    I am still, Lord. I am listening. You speak to me in the silence, moving my heart and stirring my soul to wonder, and joy. You restore me with Your All-Encompassing Love. You hold me in Your Merciful Arms. I wait in You. I surrender to You. And I receive from You, drawing each breath, which is surely Divine CPR. You are my Guide and Comfort. You are my Goal. I love You.

    Amen.

Dearest Creator,

    I am in awe of the Astounding Glory that is You. You are my Hope, You are my Savior and the Foundation upon which I exist. What have I to fear, as You, the Divine Lord of All, are my God?

    Though darkness or disappointments may surround me, and the world may seem huge, cold, and callous, You keep me close. When I am weary, You let me rest in You. When I am sad, You ease my sorrows. And when I am too troubled even too pray, when my mind will not let go of the worries of my heart and cannot focus on You, You remain, holding me, tending me, loving me. My God, how Great is Your Love! I thank You!

    Amen.

Dearest, Most Merciful Master,

    Thank You for the gift of food. It is by Your Loving Hands that we are nourished. The bounty of the Earth is Your creation, here to sustain us as we travel life's journey. Let us never forget, Dearest Lord, that there are those who are unable to find, grow, or obtain enough food to survive.

    Then let us be charitable, sharing with those in need. Put aside our judgmental natures and shine into us the bright Light of Compassion. Remind us that what we do unto another of Your children, we do unto You. Let our hands be directed by Your Hands, tenderly offering of gifts of nourishment to our brothers and sisters who are hungry. Let our actions reflect our love for You, and Your Amazing Love for all of humankind.

    Amen.

Dearest, Almighty Creator,

    Thank You for Your Infinite Mercy and Patience. You are always Present, Loving us, Caring for us, quietly urging us to open our hearts and surrender to Your Compassionate Guidance. As we do, and as we become silent before You, we hear Your Sure and Certain Voice speaking to us. "Do not be afraid," You tell us. "I am Your God. You are my dear child. Lean into me." We may hesitate. We may struggle with uncertainty. Yet when we finally release our hold and give ourselves over to You, we are overcome with Perfect Peace. And then, at last, with joy and thanksgiving we can answer You, "I am not afraid, my God! I am not afraid!"

    Amen.

Dearest, Divine Master,

    We thank You for the precious gift of music. The natural world is filled with melodic tapestries – the songs of bird and insects. The rustling of grasses and rushing of waves. The intimate beatings of our hearts. You have blessed us with the ability to create and enjoy music with voices and instruments. Music can help us celebrate. It can ease depression and pain. Music can inspire our minds or help calm the storms of our souls. Music can even draw us closer to You.

    Our connection to music is innate. Babies to react joyfully and naturally to music; it fills their bodies with an exuberant need to express what they feel. And this gift is life long. Therefore, Precious Creator, let us embrace and appreciate the wonder of music. Let us be thankful for this gift. And as the Spirit moves us let us, with melodies and harmonies, praise You for Your Wisdom and Love.

    Amen.

Dearest God,

Thank You for the gift of time. While none of us knows how long we have to live on this Earth, we know that each day, each minute, gives us a chance to do something to share Your Love and Peace. Time is not our enemy but an opportunity. Awaken our souls to the reality and wonder of now. As we strive forward let us never forget the Perfect Goal You place before us – to offer compassion and understanding to all we meet along the way. And whether our lives are completed today or years from now, we will leave the world a sweeter place.

Amen.

Dearest, Most Loving God,

How is it that You know me, Eternal Father? How is it that I, one of countless souls in Your vast and Perfect creation, am in Your Thoughts every moment of every day? Sometimes I feel as small as a grain of sand on a vast beach, a minor player in a Universe beyond my comprehension. I think of the fields and forests, seas and rivers, mountains and plains, towns and cities, and nations and worlds, and am overwhelmed by the limitless, breath-taking miracle all of You have created.

Yet then, My Creator, I wonder how I could I ever doubt that You know me? Your Knowing is without end. Your Wisdom and Power are without measure. Greater than anything that ever was, is, or shall be, is the Mind of God. How could I not know that You, who have imagined and created all there is, would not have me in Your Mind, also? That You, whose Will is to share Love, would not also share it with me?

Amen.

Dearest Almighty Father,

My soul is at peace, for what can truly threaten me, as you are God? Your Compassion is more certain and more powerful than any trial. Thank You!

Amen.

Dearest, Divine Friend,

    Thank You for the precious and exhilarating gifts of curiosity, wonder, and learning. Life is an opportunity to experience, to discover, and to grow. As we move from day to day, loving You and each other, we stand in awe of the intricacies of creation. We are amazed at its glories.

    You have blessed us with a desire to investigate our world and the worlds beyond us, to seek, and to understand. We marvel at each new discovery. We know that nothing ever revealed could in any way threaten You, but rather all knowledge serves to glorify You all the more. You are the Designer, the Creator, the Sustainer of the Universe. All Praises to You for inviting us to explore Your Astounding Handiwork.

    Amen.

Dearest Holy One,

    Thank you for the wonderful gift of laughter. When we laugh long and freely we emerge refreshed, released of stress, and even healthier. Laughter can increase our happiness, reduce our pain, relax our bodies, and even help protect our hearts. All this is part of Your Amazing, Loving Plan.

    It is Your Will that we enjoy things that are funny. Unexpected, hilarious moments, comments, or actions catch us by surprise. They may be ironic, outrageous, endearing, or just plain wacky, and they give us a chance to find the flip side of sorrow, to loosen the tight bands of anxiety. Laughter can ease conflicts between Your people, for laughing together is an amazing bond. What an incredible, uplifting gift! Let us laugh, Lord, and laugh with us!

    Amen.

Dearest Lord,

Thank You for times of solitude. Life can be loud and hectic. It often moves so fast that we feel our hearts pounding and our thoughts racing. We are busy with our day-to-day tasks and it may seem as though we are pushed from place to place, duty to duty. Yet there are also times throughout the day in which we are able to stop and be still. These times, whether a minute or an hour, are precious and necessary. We are able to give ourselves to you in private communion and prayer. We sense You around us. You touch our hearts and they rise in joy, adoration, and thanksgiving. We are assured, yet again, of Your Steadfast Mercies. We love You!

Amen.

Dearest Almighty God,

When I sit and think of You, I am so awe-struck I can barely breathe. While scientists ponder whether there is microscopic life beneath the surface of Mars, You already know. While they send craft out to the far reaches of our solar system and beyond in hopes of finding out what is there, You already know. When we stare up at the billions of stars and galaxies in a night sky, and try to imagine the vastness of space, grasp the enormity of time, and fathom the beginnings of it all, You already know.

You know because You, Most Glorious Father, are the Author of it all. You, in Your Perfect Power and Authority, have willed it to be. You are the Mind that conceived it, the Hand that created it, and the Love and Power that sustain it. And then to realize that, amid all there ever was, is, and will be, within the immeasurable expanse of creation, You know and love me and each of Your children completely and without hesitation, I am astounded. I love You, my God!

Amen.

Prayers for Forgiveness

Pray when your heart is torn by ill works you have performed or good works you have withheld. Pray when you are grieved by harmful words you have spoken or loving words you have kept to yourself. Pray when you are heartily sorry for angry, hateful, or selfish attitudes you have held against your brothers and sisters. Pray to our Loving Father. He will hear your regret and your anguish. He will you discover what you might be able to do to repair the harm you have caused. God is a God of reconciliation and forgiveness.

Dearest Creator,
    I pray that You will forgive me when my faith is shaken and my trust is weak. My God, You have never forsaken me, You have never left my side. You have always been there for me to cry to, lean on, and draw strength from. Yet at times I feel alone and frightened. I feel darkness closing in around me. I lose hope that You will sustain and help me. Turn my face back to You, my God. Take my hands away from my eyes. Show me yet again, the Perfect Love You offer. Let my heart rejoice and trust in You once more!
    Amen.

Dearest Creator,
    I pray that You will forgive me when my faith is shaken and my trust is weak. My God, You have never forsaken me, You have never left my side. You have always been there for me to cry to, lean on, and draw strength from. Yet at times I feel alone and frightened. I feel darkness closing in around me. I lose hope that You will sustain and help me. Turn my face back to You, my God. Take my hands away from my eyes. Show me yet again, the Perfect Love You offer. Let my heart rejoice and trust in You once more!
    Amen.

Dearest, Most Merciful Master,

    I kneel before You, Beloved Creator, my hands trembling. I am heartsick; I am truly sorry. I pray fervently that You will forgive me of my selfishness, pride, laziness, and fear. Forgive me for doing those things You did not want me to do, and not doing those things You wanted me to do.

    I rise before You, Perfect Father, my hands pressed to my heart. Thank You for Your forgiveness, for hearing my prayer and drawing me upward into Your healing Embrace. Thank You for knowing me, caring for me, tending to me, strengthening me.

    I stand before You, my arms outstretched and my hands open to You, trembling with awe and joy, amazed that You know me and love me, assured that You are with me always. You are the Lord of the Universe, You are the Author of Life. You are greater than our greatest hopes, more loving than our deepest longings. I praise You. I thank You!

    Amen.

Dearest God,

    Forgive us. We have made unfair assumptions about our brothers and sisters, often without even knowing them. In traffic, on the sidewalk, on a bus or train, in the store, park or apartment building, wherever we have been, our minds want us to fear or disregard someone because of the way he or she dresses, or stands, or speaks. Our minds want us to see only the clothing, the age, or facial expression, to only hear the accent or the grammar, to judge based on our own prejudices instead of Your love.

    It is true that there are dangerous people in Your world. We must be aware and alert. But we can't let that caution lead us to dismissing one another. We can't presume to know what is in another's heart. Help us see beyond the exterior. Help us realize that we are all Your children.

    Amen.

Dearest, Most Loving Creator,

    We are deeply sorry for our actions and attitudes that spring from arrogance and pride. There is no one more valuable or more lovable than any other in Your Sight. How is it, then, that we could possibly imagine ourselves as having more importance than someone else? How could we mean to place ourselves above or look down at another?

    Our talents and skills are Your gifts to us. Our places and circumstances of birth, indeed our very makeups are from Your Hand. Therefore, should we boast? Never! Instead, we should look at each other through the eyes of love, humility, and appreciation. All Your children are equally valuable, regardless of education, wealth, or appearance. We should praise You for the Wisdom and Care with which You have created us. Help us do better.

    Amen.

Dearest, Most Tender Lord,

    Forgive me for the things I did today that I should not have done. The selfishness that kept me focused solely on myself and kept me from seeing what I might have done to make the moment better for another of Your children. I was distracted. I was too busy and self-absorbed. I was worried and irritable.

    Yet, my God, You are never too busy for me. You watch me, listen to me, and surround me with Your Love always. Help me rise up out of myself. Even as I do the tasks I have each day, help me see the world not through the spotlight of my own interests but through the floodlight of Your Compassion.

    Amen.

Dearest Lord,

    Forgive me for things I have done that have hurt my brothers and sisters. Grant me clarity and compassion so that I may help heal those I have harmed.

    Amen.

Dearest Almighty, Eternal God,

Forgive me when I let worry overwhelm me. I know that worry is our mind's way of letting us know there is a situation we need to address. It tells us there is something we should examine and let go or examine and then take action. Yet worry is only to serve as an alert. Like fear, it can take over. It can destroy our happiness and drive us down into the dust. It can leave us feeling hopeless and utterly alone.

This is not Your Will, Precious Father. You ask that we look to You, reach out to You, and find our strength in You. You ask that we not hold onto our worries, but instead put them into Your Almighty Hand. You will help us let them go or You will help us deal with the worrisome situation. Let us trust in Your Wisdom and Compassion.

Amen.

Dearest God,

I kneel before you, my hands outstretched, my soul heavy with regret. I have said things I should not have said and have not spoken up when I should have done so. I have done things I should not have done and have not acted when I should have done so. Oh God, who has loved me from the beginning and has held me with a Most Tender and Merciful Regard, I have not obeyed Your Perfect Will for me. I have turned my face from You, giving into selfishness and impatience. I am wracked with grief. I am utterly, wholly sorry.

Forgive me, Father! Remind me that listening to You, walking with You, and accepting Your lead is the most precious joy there can be found. Embracing Your Law of Love brings clarity, hope, strength, and healing to my restless heart. Loving You and following You is truly my soul's desire. And it is a blessing that reaches well beyond myself. To You be all Praise and Honor. Now and forever.

Amen.

Dearest Father,

When I have offended another, give me the wisdom and compassion to go to the one I offended, admit my mistake, and ask forgiveness. Help me to overcome the fear of feeling weak or in the wrong, for every person who has ever lived has been weak and in the wrong. It is in admitting our wrongs that we can stand up and do better. May my actions help heal any anger or resentment that was created because of my offense. Thank you.

Amen.

Prayers for Each Other

It is good to pray for one another, for in doing so we open our hearts and souls to each other in the presence of the Creator; we share each other's joys and pains, sorrows and terrors. We offer all things up to our Father and ask for His intervention, help, comfort, and mercy.

Let us pray especially for those who cannot pray, when hearts are broken, exhausted, and confused, when there is such pain that the mind and spirit seem overwhelmed and incapable of reaching out. We should be the voices for these dear one, praying in their stead, speaking to God with compassion and faith. Praying for others is a gift of selflessness. It puts our minds and spirits in empathetic, sympathetic communion with another.

Dearest God,

Hold close those who are anxious. Breathe into them the breath of calm, of relief. Let them know that You are with them and that the storm will not last. Send to them a friend who will sit or stand with them, and help them move from fear into peace under Your Almighty Guidance.

Amen.

Dearest God,

Look with mercy upon those who are filled with hate. You know their reasons even if we do not. Send us, on Your behalf, to share with them Your Kindness and Understanding. May their hatred and be replaced by peace. May those who hated be freed to look up and know You. Help us help our sisters and brothers, who are all Your children.

Amen.

Dearest Almighty Father,

We pray for those who are ill. Keep close to them and comfort them. Through the pain, exhaustion, and distress, whisper to them that they are loved and that You are there as their Anchor and Unfailing Hope. Ease their agonies and soothe their brows with Your Precious and Loving Hand. Bless them, Merciful Lord, and bring them back into health. Your Will be done. We love You.

Amen.

Dearest Gentle, Almighty Lord,

We pray for those who have lost their jobs. Be with them, reassure them, and strengthen them during this dark time in their lives. Encourage others to share with them happily and humbly so they will never been without food or shelter. And we beseech You, Great and Merciful God, to show the unemployed a new path, a new door that is bright and open for them. Reveal to them new opportunities for honest work.

Amen.

Dearest, Loving God,

We pray for Your children who are depressed. Enfold them in Your Compassionate Arms. Whisper to them that they are loved and that there is purpose beyond the shadows of distress. Guide loving people to them – caring friends and competent professionals who can help diagnose and treat the ailment with kindness and understanding. Strengthen them all. Bless them all.

Amen.

Dearest Creator,

We pray for those who are seeking You but are having trouble, for those who sense there is something greater beyond ourselves yet cannot quite open their minds and hearts enough to discover that You are real. Bless their search, Father. They are Your dear children who need You. As they reach out, as tentative and hesitant as it may be, shine Your Merciful Light upon them. Move to them, Beloved Creator. Do not let them agonize for long but draw them to You. Hold them and comfort them. Thank You.

Amen.

Dearest God,

As I go about my life today, open my eyes to others around me who are weary or hurting. Someone needs an encouraging word. Someone needs a caring smile. Someone needs me to be patient. These simple actions can help heal a wounded heart, lift a spirit, and ease a mind. All because these are what You would have me do. It is Your Love I share when I look beyond my own cares and offer the gift of kindness to others. Bless You for reminding me of this.

Amen.

Dearest Eternal, Glorious Lord,

Be with those who feel hopeless, oh God! You know them perfectly. You know the circumstances that have weighed them down, crushed them, and left them panting against the Earth. We know You love them with an unfailing Love. We offer this earnest prayer, that You will not let them suffer long. That You will breathe into them the astounding, beautiful Breath of Hope and Relief. That these precious, wounded ones will be filled with a rush of Divine Renewal that lifts their bodies to their feet in joy and moves their spirits to their knees in thankfulness. You are Hope of the hopeless, Help of the helpless. You are our Savior. Thank You. Thank You.

Amen.

Dearest Heavenly Father,

    We pray for those who are suffering through illness or injury. The gift of life is filled with joys and heartaches, peace and torment, communion and separation. We know that in life we will all face struggles – some mild, some almost unbearable. We also know that one reason You have created us is to care for one another. It is compassion for our brothers and sisters who are in pain that compels us to lift them to You in prayer, asking You, Blessed Lord, to place Your healing hand upon their heads. Draw them close in Your Merciful, Almighty Arms. Soothe their bodies and their spirits. Remind them that You are always with them and always love them. Surround them with caring, loving people who can tend to them during their sickness or wounds and can help speed their recovery. Bless them, Father. We thank You. We love You.

    Amen.

Dearest God,

    We pray earnestly for those who struggle with addictions. You have created us with needs, hopes, and longings. Yet sometimes our seeking sends us into treacherous places where we become tangled in vicious tripwires. They cut us, tear us, and keep us in their destructive grips. We pray for these, Your precious children, who cannot see their way out of the blinding darkness. We lift them up to You – the hopeless, the defeated, the anxious, the alienated – those who seem lost to the world but who are never lost to You.

    We pray You will send to them brave, caring persons who can help them loosen the dreadful grip of addiction and guide them back into the light of life. We pray, Father, that You will move around them all and comfort them with Your Loving Care. Even as they fight this powerful enemy, breathe into them the Breath of Hope and Strength. You, our God, are our Salvation and Eternal Joy. We praise You. We thank You.

    Amen.

Dearest Almighty Friend,

    Help all who feel worthless. Open their hearts and pour in your Mercies that they might rise anew into this day, certain of their value to You and to the world. Let them know they are never unloved or unwanted. Let them know You.

    Amen.

Dearest Heavenly Father,

    Help those who serve as caretakers for those unable to help themselves. Though such service is done in selfless love, it is often exhausting and disheartening. Remind the caretakers that they are tending Your beloved children, and that each merciful act is an expression of Your Love. Remind them that You are with them and will strengthen them even through the darkest moments. Bring to them others who can join in to make the task lighter. Speak to them in Your still yet Almighty Voice. Let them them know that You love both the helpless and the helper equally with profound Love. Assure them that the mercies they share are gifts not only to the one in need, but precious gifts to You, also.

    Amen.

Dearest and Most Loving God,

    Take to Your Heart those who, on this day, pass from mortal life to Life Eternal. Hold these precious souls in Your Merciful Arms, drying every tear, banishing every fear, and blessing them with the profound wonder and joy of Your Perfect, Unconditional, Eternal Compassion.

    Comfort those who have lost a loved one this day. Though their pain and grief is deep, assure them that life on Earth is just part of the experience You have planned for us. Remind them that love never dies. Let them know, in Your quiet, All-Powerful Voice, that when life is done and worldly distractions fall away, we will all be drawn to You in precious Communion, where we will rejoice in glorious ecstasy and be with You forever.

    Amen.

Dearest, Most Loving God,

We pray for those who struggle in poverty. Life can be difficult, the workings of human society unpredictable and often harsh. While You have provided everything we need, while Your Almighty Hands have spread before us the life-sustaining gifts of Your Mercy, the greed of some have left others without. They are the hungry and homeless. The hopeless and lonely. Some have lost their jobs. Some have lost their confidence.

If we can share a meal, a coat, some of our income, a word of encouragement or direction, a blessing, a fervent prayer, then Father, let us not hesitate to do so. For in sharing what we can, we put Your Love in action. In humbly caring for those in need, we learn the deeper message of Your Will. And You shall hold us. And we shall all be blessed.

Amen.

Dearest Lord,

We pray for all those who feel barren, empty, and cold. We lift these dear ones to You, our Father, beseeching Your Blessing upon them. Surround them with Your Warmth and Power. Let them know that struggles and heartaches are not forever but that Your Help and Love is. Hold them close, that they might release their agonies into Your Hand and find the Peace of Your Compassionate Power. Send to them loving people who can encourage them. For we have all felt the winter of our souls; we know the cold emptiness of doubt and worry. We are on this human journey together, facing both its darkness and its profound beauties. Help us comfort each other through the stark and bitter times. Calm and comfort us with Your Blessed, Healing Touch.

Amen.

Dearest God,

We pray for those who are afraid. There is much in this world that is frightening. Help those who are hesitant to step out into life. Place Your Hand upon their hearts and minds, and whisper to them that You are with them, always. Breathe into them the Divine breath of Hope and Courage.

Amen.

Prayers for Strength, Help, and Guidance

God, who created you and loves you knows your pains, fears, uncertainties, and sadness. He longs to hear from you. The Mind and Heart and Love of God are more glorious and vast than the Universe He created, yet He is as close to you as your heartbeat, your breaths. He is here for you.

Dearest Eternal Father,

Walk with me today. I need You every moment of my life. I need You to hold my hand and show me the way. I will praise You as we walk. I will tell You my sorrows and disappointments, and give them into Your Hand. I will rejoice with You and share my joy and wonder with You, my God, my Dearest Friend, my Most Beloved Creator. Let me know You are with me. Take me forward, surrounded by Your blessed Peace, Your glorious Love.

Amen.

Dearest Lord,

Humble us, bless us, strengthen us, and lead us in the paths of love, charity, compassion, understanding, and forgiveness. You are our Heart's greatest desire, and in You we trust. May the days we live and the tasks we do be of value. Thank you.

Amen.

Dearest God,
    Sit with me and let me sit with You. You are Greater than anyone can imagine, yet in Your Perfect Wisdom You have created me as I am and You love me as I am. Let me be silent with You. Let me be still. Then let me tell You my troubles and fears. Let me sigh and grieve. Hold me through it all. Remind me that as Almighty and Perfect as You are, You have never lost thought of me. As amazing as it is, I am dear to You. It is Your Will, Your Joy, to love me. It is Your Will, Your Joy, to breathe into me the blessed breath of renewal. You, my Creator, give me a Peace that passes understanding. I love You!
    Amen.

Dearest, Most Loving Creator,
    There are times when we feel very distant from You. We feel worried and burdened, stressed and afraid, angry and disillusioned. We reach about in the darkness, but cannot seem to find Your Hand. We long for You, we cry to You, and yet we feel alone and lost. We thirst for Your Precious Presence, yet feel abandoned.
    Remind us, Precious God, that You are always there. You have gone nowhere. Help us, Compassionate Master, to sit in quietness and let the fog lift. Remind us to be still and know that You are God. While pains and troubles are temporary, You are Eternal. And we are Yours now and forever more. You are our constant Help in time of need. Your Love is greater than any agony, any trial. Thank you. Thank you.
    Amen.

Dearest God,
    Be with us even when our thoughts stray far from You. Life is difficult. Often we are overwhelmed and angry at all we must do. Yet we need You. Ease our hearts, Father. You are our Hope.
    Amen.

Dearest Lord,

While so many believe that true power is in the physical, the financial, or the political, we know that the truest power is found in love, understanding, compassion, and forgiveness. Those who walk forward with You, filled with Your Love, Your Understanding, Your Compassion, and Your Forgiveness, shine a light into the bitter darkness of hated, selfishness, cruelty, ignorance, and arrogance. Those who speak out courageously in the voice of love and understanding, who act boldly with compassion and forgiveness, are instruments of Your Blessed, Perfect Peace. In this is Divine Power, Your Power. Help us to be these people.
  Amen.

Dearest God,

Comfort me in this dark hour. I feel lost and helpless. I have little strength to handle the hardships that swirl around me and try to drown me. You are my Hope and my Help, oh God. You are my heart's Desire, my Savior, my Lord. Surround me with Your Mighty and Merciful arms; draw me close to Your Heart and hold me that I might fear no more, and might weep no more. Most Compassionate Master, I trust in You with all my being. I praise You for Your Tender Loving Care. Thank you. Thank you!
  Amen.

Dearest God,

Open the eyes and ears of our hearts, Father. Let us see and hear the beauty of Your world, the preciousness of Your creation, the value of every human being who shares this life with us. Let us know that You see each and every person as You see us – valuable, worthy, in need of love and understanding. Let us love as best we can, in action and in word. Let us not withhold that which You have given us.
  Amen.

Dearest, Most Loving Lord,

Help us to appreciate our bodies. We often dismiss them as not attractive enough, young enough, fast enough, strong enough, "good" enough. But, Our Father, You have given them to us as a gift. It is through our bodies and the senses they provide that we are able to experience the world around us and to be aware of others. It is our bodies that take the food we eat and turn it into the energy we need from day to day. It is our bodies that provide us with the blessed, healing experiences of touch, sight, smell, hearing, and taste.

Let us not hate these physical vessels in which you have placed our spirits, Dear God. Rather, help us take care of them as best we can. Help us rise above our preoccupation of what we should look like, and focus rather on what we, while here on Earth and in our bodies, should do to follow Your Guidance and share Your mercies.

Amen.

Dearest Creator,

Help me set aside time today to listen to You. Show me to a quiet place for a few minutes, somewhere I can sit and be still in Your Presence. Let me wait patiently in the silence. Let the thoughts and worries that have troubled me fall away and be gone. Let me willingly give my mind, heart, and soul up to Your Power, Glory, and Mercy. And then, Beloved Lord, I will be open to receiving Your Blessed Message to me. It may come in words. It may be revealed in images or impressions. Yet however You speak, I will know it is You, for everything You tell me or reveal to me shall be based in Love and rooted in Compassion. I will rejoice in the rush of joy or the calm relief that fills me in those minutes. I will know, yet again, that You are my Almighty God and I am Your child. And I will take Your Message and Your Peace out into the world with me.

Amen.

Dearest Lord,
   Be with us when we feel weak. You are our Strength and our Assurance. You are our Lord and our Comfort.
   Amen.

Dearest God,
   I am afraid. You know my fear. You also know that all will be well. Help me be sure of that in my soul. Help me unclench my heart and hands and give my fear to you, Lord, that you might, with your Loving Breath, blow it away. Thank you.
   Amen.

Dearest, Almighty God,
   We pray for help in dealing with difficult people. Our first reactions are often to shove back, to argue, or to dismiss. Remind us that we are all Your children. We cannot know the fears, wounds, and angers of those who irritate or frustrate us. All we see is the rudeness or coarseness, the unkind or thoughtless words and actions. Yet You see everything wholly and perfectly. You have created them as You have created us. You know them as You know us. You love them as You love us. It is Your will that we not lash out but to be patient, to bless them with prayers and forgiveness, to realize that they are in great need of understanding. While we may not see a change in them, let us be certain that love is never wasted; that the forgiveness and compassion is, indeed, the beginning of their healing.
   Amen.

Dearest Lord,
   It is late. The night is quiet. Let me be still and silent and know that You are God. Let me marvel in the certainty of You, and the Blessed Peace of Your Might. Let me listen to You. Let me listen for You. Let me rest.
   Amen.

Dearest, Most Glorious Father,

Help us to listen to You more than we listen to ourselves. Our minds are so busy planning, problem solving, creating, imagining, worrying, and regretting. All of this mental activity is part of life – some constructive, some destructive. Be our focus, Beloved Master, so that when our thoughts get tangled and we feel confused or disheartened, we can stop, be silent, and reach out to You. You are the Clear Light of our being. You are the Calm and Perfect Truth that we long for and seek. We are created for You, for this. Speak to us as we let our minds go still. Clear away the shadows, Precious Creator. And lead us onward.

Amen.

Dearest, Compassionate Lord,

The night was long and restless. I awaken, weary and anxious. Some of my worries are vague tensions that cling to my heart and knot in my mind. You know my heart, my mind, my fears, my frustrations. Let me put them into Your Almighty Hands, trusting completely in Your Love and Power. You offer to help me carry my burdens, time and again. But I often cling to them, unable or unwilling to be still, to lean into You, and to give them up to You. Help me trust You and remember Your promise to be my Strength. Help me step back to see my life more clearly, to know that while struggles are part of my journey, You are here and will help me carry my burdens. And in doing so, You also carry me.

Amen.

Dearest, Most Glorious Creator,

Tend to our spirits, our Father. Help us learn from the sting of disappointment, the pain of misunderstanding, and the hurt of betrayal. Teach us to rise above and beyond these feelings, because they keep us from loving You and loving others as You would have us love. Let us rest in You and be strengthened by Your Grace and Mercy. In this may we then stand again, strong in faith, hope, and assurance, filled with compassion and charity toward our brothers and sisters.

Amen.

Dearest, Merciful Creator,

Be with me in this moment. In the urgency of the day, in the spinning of the world around me, in the turmoil of fears and uncertainties, I need Your Hand to give me peace. I need Your Touch to assure my soul that all is well. Some day, Compassionate Lord, I will be with You without the distractions of the world, close with You forever more. But until then, let me embrace this precious gift of living, this experience that You have put before me, and trust You will guide me each step of the way. I thank You. I love You.

Amen.

Dearest Lord,

Humble us before You. Remind us that haughtiness, arrogance, and selfishness separate us from our brothers and sisters, and turn our hearts away from You. Teach us patience and gentleness, love and understanding. Help us let go of our desire to be critical of others in an attempt to raise ourselves. Forgive us our heartless actions. Fill us with the courage and compassion to live each moment as You would have us live.

Amen.

Dearest God,

Even in times when it seems You are far from us and we are struggling alone through the turmoil and darkness of life, let us never lose faith and certainty that You are always near. Though our hearts may be weary and our minds overwhelmed, when the world is so noisy we can barely hear our own voice or our own thoughts, remind us that You are with us – before us, behind us, beside us, beneath us, and above us, hearing our prayers, holding us close. Here to renew us and give us peaceful rest. Help us learn to let go and let You help us. You are our Father, our God, our Loving Eternal Master. We praise You. We love You. We need You.

Amen.

Dearest God,

 The day is new. So much is ahead. My journey awaits. Hold my heart as I hold Your hand, and guide me in the paths of Compassion and Courage. I love You!

 Amen.

Dearest Almighty Father,

 The day has been difficult. Disappointments darken my spirit. Burdens weigh heavy on my heart. The same trials hound me, over and over, and I feel I have lost my ability to change things for the better. I feel angry. I feel helpless. I feel weak. I know that life is filled with challenges. I know, too, that You are here to be my Guide and Help. Yet I feel worn out. I sense I have let others down and have let You down. Forgive me my lack of trust. As I kneel before You, Breathe into me Your Divine Breath of Renewal. Help me surrender my troubles to Your Tender Care. Assure me, yet again, that You are my Merciful Creator. Remind me that I need only do my best with Your Guidance and give the rest into Your Hand. Then my soul shall be at peace. I shall sleep in Your Loving Arms and arise with joy and thanksgiving to face a new day.

 Amen.

Dearest, Most Compassionate Father,

 Humble our hearts, Lord. There are times when we find ourselves puffed up and feeling superior to others, though we know this is not Your Will. You desire us to be confident, to act and speak out courageously for understanding, peace, and justice, yet it is not Your desire for us to be arrogant. Correct us when we lose our humility. Remind us that You do not put any of us above another, for You love each of us equally. We want to follow Your Perfect Lead. Teach us, Almighty Master. Gently, firmly, open our hearts to Your Loving Guidance. Then we shall be truly blessed, and we shall be freed to bless each other.

 Amen.

Dearest Lord,

Remind us that forgiveness brings peace; that forgiveness has the power to heal both the offender and the offended. We know how it feels to have the burden of sorrow and regret pushing down on our shoulders. It clouds our minds and torments us in the darkest hours of the night. It causes us to hold back, to look upon the world with distrust and uncertainty. It can even affect the health of our bodies.

Yet when we are forgiven, Merciful Father, the light fills our spirits and the air is fresh and sweet again. Our hearts, which had beat hard and painfully in our chests, swell with relief and joy. In remembering this, may we also be forgiving of our neighbors. They, too, suffer as we have. They, too, long for the precious gift of pardon. This gift is within our power.

Amen.

Dearest God,

Be the Pillow beneath my head, the Warm Blanket over my body, the Comforting Shadows that fall around me, the Sweet Scent of Evening Air, and the Precious Song that sings me to sleep.

Amen.

Dearest Heavenly Father,

The day has been difficult. I have been battered by thoughtless words and actions. I have witnessed people lash out with hateful and hurtful comments. I have felt myself struggling within a sea of human angst, distrust, and discord. I lift my troubled heart to You, Most Compassionate God. I need Your Refuge. I need to draw close to You. I agonize and worry, question and despair. Yet You are here, always close. You ask that I lean into You and be still, for it is within that Precious Communion that You heal me. In Your Embrace, my soul sings out in rapturous joy, assured of Your Mercy, Authority, and Profound Love. It is there that, restored and renewed, I shall begin again with You by my side.

Amen.

And now may the Creator of all speak to our hearts and say, "My Dearest Children, All Shall Be Well." And may all who live and breathe, may all that have form and being due to the Loving Will of our Creator, lift our hearts and reply, "Amen!"

Amen.

www.ingramcontent.com/pod-product-compliance
Lightning Source LLC
Chambersburg PA
CBHW071655090426
42738CB00009B/1527